LOUIS XIV

Louis XIV ruled France for more than half a century and is typically remembered for his absolutism, his patronage of the arts and his lavish lifestyle — culminating in the building of Versailles. This original and lively biography focuses on Louis' personal life while keeping the needs of the history student at the forefront, featuring analysis of Louis' wider significance in history and the surrounding historiography.

An analytical account of Louis' life, this study proposes that the Sun King's reign and legacy cannot be fully understood without a detailed investigation of Louis' private life and personality, including his upbringing and his many lovers. Louis' relations with his closest family set the tone for the treatment of his French subjects and for his foreign policy towards the rest of Europe.

This book balances the undeniable cultural achievements of the reign against the realities of Louis' egotism and argues that, when viewed critically, Louis' rule (1643–1715) personified the disadvantages of absolute monarchy and inexorably led to social and political blunders resulting in the suffering of millions. Richard Wilkinson demonstrates that while Louis excelled as a self-publicist, he fell far short of being a great monarch.

This up-to-date and accessible biography is essential reading for all students and those with a general interest in one of history's most colourful rulers.

Richard Wilkinson studied at Cambridge and gained his doctorate at Hull. He was Headmaster of Scarborough College and King Edward's School, Witley. Now retired, he teaches history at Marlborough College summer school. His previous publications include *Louis XIV, France and Europe 1661–1715* (2002) and *Years of Turmoil* (1999).

ROUTLEDGE HISTORICAL BIOGRAPHIES

SERIES EDITOR: ROBERT PEARCE

Routledge Historical Biographies provide engaging, readable and academically credible biographies written from an explicitly historical perspective. These concise and accessible accounts will bring important historical figures to life for students and general readers alike.

In the same series:

Bismarck by Edgar Feuchtwanger
Neville Chamberlain by Nick Smart
Oliver Cromwell by Martyn Bennett
Churchill by Robert Pearce
Edward IV by Hannes Kleineke
Gladstone by Michael Partridge
Henry VII by Sean Cunningham
Henry VIII by Lucy Wooding
Hitler by Martyn Housden
Jinnah by Sikander Hayat
Lenin by Christopher Read
Martin Luther King Jr. by Peter J. Ling
Martin Luther by Michael Mullet
Mary Queen of Scots by Retha M. Warnicke
Mao by Michael Lynch
Mussolini by Peter Neville
Nehru by Ben Zachariah
Emmeline Pankhurst by Paula Bartley
Richard III by Ann Kettle
Franklin D. Roosevelt by Stuart Kidd
Stalin by Geoffrey Roberts
Trotsky by Ian Thatcher
Mary Tudor by Judith Richards

DEDICATION

For Martin, Stephen, Catherine and Peter

CONTENTS

LIST OF PLATES AND FIGURES   vii
ACKNOWLEDGEMENTS   viii
CHRONOLOGY   ix

1   **Introduction**   1

2   **The Rising Sun, 1638–61**   10

3   **The king and his subjects**   34

4   **The king at work**   55

5   **Culture with a purpose**   82

6   **Relations and friends**   98

7   **The world at his feet: foreign policy, 1661–84**   122

8   **Louis XIV and religion**   143

9   **Nemesis: foreign policy, 1684–1715**   168

10   **The Sun King and his people, 1684–1715**   197

11   **Conclusion**   215

GLOSSARY   232
FURTHER READING   234
NOTES   240
INDEX   250

LIST OF PLATES AND FIGURES

PLATES (BETWEEN PAGES 146 AND 147)

1 King Carlos II of Spain
2 Louis XIV in royal costume
3 Louis, painted unflatteringly at age 68
4 Cartoon of Louis by William Thackeray
5 Madame de Montespan
6 Françoise Louise de la Baume le Blanc, duchesse de Vaujour
7 Françoise d'Aubigné, marquise de Maintenon, and her niece
8 François-Henri de Montmorency-Bouteville, maréchal-duc de Luxembourg
9 Anne of Austria
10 *The Baker's Cart*, by Jean Mitchelin, 1656

FIGURES

1 Bourbon family tree and the Spanish succession   xi
2 French expansion under Louis XIV   xii
3 Louis XIV's palaces   xiii
4 The cabals   xiv

ACKNOWLEDGEMENTS

I am grateful to John Alderson, Douglas Dales, John Elliott, Peregrine Horden, Catherine and Dean Petters, Geoffrey Treasure and Peter Wilkinson for reading chapters of my book. Their corrections and improvements have been invaluable. Jacques Courrégé, Rodney Dingle, Christopher Eames, Wendy Gibson, Nicholas Henshall, Stanley Josephs, Robert Knecht, Anthony Levi and Roger Macdonald have helpfully answered my letters. Boris Anderson, Simon Dixon, Margaret and Derek Hoyle, Roger Mettam and Philip Spencer have discussed Louis XIV with me. I have been grateful to them for their valuable time. I have enjoyed working for Victoria Peters, Senior Editor (History), Emma Langley and Alan Fidler at Routledge. The staffs of the following libraries have been invariably patient and helpful: the Bibliothèque Nationale, the Bibliothèque Mazarine, the Prado, the British Library, the Institute of Historical Research, Doctor Williams' Library, the Birmingham University Library, Leyburn Public Library. Three people have been outstandingly supportive. Robin Briggs has corresponded at length, has welcomed me to All Souls on three occasions and has allowed me to read his unpublished article on the Jansenists. I have so much appreciated his guidance. Robert Pearce, Series Editor for Routledge Biographies, has been unfailingly encouraging. He has read my text several times, all the while making constructive comments. My wife, Ann, has read chapters, corrected my spelling and taste, and has dug me out of several, self-inflicted computing potholes. Martin, Stephen, Catherine and Peter have helped me in all sorts of ways. Without being a dynast in Louis XIV's class, I dedicate this book to them in love and gratitude.

Chronology

1638	5 September. Birth of Louis the dauphin to Anne of Austria
1640	Birth of Philippe (Monsieur) to Anne of Austria.
1642	Death of Richelieu
1643	14 May. Death of Louis XIII. Accession of Louis XIV. Battle of Rocroi.
1647	Louis survives smallpox
1648	Treaty of Westphalia ends war between France and the Empire
1648–53	The Fronde
1651	7 September. Louis comes of age
1654	7 June. Louis crowned at Reims
1658	Louis contracts typhoid. Affair with Marie Mancini
1659	7 November. Treaty of the Pyrenees ends war between France and Spain
1660	9 June. Louis marries Marie Thérèse
1661	March. Death of Mazarin. Beginning of the personal rule
1661–7	Louise de La Vallière chief mistress
1661–4	Fall of Fouquet. Colbert controller-general
1665	September. Death of Philip II of Spain. Accession of Carlos II
1666	January. Death of Anne of Austria
1667	May. The War of Devolution
1667–81	Madame de Montespan chief mistress
1668	May. Treaty of Aix-la-Chapelle ends War of Devolution
1670	Secret Treaty of Dover between England and France
1672	April. Outbreak of Dutch War. William of Orange comes to power
1678–9	Peace of Nijmegen between France and the Dutch Republic
1679	Affair of the Poisons. Chambre Ardente established
1679–83	The Reunions
1680	Paris hails 'Louis the Great'
1681	French seizure of Strasbourg
1682	The court moves to Versailles. Assembly adopts Gallican Articles

1683	Deaths of Colbert and Marie Thérèse. Louis marries Mme de Maintenon
1684	Truce of Ratisbon
1685	October. Edict of Fontainebleau: Revocation of the Edict of Nantes
1686	League of Augsburg formed. Operation on Louis' anal fistula
1688	Nine Years War. William of Orange invades England
1689	French devastation of the Palatinate
1690	Battle of the Boyne
1691	Death of Louvois
1691–2	French victories at Steinkirk and Neerwinden. Louis' capture of Namur
1697	October. Treaty of Ryswick concludes the Nine Years War
1698	October. First partition treaty
1700	March. Second partition treaty. November. Death of Carlos II. Will accepted
1701	September. The Grand Alliance of The Hague
1701–14	War of the Spanish Succession
1702	Death of William III. Accession of Anne to the English throne
1704	Battle of Blenheim
1705	Papal bull *Vineam Domini*
1706	Battle of Ramillies
1708	Battle of Oudenarde
1708–9	Severe winter. Louis' appeal to the nation
1709	Battle of Malplaquet
1711	Death of Monseigneur the Grand Dauphin
1712	Deaths of the ducs de Bourgogne, Bretagne and Berry. Victory at Denain
1713–14	Treaties of Utrecht and Rastadt end the War of the Spanish Succession
1714	Papal bull *Unigenitus*
1715	1 September Death of Louis XIV

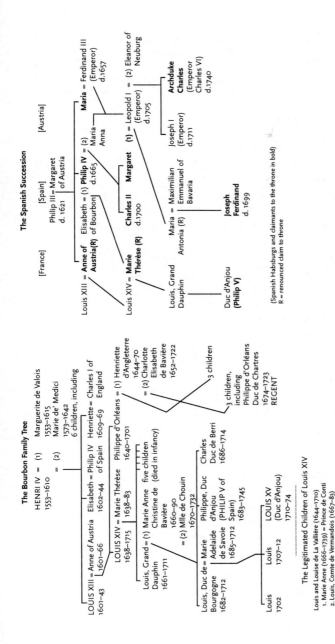

Figure 1 Bourbon family tree and the Spanish succession

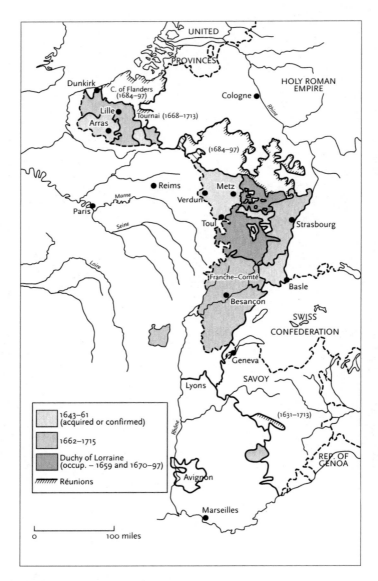

Figure 2 French expansion under Louis XIV

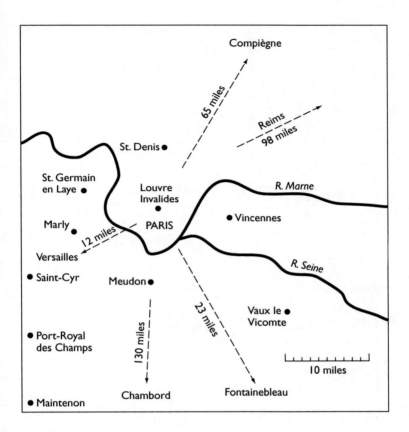

Figure 3 Louis XIV's palaces

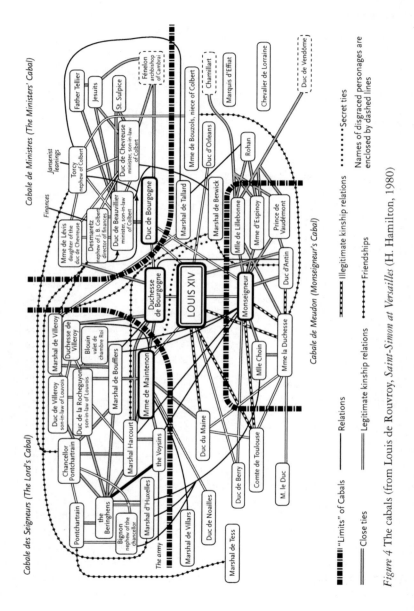

Figure 4 The cabals (from Louis de Rouvroy, *Saint-Simon at Versailles* (H. Hamilton, 1980)

Cabale des Ministres (The Ministers' Cabal)

Cabale des Seigneurs (The Lord's Cabal)

Cabale de Meudon (Monseigneur's Cabal)

Fénelon archbishop of Cambrai

Father Tellier

Jesuits

St. Sulpice

Chamillart

Marquis d'Effiat

Chevalier de Lorraine

Duc de Vendôme

Mme de Bouzols, niece of Colbert

Duc d'Orléans

Rohan

Torcy nephew of Colbert

Duc de Chevreuse minister; son-in-law of Colbert

Jansenist leanings

Mme de Lévis daughter of the duc de Chevreuse

Desmaretz nephew of J. B. Colbert director of finances

Duc de Beauvillier minister; son-in-law of Colbert

Duc de Bourgogne

Marshal de Tallard

Marshal de Berwick

Mlle de Lillebonne

Mme d'Espinoy

Prince de Vaudémont

Finances

Duchesse de Bourgogne

LOUIS XIV

Monseigneur

Duc d'Antin

Marshal de Villeroy

Duchesse de Villeroy

Blouin valet de chambre Roi

Marshal de Boufflers

Mme de Maintenon

Mme la Duchesse

Mlle Choin

Duc de Villeroy son-in-law of Louvois

Duc de la Rocheguyon son-in-law of Louvois

Chancellor Pontchartrain

Marshal Harcourt

the Voysins

Duc du Maine

The army

Pontchartrain

Bignon nephew of the chancellor

Marshal d'Huxelles

Duc de Berry

Comte de Toulouse

M. le Duc

the Beringhens

Marshal de Villars

Duc de Noailles

Marshal de Tess

▮▮▮ "Limits" of Cabals   —— Relations   ▬▬▬ Illegitimate kinship relations   •••••• Secret ties

—— Close ties   —— Legitimate kinship relations   ••••• Friendships   Names of disgraced personages are enclosed by dashed lines

1

INTRODUCTION

VIGNETTE: THE SUN HAS PUT HIS HAT ON

It is a spring afternoon at Versailles in 1683. Against the gorgeous back-drop of his newly completed palace, the Sun King, having spent the morning with his councillors, is now coming out to play. As his por-traits testify, Louis XIV is the picture of health, expensively dressed in plumed hat, greatcoat, cravat, and buckled riding boots. He exudes confidence and self-satisfied good humour as he swaggers into his gar-dens, twirling his moustache and swinging his cane. Although only five feet four inches, he compensates for his lack of height not merely by his high heels and enormous wig, but through sheer presence and magnetic personality – like another powerful little man, David Lloyd George, who looked 'eight feet tall', according to a susceptible female observer. Where is Louis going? Possibly to hunt the deer, scuttling away into the greenwood that initially attracted Louis to his beloved Versailles. Possibly to shoot partridges, for he is a crack shot. Possibly to stroll round his estate, admiring the fountains and lakes, the flower beds that he has designed and in which he delights, but not forgetting the vegeta-ble gardens where he can display his considerable expertise.

Louis is not alone. Far from it. An immense crowd of courtiers, noblemen, ecclesiastics, lackeys and courtesans surround their king, jos-tling and shoving to get near him, running ahead in order to take up an advantageous position where they hope to be noticed, even better to be addressed however briefly by the monarch, possibly clutching a petition to thrust into his hand. Primo Visconti, the Italian man-of-affairs, described the scene like this: 'It is a wonderful sight to see the king surrounded by courtiers, valets and so forth, all in a melée of confusion, running and chattering noisily around him. It reminds me of a queen-bee, when she goes out into the fields with her swarm.'[1]

Questions immediately come to mind. Was this what the king wanted? Why did this swarming crowd shove and jostle? Was there no danger of untoward approaches to the king – even assassination? After all both his grandfather Henri IV and *his* predecessor Henri III had been stabbed to death. These questions will be addressed in the pages ahead.

For now, suffice it to say that Louis was a supremely sociable man who loved to be the centre of attention. He had no objection to crowds provided they were there on his terms. As for his swarming acolytes, they too were there because they wanted to be. Part of Louis' skill was to make it worth while for his subjects to associate with him. 'Sire', exclaimed the marquis de Vardes, 'When one is away from you, one is not only wretched, one is ridiculous.' And assassination? Never out of the question, for Henri IV had been the best-loved king in French history – yet he had fallen victim to the seventeenth-century equivalent of a suicide bomber. Louis was not in fact a risk taker. His soldiers were never far away at Versailles. Furthermore, that jostling crowd would all be familiar to the Sun King and his minders.

Not that assassination seemed likely in 1683, when Louis was in his pomp, recently hailed by the city fathers of Paris as 'Louis the Great' after the successful Dutch war, admired and respected throughout Europe as the personification of monarchical professionalism. Why should anyone *want* to kill him? Not only France but Europe looked to the Sun King for leadership. His effulgence blazed brilliantly, not only politically but in the social and cultural spheres as well. Louis the Great? He was Louis the Greatest!

ABOUT THIS BOOK

This is a book about a man's life. The man is Louis XIV, a remarkable individual and a remarkable king. While he dedicated himself to the task of ruling France for over half a century, this book is not a history of France though clearly Louis must be placed in his historical context. It is primarily concerned with a fascinating human being, who, like the rest of us, was a mixture of good and evil, acquainted with both success and failure. I shall pinpoint his mistakes as well as his successes, his defects as well as his qualities. 'He who judges Louis XIV, judges himself.'[2] This may well be true. So be it! I shall not be deterred from assessing not only Louis' achievements but also the man. Unlike some biographers who rate Louis as 'a great king and a great man', I reckon that he was flawed; 'great', maybe, in some respects, but far from 'great' in others. My chief objective, however, is not so much to judge Louis as to understand him, to understand his attitudes and aspirations and to identify the personal and political handicaps under which he operated. I shall try to get to know Louis XIV and to make him live, to establish what sort of a man he was, as well as what sort of a king.

This objective is surprisingly hard to achieve. My vignette chosen to introduce Louis to the reader highlights the problem. Always on show from dawn to dusk, always surrounded by crowds of people, the centre not only of French but of European scrutiny, described by innumerable contemporary diarists, journalists and official observers, Louis remains a surprisingly distant figure. His own cousin's son, the duke of Berwick, and one of his most successful generals, who was frequently in the Sun King's presence, remarked: 'It must be acknowledged that no prince has ever been so little known as this one.'[3] One of his victims allegedly wore an iron mask. Louis could rightly be described as 'the man in the golden mask', gold being the colour of Apollo, the sun god, with whom he deliberately identified himself. The essence of his professionalism was to give nothing away, not to divulge what lay behind the magnificent exterior. Did he ever let his guard down? Hardly ever, and then only to his nearest and dearest, who tended to be infuriatingly discreet.

This elusiveness makes the biographer's job difficult if the attempt is made to depict the whole man. Indeed, some historians, it seems to me, have virtually given up in advance, contenting themselves with analysis of his public persona and his professional achievements only. Such an approach for me would be a cowardly evasion. I intend to get behind the golden mask if at all possible. This is my excuse – if excuse is needed – for concerning myself with Louis' private life. This includes his sex life. Some historians tend to adopt a dismissive attitude to anyone who pries into Louis' relationships with his wives and his mistresses on the grounds that the serious scholar should be above court tittle-tattle. But one knows a man by his friends, his enemies – and his lovers. Given that Louis is so very elusive, no avenue should be unexplored, and that, to my mind, includes the bedroom and the backstairs.

Like the rest of us, Louis was the product of heredity and environment. In his case there are problems with both when it comes to historical interpretation. These will be addressed in Chapter 2. If Louis came to the job with baggage, so did the country he was to govern. The French people form the subject-matter of Chapter 3. Chapter 4 shows the Sun King at work, Chapters 5 and 6 at leisure, including his private life. The fundamental stumbling block in Louis' career was his foreign policy, which in practice meant war. However, he exacerbated his problems abroad by creating difficulties at home, especially with regard to religion. So the chapters on foreign policy – 7 and 9 – envelop a chapter on the Sun King's religious aims, achievements and mistakes. Chapter 10 examines the impact of Louis' reign on France. Lastly we witness the king's harrowing and courageous death, a fit occasion for a final assessment of the ruler and the man, set against his time and his nation's history. Louis' contribution to the evolution of France can profitably be assessed here.

LOUIS XIV – FOR AND AGAINST

Such a high-profile figure as Louis XIV has always provoked controversy. The final section of this introduction will survey the contrasting approaches both of contemporaries and historians to the Sun King's personality, policies and achievements. This exercise will clarify the unavoidable issues of Louis' life, which no biographer can reasonably ignore.[4]

Certainly, in the first part of Louis XIV's reign, French contemporaries were favourably impressed by their king. And they said so, frequently and noisily. For instance the sonorous court preacher Bossuet, bishop of Meaux, advocated the divine right of kings in general and Louis in particular, and the subject's duty to obey. Paul Pellisson, a devoted hack who helped Louis write his memoirs, concluded his panegyric like this: 'If it had been possible for me, while dazzled by the brilliance of a great king, charmed by his virtues, and imbued with his goodness, I would have praised him a thousand times more.' Dramatists, poets and analysts heaped incense on the king's altar with a trowel. Historians disagree as to how much Louis liked to be flattered. This was to some extent government policy, reflecting the necessity of maintaining the king's image – or his *gloire,* to use the contemporary term. 'Nothing matters more than the maintenance of Your Majesty's *gloire',* according to Louis' minister in charge of publicity, Jean-Baptiste Colbert. Nevertheless Louis was too intelligent and had too-developed a sense of the ridiculous to take all this flattery at face value. 'I would praise you more if you praised me less', Louis remarked to the dramatist Racine. Perhaps Louis liked praise, provided that it stopped short of flattery. It is a fine distinction. In truth, he received plenty of both.

On the other hand, towards the end of the reign when disaster devastated both the French economy and the French armies, French critics laid into the Sun King. Highly unflattering pamphlets circulated, alleging, for instance, that Louis was senile, dominated by his wife whom he was sexually incapable of satisfying and unable to prevent national meltdown. Two remarkable figures in particular damned Louis. First, Fénelon, the archbishop of Cambrai, blamed Louis for initiating the wars that ruined France and for having no concern for his people's welfare. Second, the duc de Saint-Simon castigated the king for succumbing to flattery, appointing ministers whose only qualification was their obsequiousness, and leading his country into the abyss of bankruptcy and defeat. Others joined in, for instance Louis' specialist in siege warfare, Marshal Sebastian Vauban, who pleaded for a more just system of taxation, in order to relieve the suffering peasantry, doomed by the expense of Louis' wars, so heedlessly provoked. Interestingly Louis himself, on his deathbed, confessed to many of these charges.

During the eighteenth-century Enlightenment, writers continued to disagree about Louis XIV. Montesquieu and Saint-Pierre blamed him for the sufferings of the people. Voltaire, on the other hand, was devoted to the Sun King's memory:

> It seems to me that one can hardly view all his works and efforts without some sense of gratitude, nor without being stirred by the love for the public weal which inspired them. Let the reader picture for himself the condition today, and he will agree that Louis XIV did more good for his country than twenty of his predecessors.[5]

While Voltaire had a barely concealed agenda in praising Louis XIV – he enjoyed contrasting him with Louis XV – his familiarity with the world that Louis created must command respect.

Historians writing after the Revolution were, like the rest of us, influenced by the world they lived in, but perhaps especially so. Guizot, for instance, labouring to preserve the July Monarchy, hailed Louis XIV as a great architect of the French bureaucratic state. Lavisse the democrat, on the other hand, felt that Louis was consumed with pride and arrogance and that he betrayed France with his addiction to absolutism. Even in the military context, 'he had the abilities of a good staff officer, but neither the mind of a general nor the heart of a soldier'. In the twentieth century Roland Mousnier saw Louis XIV as a revolutionary social leveller, bringing the aristocracy down to the bourgeoisie in preparation for the coming of social democracy. Mousnier likewise stressed Louis' revolutionary creation of an administrative state. Pierre Goubert, on the other hand, is a distinguished example of the *Annales* school of French historians who emphasise social and economic factors severely limiting Louis' freedom of manoeuvre. Against this background, did the king *matter* so very much? Goubert concludes that, in a negative way, Louis certainly did matter, if only because of his addiction to war in pursuit of his own *gloire*. Despite his determination not to judge the Sun King, Goubert is refreshingly critical, especially for a Frenchman.

A number of Anglo-American historians have developed Goubert's approach by questioning the validity of the whole concept of absolutism.[6] Led by Roger Mettam, a number of meticulous researchers into the histories of outlying provinces have demonstrated the extent to which Louis ruled through attracting the cooperation of the governing classes. Instead of dominating the aristocracy by replacing them with the intendants, as used to be believed, and imprisoning the nobility at Versailles, Louis exploited clientage and patronage by establishing a community of interests between the crown and local big-wigs. Similarly, far from bullying the local estates and the parlements, the crown did a deal with them, preserving the interests of the office-holders who had responded to Mazarin's provocation by triggering the Fronde revolts that tore France apart (1648–53). In this context, 'absolutism' appears to be meaningless, or, as Nicholas Henshall has argued, a myth. David Parker, who accepts the reality of French absolutism, concedes that Louis XIV operated through compromise and concession. This revisionism has provoked a backlash. John Hurt has highlighted Louis XIV's successful aggression against the parlements, while John Lynn and Guy Rowlands have charted Louis' creation and domination of his huge army that gave him a considerable monopoly of violence within France. Anette Smedley-Weill claims that the intendants successfully imposed royal authority in the later part of the reign, although perhaps she underestimates the practical realities facing the crown, which has always been the essence of the revisionists' case. Here no biographer can duck the challenge to come down on one side or the other.

François Bluche certainly has no problem with taking sides. He wholeheartedly admires and defends the Sun King, adopting a frankly nationalistic deference towards a great French hero. Perhaps significantly, he mentions virtually no Anglo-American authors in his detailed and sympathetic treatment of the Sun King's reign. Bluche personifies the French inclination to assume that France's seventeenth-century rulers – his predecessors cardinals Richelieu and Mazarin as well as Louis XIV – were up to the job. To a great extent this French nationalist enthusiasm has concentrated on Louis' *cultural* conquest of Europe, going back to Chateaubriand who praised Louis rather than Napoleon as the enabler of civilisation: 'It is the voice of genius of all kinds which sounds from the tomb of Louis: from the tomb of Napoleon only the voice of Napoleon is heard.'[7] Is this fair to either Louis or Napoleon? 'We incorrigibly patriotic Frenchmen should not be in too great a hurry to proclaim a triumph of the French spirit', admits Pierre Goubert. Bluche, however, follows John Wolf and Ragnild Hatton in justifying Louis XIV's foreign policy as well, where one might think that the king was most vulnerable. Bluche claims that Louis' territorial acquisitions were fundamentally defensive. He blames William of Orange and the emperor Leopold for initiating the later wars in which Louis became involved. All that Bluche will concede by way of criticism is that Louis' religious policies were seriously flawed, 'inevitable rather than justifiable'.

A more balanced French work is J.-C. Petitfils' biography. He argues that Anglo-American revisionists have gone too far in rejecting absolutism. He establishes Louis' success in building up royal power, but he regrets that Louis ducked the challenges of reforming law and taxation. He points out that on his deathbed Louis accepted the charge of irresponsible war-making. On the other hand he acquits Louis of another of the charges against his excessive expenditure – being too fond of building.

Relatively speaking the cost was small, and the enhancement of French cultural prestige immense.

English historians no longer adopt the Whig tradition established by Macaulay, Trevelyan and Ogg in placing Louis XIV in an apostolic succession of absolutist demon-kings, threatening representative liberty with their frenetic aggression: Philip II, Louis XIV, Napoleon, Kaiser Wilhelm, Hitler … As long ago as 1906, Lord Acton recognised the Sun King's merits: 'Lewis XIV was by far the ablest man who was born in modern times on the steps of a throne. Few men knew how to pursue such complex political calculations, or to see so many moves ahead. He was patient and constant and unwearied.'[8] Geoffrey Treasure and Ian Dunlop broadly accept the revisionist picture of a king cleverly manipulating local aristocratic factions in the interests of France. Robin Briggs, while accepting Louis' considerable achievements against the general background of early modern France, believes that he could have done so much more had he been less of a blinkered conservative, a product of his age in the worst sense of the term. Louis' most recent English biographer, Anthony Levi, attributes the king's aggression to insecurity, based on his awareness that he was Mazarin's son, not Louis XIII's – a thesis he vigorously defends, but which other historians for the most part reject.[9] Antonia Fraser's study of Louis and his mistresses depicts Louis in an attractive light – a man whom his lovers adored every bit as much as he adored them.[10]

The books surveyed here, which are but a fraction of the works devoted to Louis XIV's reign, testify to the continuing fascination of the Sun King and the widely diverging conclusions reached both by contemporaries and historians. Indeed, the intrepid biographer must feel like the writer of the epistle to the Hebrews who was 'encompassed by a great cloud of witnesses'.[11] Nevertheless one 'must run the race that is set before us', which means facing the issues that in particular demand our attention.

So how powerful *was* the Sun King, whether one uses the term 'absolutism' or not? Was his foreign policy devised for his own glorification or in the true interests of France? How responsible was he for the massive loss of human life and physical suffering caused by the wars in which France was involved? Was Louis a reformer who modernised France so far as was possible in the circumstances? Can he take credit for the outflowing of French culture that dominated the civilised world? While there are few, if any, defenders of Louis' religious policies, can we at least understand what he was trying to do? As for the man himself, many historians from Lavisse to Briggs describe him as 'mediocre'.[12] Will that really do? What was he like as a human being? Was he basically a nice man if you *could* get to know him? What really lay behind the golden mask? Nobody seems to be quite sure.

Perhaps the road to salvation for the biographer is to become immured as much as possible in the seventeenth century. This is easier said than done. As Robert Darnton observes:

> Other people are other. They do not think the way we do. Nothing is easier than to slip into the comfortable assumption that Europeans thought and felt three centuries ago just as we do today – allowing the wigs and wooden shoes. We constantly need to be shaken out of a false familiarity with the past.[13]

This is well put. The word that sums up the problem is *mentalité* – the unwritten attitudes and assumptions that distinguish Louis XIV's contemporaries from our own time.

For instance, my opening vignette could have featured the Sun King seated on his *chaise percée,* surrounded by courtiers – incidentally, another scene also described by Visconti. Louis' *chaise percée* was his portable commode, his lavatory, on which he relieved himself while dealing with petitions and state business. This scenario may strike us as demeaning, distasteful and absurd – though if anyone could bestow dignity on the event it was Louis. But we live in the age of the lockable water-closet when privacy and self-withdrawal are the natural setting for 'calls of nature'. In the early modern period it was not so straightforward. A monarch required assistants to prepare his commode and enable him to be cleaned up while his urine and excrement were removed. As a recent historian remarks: 'In France the king was not even left alone when he relieved himself, as the "groom of the stole" attended to wipe the royal bottom'.[14] The point is that the more intimate the service, the greater the honour – that was the contemporary *mentalité.* So there was actually competition to assist the king on his *chaise percée,* however strange this may seem to us. As the novelist L.P. Hartley wrote in *The Go-between,* 'the past is another country – they do things differently there'. Our ambition must be to enter that strange, faraway world.

2

THE RISING SUN, 1638–61

Louis XIV was born at the royal palace of Saint-Germain-en-Lays on Sunday, 5 September 1638. He was, like the rest of us, the product of heredity and environment. Yet, as this chapter will show, this is not a straightforward story. Doubts have been cast on Louis' paternity, while the environment in which he grew up was so traumatic that it is a mystery how he emerged so well balanced and self-confident. He was supposedly the son of Louis XIII and Anne of Austria, but his parents were spectacularly incompatible, experiencing a distant, disfunctional relationship - hardly the basis for a stable home background.

Louis XIII was damaged goods. His physical health had been wrecked by his doctors, his mental health by his father, the popular and charismatic Henri IV. Not only was young Louis chastised mercilessly, but his father's assassination in 1610 thrust him at the age of eight into a vicious and unstable world which his mother, the regent Marie de Medici, failed to control. Patronised and ignored, Louis lacked self-confidence, forever hoping to emulate his father whose military and sexual exploits were legendary. 'Do I stink like my father?' he asked hopefully. He became an unhappy, inhibited, merciless ruler, whose nickname 'Louis the Just' reflected his people's respect rather than their affection. He forfeited popularity by accepting the domination of his chief minister, Cardinal Richelieu. Louis proved incapable of establishing any sort of a relationship with his wife, the Spanish princess Anne of Austria.

Although a result of Habsburg inbreeding, Anne was surprisingly normal and well balanced. But she lacked the sympathy and tact to win the affection and trust of her strange husband. After three miscarriages, a fourth pregnancy ended when Anne fell on the Louvre's highly polished floor during a romp with her court ladies – irresponsibility that Louis could not forgive. She infuriated her husband by flirting with the English king Charles I's favourite the duke of Buckingham. Fifteen years of cold war followed. Louis despised and terrified her, while she corresponded with his enemies, both at home and abroad. If she had known any state secrets, she would have betrayed them. Husband and wife seldom met socially, let alone sexually.

So Anne's production of a child within a fortnight of her thirty-seventh birthday in the twenty-third year of her marriage and sixteen years after her last pregnancy is indeed a mystery. The story goes that one stormy night in December 1637 the king was prevented from reaching his destination by floods and gales that swamped the roads and blew out his guards' torches. With nowhere else to go Louis found refuge at the Louvre where, as it happened, his wife was staying. His own suite was being refurbished, so that the only bed available was his wife's. A few weeks later she announced her pregnancy.

So much depended on the outcome that Louis committed the nation to the good offices of the Virgin Mary – a confusion of religion and politics for which he was rebuked by the austere theologian Saint-Cyran. As for Anne, in trouble for corresponding with her brother the Spanish commander in the Netherlands, she feared that only a male heir would prevent her being sent home in disgrace or exiled to a nunnery. She financed a church at her convent of Val de Grace in an attempt to get the Almighty on her side. It seems to have worked. The healthy, chubby boy, weighing nine pounds, to whom she eventually gave birth, was hailed as *le dieudonné* (the gift of God), the Sunday child, a miracle indeed. 'Painters, hurry to paint him while he is still little, because when he grows you won't manage it!', was a typical example of public enthusiasm.

The widespread rejoicing – bells, fireworks, bonfires, cannon and the like – was not quite unanimous. For the king's brother, Gaston, duc d'Orléans, the happy event was a disaster. The personification of irresponsible disloyalty, 'he entered into conspiracies from lack of will, and crept out of them for lack of courage' (Richelieu). He had looked forward to succeeding his sickly brother and marrying the queen. So he now insisted on meticulous inspection of the infant's masculinity and health, remarking that, while he was satisfied that the baby had emerged from his sister-in-law's belly, he was not so sure how it had got there.

Scurrilous rhymes circulating in Paris repeatedly questioned the baby's paternity. And Louis XIV's recent biographer, Anthony Levi, is convinced that Cardinal Mazarin, Anne's lover, future chief minister and possible husband, was the father. Levi believes that Louis XIII was impotent and that Anne's earlier pregnancies had also been the results of infidelity, for instance with Buckingham. He thinks that Louis XIV resembled Mazarin rather than Louis XIII in looks and ability and that his future 'insecurity' was due to his awareness that he was illegitimate. Levi has to do some fancy footwork with dates to get Mazarin in the right place at the right time. But his greatest challenge is to square Louis XIII's suspicious vindictiveness with acceptance of his wife's pregnancy. Levi has to argue that it was all Richelieu's idea and that he sold the plot to the king as the only way to defeat Gaston's ambitions and guarantee the dynasty's survival.[1]

Few historians to my knowledge have been convinced by Levi. The greatest stumbling block is how the story, if true, never progressed beyond the gutter tittle-tattle, which was no more credible than the pornographic nonsense about Marie Antoinette in the 1780s. Nor is it easy to square the story with Louis' adulatory references to Mazarin in his memoirs. Even so, there have been several examples of more or less certain royal illegitimacies. James I of England was widely believed to be David Rizzio's child, hence his brains – his supposed father Lord Darnley being virtually certifiable. 'Of course he's Solomon, he's David's son!' quipped Henri IV. Louis' Valois predecessor, Charles VII, was probably not the son of the mad king Charles VI whose wife was notoriously promiscuous. And there have been suggestions of dubious royal ancestry in modern times. Interestingly Louis' foreign minister, Loménie de Briennes, once drew his attention to a rumour that Richelieu was his father, prompting the magisterial reply: 'If I am Richelieu's son, I owe him even more than I do already. All that matters, however, is that I am king and the son of a very great queen.'

Whether or not historians have been too quick to dismiss Levi, he does attempt to answer a real question: how does one explain Louis XIV's aggressive and inconsistent behaviour, both as a man and as a statesman. 'Insecurity based on awareness of his own illegitimacy' – Levi's answer

– may be psychobabble based on dodgy history, whereas many would argue that losing his father early in life so that he became king in name only is a much better answer. Still, Levi highlights a problem that any biographer of the Sun King must address. On balance, I believe that there are more convincing explanations of Louis' conduct and that the 'official' version of Louis XIV's paternity is probably correct.[2]

So what did Louis XIV inherit from his parents? Actually he most closely resembled his Bourbon grandfather, Henri IV, displaying his sociability, sexual prowess, self-confidence and political skill. And with due respect to Levi, Louis XIV's swarthy complexion and prominent nose were typically Bourbon. He inherited his mother's good health and hearty appetite. Born with two teeth, he demolished eight wet-nurses, prompting the Swedish ambassador to remark, 'Let France's neighbours beware such precocious greed.' Let women beware too! From his mother he derived a passion for smart clothes and jewellery, and from her grandfather, Philip II of Spain, his conscientious capacity for hard work. He resembled both parents in their piety and love of music.

When we turn to environment there is no doubt that Louis XIV had a torrid childhood. The birth of an heir and the arrival of another miracle child two years later – Mazarin's doing again according to Levi – did not bring the parents any closer. Quite the reverse. Louis XIII detested his children, inevitably provoking their fear and distrust. In September 1640 when Louis was just two, his father wrote: 'I am most displeased with my son. As soon as he sets eyes on me, he yells as if he were looking at the devil and always cries for his mother.' The king's solution was to take the boys away from their mother – a proposal that reduced Anne to desperation. Little Louis had to be coached into being polite to his ogre of a father. In fact the two-year-old had to plead for forgiveness so as not to be taken away from his mother. No wonder that in later life Louis XIV seldom referred to his father, preferring to model himself on Henri IV.

When Louis XIII succumbed to tuberculosis and to his doctors' 'cures' ('I am one of those unfortunate people who are treated by the medical profession', he wrote), his elder son was officially baptised with Mazarin as godfather – two years early, due to his father's illness. 'What name have they given you?' whispered the dying man. 'I'm Louis XIV', replied the boy. 'Not yet – but you soon will be.' In the distance laughter could be heard. 'That will be the queen', Louis XIII wrongly surmised. In fact Anne was devastated by her husband's death. Although a lover of cleanliness, she nursed him through the malodorous tubercular diarrhoea that finally carried him off – or it may have been Crohn's disease that killed him.

Distrusting Anne's loyalty to France, Louis XIII tried to limit her freedom of manoeuvre by making her one of a regency council of five. But the four-year-old's first public engagement as king was to request the lawyers in the Parlement of Paris to overturn his father's will. Lifted on to a stack of cushions, often glancing anxiously at his mother, he managed to lisp his much-rehearsed lines: 'Gentlemen, I have come to see you so as to express my affection and goodwill towards my Parlement. My Chancellor will tell you my will.' The 'king's speech' that the chancellor read out requested the cancellation of Louis XIII's will in favour of Anne as sole regent – a proposal that the lawyers were glad to endorse, seeing here a welcome recognition of their own authority. They were well aware that across the Channel parliament – although a different institution from French parlements – had demolished Stuart monarchical power and was now making war on Louis' uncle, Charles I.

For eleven years authority was exercised on behalf of France's child king by two foreigners: Anne, the Spanish princess, and her chosen chief minister, the Sicilian careerist Giulio Mazarini – or Jules Mazarin as he was called in France. Privately conversing in Spanish, they navigated the French language and French politics with uneven success. On the face of it, for the next five years they played a weak hand badly. In truth it was never easy.

Mazarin was cleverer than Anne.[3] His charm and wit had fascinated Richelieu, whose client he became. 'The cabbage-chopper', Richelieu called him, referring to his not particularly aristocratic background. He was basically an adventurer, a gambler who cheated, an arriviste who in French eyes never arrived. Having originally made his career as a papal diplomat, Mazarin's strong suit was foreign policy. He devoted himself to bringing the long war between France and the Habsburg Austrians and Spanish to a satisfactory conclusion before the money ran out. He only half succeeded. His domestic policy was even less impressive. For instance, a noble uprising led by Henri IV's bastard, the duc de Beaufort, was survived with difficulty. While Richelieu would have persuaded Louis XIII to execute the ringleaders, Beaufort was merely imprisoned and indeed, to be fair to Mazarin, lived to be quite useful to the monarchy later on. Mazarin meanwhile was content to murder the French language. Peasants revolted against high taxation. Office-holders led by the parlements resented the creation of new posts purely for money-raising purposes. The fact was that, due to her hopelessly inadequate system of taxation, France was punching above her weight. The war seemed interminable. Total meltdown loomed.

It was against this fraught background that Louis XIV spent his first decade. Inevitably much passed him by. Secure in the love of his mother and Mazarin, his father/godfather/step-father, fortunate in his official tutor the kind-hearted Marquis de Villeroy and in his faithful valet de La Porte, he played soldiers, learned to ride, shoot, dance and listened to fairy tales. But we have already noted the demands made of him when he was still a toddler. It was a challenge for Anne to bring up her son both as a little child and as her king. Whereas she reverently knelt before him when her husband died, she never forgot her obligation to discipline him. We get occasional glimpses of this problematic anomaly. Once on a trip to Normandy the eight-year-old defied her authority. 'You will learn that you can be spanked in Rouen just as hard as in Paris', exclaimed his furious mother. Louis immediately apologised: 'Mama, please forgive me – I promise never to do anything but what you want.' There were tears of reconciliation.

Anne was anxious to promote Louis' superiority over his brother, lest Philippe turn into another Gaston. She dressed Monsieur (as the king's younger brother was always called) in girl's clothes to discourage any political or military ambitions, unintentionally encouraging his latent homosexuality. Louis demanded his brother's obedience even when the two boys were aged four and two. Actually they usually got on well enough, enjoying a normal relationship, every now and again scrapping and quarrelling. Once they fell out over Philippe's determination to eat stew during Lent. When Philippe's hair got splashed, he flung the whole dish at his brother. On another occasion La Porte intervened:

> The King insisted on sharing a small room with Monsieur. In the morning, when they woke up, the King without thinking what he was doing spat on his brother's bed, when his brother purposely spat back on the King's bed; and the King, rather cross, spat in his brother's face, and then his brother jumped on to the King's bed and pissed all over it; the King did likewise over his brother's bed; and then, as they both had run out of spit and piss, they began dragging the bed-clothes off each other, and then started to come to

blows. I tried to stop the King, but as I could not, I had to send for M. de Villeroy who read the riot act. Monsieur got much crosser than the King, but it was much more difficult to quieten the King than Monsieur.[4]

A significant and prophetic episode. Philippe throughout life easily flew off the handle, but quickly regained his good humour, whereas Louis had greater self-control, but brooded. Actually until his death in 1701 Philippe was the only person who was able to have a row with the king. Normally on affectionate terms, though Louis patronised and side-tracked his brother from any political responsibility, they sometimes shouted furiously at each other. Yet Philippe remained loyal. They were both devoted to their mother. Louis' relationship with Mazarin at this stage is less clear. La Porte loathed Mazarin and did his best to turn the king against him. Once the little boy saw Mazarin on the terrace at Compiègne surrounded by his hangers-on. 'There goes the Grand Turk!' he shouted.

In November 1647 Louis experienced the first of his many ordeals at the hands of the medical profession when he caught smallpox. Until well into the nineteenth century royal doctors in particular weakened and often killed their patients by bleeding and purging. On this occasion the nine-year-old narrowly survived three bleedings and a drastic purge. Indeed he lost consciousness for several hours. He nearly died, and toasts were drunk to 'King Gaston'. Anne nursed him throughout his ordeal. The child showed courage and patience. Louis flagged up his recovery by asking for his favourite white pony – a present from his god-father. The pony was duly brought into the bedroom. The patient finally proved stronger than his doctors deserved.

What were the effects of those first ten years? From his earliest conscious moments Louis must have been aware that he was special, though it must all have been bewildering at times. How can you explain to a two-year-old that to ensure his mother's political survival he must placate his royal father? What went through the four-year-old's mind when he was lifted onto those cushions before the Parlement of Paris? Louis learnt fast. He loved to hear the history of the French monarchy read to him, despising the feeble kings of the Merovingian period – he would *never* be like that! One of his heroes was Louis XI, the 'universal spider', who, in the pages of Louis' favourite author Philip de Comminges, out-manoeuvred his enemies, domestic and foreign, while he restored and enlarged France after the Hundred Years War. But the king he most admired was his grandfather Henri IV – *that* was the sort of king he was going to be. *If he ever got the chance!* For the French monarchy now faced the greatest domestic challenge between the end of the religious wars in 1598 and the revolution of 1789. This upheaval was the Fronde (1648–53).

THE FRONDE

A *fronde* was a catapult wielded by Parisian urchins who aimed stones at the windows of the rich. It might seem an appropriate name for a revolt that eventually failed due to the frivolity of its leaders. But it is also appropriate because it was a sport that could turn nasty and lead not only to broken glass but broken heads. And the Fronde justified its name by beginning in Paris. It spread unevenly and erratically to the provinces, flaring up in Rouen, Aix, Bordeaux. It was a chaotic, complex affair. Because its impact on the boy king was immense, shaping his attitudes and policies when he eventually came to power, we must briefly identify its causes, nature and consequences, while also establishing Louis' own role.

The Fronde was not wholly the fault of Louis' ministers, however inept. It was a delayed reaction to the foreign and domestic policies of Cardinal Richelieu. 'The great Armand' unquestionably strengthened the position of the monarchy, as the true founder of French absolutism. Furthermore he set in train France's replacement of Habsburg Spain and the Empire as the dominant power in Europe. Had he and Louis XIII lived a little longer they would quite possibly have had an excellent chance of imposing a favourable peace settlement. Arguably, on the other hand, Richelieu did well to die in 1642 before his birds came home to roost. He has a case to answer.

Richelieu's self-aggrandisement, combined with the exaltation of royal authority (historians refer to a 'duo-cephalic' or 'double-headed' regime), alienated the nobles. His brilliant exploitation of patronage to the benefit of his 'creatures' and his relations, fully justifying his claim to be 'the best uncle in history', infuriated those who were not his clients. His use of intendants (royal troubleshooters) annoyed France's 45,000 office-holders. Taxation to fund his expensive wars bore cruelly on the peasants whose inability to pay brought down the king's troops on their heads ('fiscal terrorism' is another valid piece of historians' jargon). His French army was an ill-organised mob, which beat up friend and foe alike, but apart from the occasional triumph such as Condé's brilliant victory at Rocroi in 1643 it proved incapable of beating the Spaniards. In David Parrott's words: 'From 1635 Richelieu was waging on an unprecedented scale a war which was beyond France's military capacity to bring to a successful conclusion.'[5] In other words, Richelieu bequeathed an unpopular regime incapable of winning an unaffordable war. As Roger Mettam observes, 'At the death of Richelieu in 1642, most subjects of Louis XIII were discontented with the government ... the situation which he [Mazarin] inherited was an impossible one.'[6] While historians unanimously admire Richelieu's statesmanship, one wonders if the costs were too high and if he really deserved the admiration he demanded.

Perhaps the answer is provided by a prominent *frondeur*, Paul de Gondi: 'Richelieu I disliked but respected; Mazarin I neither liked nor respected.' With all his mistakes and crimes, Richelieu was a man of stature. When Mazarin succeeded him as chief minister, sleaze replaced style. Richelieu was an inspired propagandist, especially on his own account, whereas Mazarin was a poor communicator. Richelieu was at least French. Furthermore, he would never have made Anne's and Mazarin's mistake when they *simultaneously* alienated the aristocracy, the peasants, the city of Paris and the government's most reliable supporters, the office-holders.

Government virtually came to a standstill in early 1648 when office-holders and taxpayers went on strike. New taxation had to be registered by the Parlement of Paris, or imposed by a *lit de justice* ('bed of justice') when the crown introduced measures against which the Parlement could only remonstrate. This Parlement of Paris must not be confused with England's Parliament. Throughout France there were several parlements, entitled to register laws and taxation. Of these the Parlement of Paris was the most important. But it differed from Parliament in that its members were not elected and so could not speak for the country in the same way that Parliament could. If there was a French equivalent it was the Estates-General, which was representative of the clergy, nobles and bourgeois. But it had not met since 1615 and would not meet again until 1789.

Nevertheless the Parlement of Paris was proud of its ancient right respectfully to offer suggestions to the government in times of crisis. In

January 1648 its advocate-general, Omer Talon, tried to explain to the queen regent the plight of the people, prompting the reply: 'Shut up! I don't want to listen to you.' When new taxes were introduced by a *lit de justice*, the nine-year-old king, who was recovering from the small-pox that had nearly killed him, forgot his lines and wept. Confrontation escalated in May when the various courts of office-holders produced the Act of Union, summarising the lawyers' protests. 'They are trying to make a republic within a monarchy', snarled Anne, while Chancellor Séguier pointed out English parallels where Parliament had imprisoned the king.

Historians have generally identified a European crisis in the 1640s, affecting Spain, Italy, the Low Countries, eastern Europe and Germany as well as England and France. Certainly events in Paris now echoed England. Condé had just won another victory at Lens, prompting Louis' observation that 'the gentlemen of the Parlement won't like that'. Anne exploited the good news by arresting her enemies, emulating Charles I's disastrous attempt in England to pluck six prominent opponents. It was equally counter-productive. Like Charles's coup, it was bungled. After the popular and eccentric lawyer Broussel – who donated his winnings to the poor – had been dragged from his supper table in his slippers, the getaway coach broke down so that he was recognised by passers-by. Paris erupted.

While the crowd roared and jeered round the Louvre, little Monsieur shed tears of panic even though his elder brother drew his sword to pro-tect him. The deservedly unpopular Chancellor Séguier was chased into a friend's house where he cowered in a broom cupboard. The queen's *bête noir*, Paul de Gondi, the future Cardinal de Retz and archbishop of Paris, had to broker a truce. He was a slightly absurd figure with a mon-umentally high opinion of himself, a combination of Mr Pooter and Mr Toad on whom the exceptional circumstances of the Fronde conveyed a spurious importance. Louis never forgot or forgave his presumption in imposing terms on the queen. Anne ground her teeth, released Broussel and summoned Condé. In January and February 1649 he besieged Paris and defeated Gondi's scratch force with contemptuous ease – 'a war of chamber-pots' Condé called it. An uneasy peace was concluded at Saint-Germain.

Paris, however, seethed with hatred of the government in general and Mazarin in particular – hatred expressed in the scurrilous poems known as the *Mazarinades*. This genre was launched by the poet Paul Scarron, whom we shall meet again. His *La Mazarinade* credited Mazarin with what the French were pleased to call 'the Italian vice'.[7] The queen was also lampooned. In July 1649 rioting printers saved Claude Marlot from the gallows. He had just published *la custode du lit de la reine* (the guardian of the queen's bed), containing the following: 'Townsmen, don't doubt it any more; it's true that he fucks her.'[8] As well as being accused of every imaginable vice, including raping the queen and buggering the king, Mazarin was alleged to have deliberately prolonged the war in order to remain in office and enrich himself. Worryingly he was compared to Marie de Medici's Italian favourite Concini, whose corpse was torn to pieces by a Parisian mob (1617) after Louis XIII had arranged his murder. Meanwhile, Parisians remained devoted to the king. Anne had twice removed him from their midst, but in order to prevent a third exodus Gondi surrounded the Palais-Royal in February 1651 thus enabling hundreds of the king's subjects to file through the royal bedroom to check that he was still there. They gazed at Louis, who pretended to be asleep while his mother kept watch like a tiger guarding her cub. The shame of it! It must have been as frightening for the little king as humiliating for the proud Habsburg princess.

Anne and Mazarin badly needed allies. Now, however, Condé sulked because his services were not sufficiently recognised. He was the quintessential *frondeur*, selfish, irresponsible, unreliable, all the more dangerous because he was also intelligent and well educated, a soldier of genius with serious intellectual interests. He stood for a real principle – that the way forward for France was not the royal absolutism that Richelieu had initiated but cooperation between crown and nobility. With bulbous eyes and hooked nose, he was a terrifying figure, stinking of mud and blood. When he intrigued against the crown with his brother Conti and brother-in-law Longueville, Anne and Mazarin went for broke. They arrested the three noblemen, imprisoning them at Le Havre. It was a gamble that failed. 'Alas, Madam, you have insulted princes of the blood', exclaimed the loyal parlementaire, Matthew Molé. The patronage ties that enabled the princes to dominate Normandy, Burgundy and the Loire valley operated in their favour. France proved ungovernable. Mazarin lost his nerve, released the princes and ran away into self-imposed exile. Condé now became impossible. Once when meeting Louis returning from a bathe in the Seine, instead of climbing down from his coach to greet the king as he should have done, he just nodded his head. Louis was speechless with rage at this calculated insult.

Now flourished the Fronde of the princes in which they lost the support of Parlement and fought against each other. For it soon became apparent that the various elements of the Fronde revolts were united only by hatred of Mazarin. His departure therefore proved to be a smart move. Once he had gone, the Fronde fell apart. All pursued their own selfish interests. Meanwhile Louis came of age in September 1651. The French people saw in him their hope for the future. For their suffering was inconceivable. Twenty thousand starving countrymen, reduced to cannibalism and decimated by plague spread by the rival armies, flooded into Paris.

Everywhere horrors multiplied. Gradually Mazarin's exactions were perceived as preferable to rape and pillage by undisciplined troops. In July 1652 Condé excelled himself. He fought his way into the city through the Faubourg Saint-Antoine. His success was made possible by the treachery of Gaston's daughter, la Grande Mademoiselle, a plain, stupid young woman who expressed her intention of marrying the king and becoming queen. She turned the guns of the Bastille on the royal army. 'She has killed her husband!' exclaimed Mazarin, who had prematurely returned from exile. Condé's troops massacred over a hundred Parisians and roughed up a priest who tried to mediate. Paris had had enough of him. Condé could see that the game was up and departed to serve the king of Spain, adding treachery to his misdemeanours. Louis and his mother received a rapturous welcome when they returned to the city. Mazarin tactfully went into exile again before returning in autumn 1652. Apart from a republican revolt in Bordeaux and persistent pamphlet warfare by Gondi's clerical supporters in Paris, the Fronde was over.

In more senses than one Louis grew up during the Fronde. In 1648 he was a tearful little boy. In 1653, though barely fifteen, he was a masterful young man. That he came through the ordeal says much for his resilience. Consider. Louis was twice chased out of his capital, forced to take refuge in unheated, unfurnished palaces in the depth of winter, jostled by crowds, his bedroom invaded while he pretended to be asleep, betrayed by his own family, bombarded by his cousin, insulted in pornographic verse. He had seen his mother humiliated, his godfather driven into exile, his troops opposed by princes of the blood. Yet he proved indestructible. Furthermore, Louis did more than survive. He was his supporters' trump card. He was the king. His dignity, poise and good looks won the day.

Why did the *frondeurs* lose? Many explanations have been advanced. They produced no Pym, no Cromwell. They developed no ideology, religious or political. Anne and Mazarin eventually got their act together, learning from experience, making concessions when necessary but acting decisively when the time came. But the key factor was Louis. He was clearly the only answer to dissension and violence. To be successful a rebellion has to target a royal, male, adult, culpable bungler. Charles I, Louis XVI, Nicholas II are classic examples.[9] A female regent and a foreign chief minister are too transient to perform this role, even though no one could be more unpopular than Mazarin. When the king is an attractive twelve-year-old – a poppet rather than a puppet king – you haven't a hope, provided that he keeps his nerve and plays his part. This Louis did, and he knew it. He completely wrong-footed the *frondeurs*. The welcomes he received while he toured provincial France with his mother culminated in his triumphant return to Paris.

Indeed, the Fronde was not all trauma for Louis. In many ways it was exhilarating. 'You have had your say: now go!' – to a deputation of parlementaires. 'I welcome you back and wish to forget your disloyalty' – this to his cousin the brilliant Marshal Turenne. 'It went like a dream' – this to his mother after he had cleverly inveigled Cardinal de Retz into the royal presence so that he could be arrested. He loved the company of his troops – for instance, when the queen and her son boosted the royal army's morale in the Loire valley and in Normandy. Louis' self-confidence was confirmed rather than wrecked by the Fronde.

Even so there remained disagreeable memories that in 1672 led Louis to expunge from the records all references to what had been a bumpy ride for the monarchy. Some of the conclusions he drew from the Fronde were mistaken. Louis took the wrong cue in blaming the Jansenists ('Catholic Puritans' sums them up). He failed to appreciate the loyalty of parlementaires such as Molé and Talon. It was a pity he turned against Paris, seldom visiting the capital for the rest of his reign. But he certainly took the right cue in his determination never to reward princes of the blood with roles in central government. He never forgot how disloyal they proved, to say nothing of their wives and mistresses. Never a man to forget names or faces, he remembered accurately those who had defied the crown. Louis' greatest political triumph was eventually to emasculate the nobility – an ambition fuelled by the Fronde.

THE LORD'S ANOINTED

In the aftermath of the Fronde the boy king's government exploited its success. For instance, despite its outrageous expense, Mazarin introduced Italian ballet at court to convey a king-worshipping, political message. Louis, who danced beautifully, enjoyed participating, especially when Monsieur, playing the role of the morning star, announced the arrival of his brother the Sun, anticipating the cult of the Sun King. More prosaically Louis visited his troops campaigning in the north-east. A particular purpose of this campaign was to drive the Spaniards 40 miles away from Reims where French kings were crowned.

Le sacré, as the ceremony was called, took place on 7 June 1654. It combined consecration and coronation. In other words Louis first acquired the special spiritual status that French kings uniquely enjoyed, involving confession, a quasi-sacerdotal anointing by the holy oil of Clovis and the reception of both the communion bread and wine normally reserved for priests. Then he was crowned by the bishop of Soissons (unfortunately the archbishop of Reims had not yet been priested), girded with the sword of Charlemagne and greeted by the lay and spiritual peers – '*Vivat rex in aeternum*' ('May the King live for ever'). Louis swore to protect his people, maintain peace at home and abroad and extirpate heresy. The fifteen-year-old behaved impeccably during the five-hour ceremony, which was only slightly spoilt by the absences of various *frondeurs* still in disgrace such as Gaston, Condé and Madamoiselle who maintained that she never wanted to go in the first place. But the queen-mother and her chief minister looked down with pride from their special balcony. The sun shone, the bells pealed, the crowds cheered, although the common people were not allowed into the cathedral until the end of the service, and then only into the nave in order to genuflect to their new king – a significant break with tradition.[10] An equally significant innovation was that the newly crowned king did not formally enter his capital. Louis never forgave Paris the Fronde.

Arcane mumbo-jumbo, it might seem to us. Or 'medieval rubbish', as Karl Marx called it. But *le sacré* meant a great deal to Louis and to his contemporaries. It established and represented the mystic union between crown, church and people. The French monarchy was believed to be uniquely Christian – hence the king's official titles 'the Most Christian King' and 'the Eldest Son of the Church'. Hence the king's alleged ability to cure scrofula by touching the sufferer. The king accepted obligations to defend and, when necessary, reform the church. As a Catholic he owed obedience to the pope, but this did not mean that the pope could interfere in the running of the French church. The church for its part accepted the king as its master, paying substantial voluntary taxes. The French people adored their king, believing him to be chosen by God and endowed with the necessary qualities at his coronation. His status was indeed almost divine and rebellion was a sin against God. The nobility saluted him as their sovereign and military commander. Theologians and philosophers vied with one another in hailing their newly crowned and anointed king.

All of these ideas were familiar to Louis but re-emphasised by the ceremony on 7 June. It was a magical experience for the serious and susceptible teenager: the gorgeous music, the swirling incense, the dignitaries of church and state kneeling at his feet – all this in the magnificent setting of the French high-gothic masterpiece where Joan of Arc had stood by her dauphin over two centuries earlier. For Louis it was the underwriting of his quasi-divine status. Contrast his hatred of republicanism and horror at the English treatment of his uncle, Charles I, who was forced to flee from Oxford disguised as a servant, who was defied to his face by Scottish theologians and English country gentlemen, and who was eventually tried and executed *in public*. Hence Louis' loathing of the Fronde.

Did he ever wonder whether God had really chosen him and had really equipped him to rule? While there were contemporaries who questioned monarchy, such doubts looked less plausible when the king was as charming, handsome and intelligent as Louis. He always had a high opinion of his own qualifications – at least until disaster struck at the end of the reign. In his memoirs – written for the instruction of the dauphin – he was to express his conviction that God always equipped kings with the necessary qualities. If he had ever had doubts as to divine favour, they would be knocked on the head by the moving and impressive ceremony in Reims cathedral. Geoffrey Treasure compares the physical and spiritual attributes of kingship to the dual nature of Christ as both man and God. It is a thought-provoking comparison in that Christians believe that Christ was without sin and therefore qualified for his Messianic role. But what if the king was inadequate? This question will occur during the history of Louis XIV's reign. But it was not perhaps in the forefront of anyone's mind on that June day.

A few months later Louis demonstrated his increasing self-confidence. In March 1655 the *surintendant de finance* Nicolas Fouquet persuaded the Parlement of Paris to reregister new taxes on legal documents. On 13 April, however, radical lawyers of the Chambres des Enquêtes decided to question the justice of these new demands. The various chambers of Parlement accordingly assembled for a joint session without informing the chief minister – provocative behaviour, if not downright illegal. The king and the chief minister were hunting stags and wild boar in the forest of Vincennes when the news came of this unexpected meeting. Louis rejected Mazarin's preference for caution, galloped the four miles into Paris and, dusty and sweating, still wearing his hunting jacket, high boots and grey hat, burst into the Gilded Hall. The astonished parlementaires were treated to the following rebuke:

> Everyone knows how much trouble your meetings have caused in my state and how many dangerous results they have had. I have learnt that you intend to continue them on the pretext of discussing the edicts which, not long since, were published and read in my presence. I have come here expressly to forbid you to do this which I do absolutely, and I forbid you, Monsieur le Premier President, to permit or tolerate this, whatever pressure Messieurs des Enquêtes may bring on you to do so.[11]

The parlementaires were stunned while their insultingly scruffy young king strode out of the chamber, brandishing his riding crop. The sixteen-year-old was clearly out of order and, when they complained, Mazarin was embarrassed. He typically opted for a fudged solution, persuading Marshal Turenne to request more money to meet the exceptional needs of the army, with which Parlement could comply without losing face. But the autocrat had shown his teeth. It was on this occasion that Louis was supposed to have made his most famous remark: 'L'état c'est moi.' He never said it. But crowned and consecrated, his self-confidence was supreme enough for him to have spoken with such self-assertion.

A poignant contrast between theory and fact so often reminded early-modern rulers that, however absolute they may have considered themselves to be, they were only too mortal. In July 1658 Louis had another joust with the medical profession. After inspecting his troops at the siege of Mardyck he caught 'marsh fever' from the atmosphere around the fortress, caused by partially buried corpses rotting in the sunshine. It was probably typhoid. Louis was bled and bled again, purged and given emetics to make him vomit. He felt so ill that he commanded Mazarin to tell him if he was about to die. But once again Louis' robust constitution triumphed over his doctors, to the immense relief of nation and court, but especially of Mazarin's niece, Marie Mancini, Louis' current girlfriend. Bluche uncharitably thinks that she saw her own fortune evaporating, but Louis was touched by the girl's grief. Actually she was by no means her uncle's favourite relative.

LOVE AND MARRIAGE

The cardinal's foreign policy was at last coming to fruition. The war between France and Spain resembled two exhausted pugilists collapsing into each other's arms. If anything the Spaniards had the upper hand, in 1656 winning a significant victory when, led by Condé, they relieved Valenciennes. But Mazarin, appreciating that France on her own could not deliver a knockout blow, brought in the New Model Army from across the English Channel. In the 1630s Richelieu had employed the Protestant king of Sweden, Gustav Adolf, to harry the Catholic Habsburgs. Now in March 1657 Mazarin did a deal with the republican, ultra-Protestant, regime of Cromwell, the regicide. What on earth did the pious young king make of his godfather's *real politique?* As a budding military expert he would certainly appreciate the excellence of the red coats. They needed twice the rations of their French counterparts, but helped Turenne win the battle of the Dunes (14 June 1657). Louis entered Dunkirk – and then handed it over to Cromwell. The Spanish were now sufficiently sobered to discuss terms for a general peace settlement.

But what terms? For Mazarin there was only one scenario – the marriage between Louis and Philip IV's daughter, Marie Thérèse. Despite the indisputable fact that Louis was the most eligible bachelor in Europe, the Spaniards played hard to get. Mazarin adopted a subtle ploy by inviting the Duchess of Savoy and her daughter Marguerite to meet the French court and be vetted by Louis and his mother. They all travelled to Lyon for this purpose. The ploy worked. Philip IV shouted: 'It cannot be allowed to happen!' – and promptly opened negotiations for his daughter's betrothal. Having served her purpose, Marguerite was packed off home with some jewellery as a consolation prize. Actually she would have made a good queen, for she was intelligent, amiable and pleasant looking. But Louis had an even better idea. For he was head over heels in love.

Louis had already been introduced to the joys of sex by Mme de Beauvais, his mother's aristocratic laundry woman, who had met the sixteen-year-old coming out of his bath and had bundled him into a sewing room where she took his virginity. Already shop-soiled, she also gave him gonorrhoea – or it could have been somebody else because there was now no stopping Louis, though his doctors tactfully pretended to be astonished at his infection. In truth, he was highly sexed, inevitably attractive to women (he *was* the king) and soon had regular mistresses.

But his love for Marie Mancini was different. If her portraits are reliable, she was pretty as well as clever and well educated. Louis appreciated her mind, her humour, her sensitivity, as well as her looks. In fact they probably never had sex. Louis knew that this was the girl with whom he wished to spend the rest of his days. He told Anne and Mazarin that he was the king and he had decided to marry her, so they had better get used to the idea. Both were horrified. Initially Anne accused Mazarin of complicity: 'I do not believe that the king is capable of such baseness [*sic*]. If he *were* to think of it, all France I warn you will revolt against you, and I will put myself at the head of the rebels to restrain my son.' But Anne was unfair to Mazarin, however tempting such a misalliance must have been for the old scoundrel. In truth, he wanted his nieces to marry well, but surely not *that* well. And the Spanish match represented the consummation of all that he had striven for. His letters to Louis prove this:

> God has established kings to watch over the ease and preservation of their subjects and not to sacrifice them for their own passions; and when such unhappy princes have appeared, they have commonly been abandoned by Divine Providence.[12]

With considerable disloyalty to his niece, Mazarin compared her unfavourably and, alas, inaccurately with Marie Thérèse: 'One may say that the Person you dote on comes nowhere near the beauty, either of mind or body, of the Princess who is to be your spouse.' And for good measure he alleged that his niece was carrying on with another man. Louis was too intelligent to believe these slurs or to take Mazarin seriously when he asserted that 'nothing is capable of hindering me from dying of sadness, should I see a person who is so closely related to me causing you so much mischief and damage'. 'Do as you like', Louis heartlessly replied, 'I shall find someone else to replace you.' Mazarin wrote to Anne in despair about the apparently unconquerable obstinacy and folly of *le Confident*, as they called Louis.

The lovers lingered in each other's company as long as they could. But at last Louis faced up to his destiny. They parted tearfully in the Louvre courtyard. Marie sobbed: 'You love me, you are the king, and yet you weep and I must go.' Louis indeed was distraught. How could he appreciate his 'official' bride when he saw her for the first time a few weeks later? While Louis was always polite and self-controlled on major state occasions, it must have been very difficult for him. For Marie Thérèse could hardly have been less like Marie Mancini.

The two courts met on the Isle of Pheasants in the middle of the Bidassoa, which divided Spain from France. Both parties remained in the half of the room that was theirs. The French party was far more informal, loquacious and spectacularly dressed than the sober Spaniards. Anne rushed forward to embrace her brother Philip whom she had not seen for forty-five years. But he coldly refused to permit such vulgar and demonstrative affection. Nor was Louis allowed to meet his bride. The nearest approach that etiquette permitted was for him to stand in the doorway. 'What a beautiful door!' the Infanta coyly remarked. Then Louis enjoyed showing off his horsemanship along the river bank while the Spaniards admired him from their barge.

Eventually the happy couple were officially introduced. The scene was captured by Le Brun's tapestry. The two kings are seen politely greeting each other. But the centrepiece was Marie Thérèse. She was a dumpy young woman with an unflattering hairstyle and poor teeth. She did not look very bright, glancing apprehensively at her unsmiling father. She was totally unprepared for her role as queen of France, intellectually still a child, a virgin in mind and body. Nobody had thought to teach her to speak French. The diarist Mme de Motteville thought that her clothes were 'quite horrible'. Her *pièce de résistance*, which fascinated the French, was a vast farthingale of a kind that French women had discarded half a century ago. Mme de Motteville called it 'a monstrous contraption, nearly circular, looking as though a number of barrel hoops had been sown inside the skirt, only barrel hoops are round whereas the Infanta is flattened at the front and at the back, widening out at the sides ... when she walks it goes up and down'.[13] Soon Maria Thérèse typically did the stupidest thing possible. She fell hopelessly in love with her husband.

The French were equally unimpressed by her father whom they thought stiff and pompous. Austere and careworn, Philip IV had spent half his life with prostitutes, the other half at the foot of the cross. Apparently he had only laughed three times in his life, and this was not one of them. Philip's digestion was reputedly so delicate that he had to resort to a wet nurse. But he did not gratify French curiosity by having a snack. He was only slightly more robust than Mazarin, who hovered in the background, desperately ill, but with the satisfaction of knowing that his life's work was done. Louis' radiant good health was positively indecent.

After two wedding ceremonies, one at Fuentarabia in Spain and the other at Saint Jean de Luz in France, Philip wept when he parted from his daughter. Marie was even more upset – and she was right to be. She is one of the saddest figures in Louis' reign. Years later she was to maintain that she had not spent a single happy day since leaving Spain, though this was a slight exaggeration. Louis was at first an ardent lover. 'Time for bed!' he exclaimed immediately after the wedding supper. 'It is too early', replied Marie, looking with pleading eyes at her mother-in-law. But they were soon officially bedded, and seemed happy next morning. The journey north through a welcoming, smiling land was an opportunity for Louis to show off his bride before their triumphal entry into Paris. Mazarin was too sickly to take part, so he and Anne watched from Mme de Beauvais' balcony. Another spectator was the widow of the poet Scarron, the inventor of the *Mazarinades.* Her praise was unstinting of the young king's demeanour. 'I believe that nothing so beautiful could possibly be seen and that the queen must have gone to bed last night very contented with the husband whom she has chosen.' Marie was not to be contented for long.

THE DEATH OF THE PILOT

Utterly exhausted, crippled with gout and stone, Cardinal Mazarin went downhill fast, dying on 8 March 1661. Badly frightened by a fire in the Louvre on 6 February, he shuffled round his picture gallery muttering to himself: 'Must I really leave all this behind?' Famous 'last words'? Well, not quite, for on his deathbed he whispered, 'the hour of mercy, the hour of mercy'. Some would say that he needed mercy. 'There goes the second cardinal,' was one satirical comment, 'heaven grant that there isn't a third!'

How should one rate Mazarin's services to the French monarchy in general and to Louis XIV in particular? Was Mazarin merely a stop-gap between Richelieu and Louis XIV, the two giants of French absolutism? Like Richelieu, Mazarin held power for eighteen years. Arguably he was the pivotal figure in the international development of seventeenth-century France. He negotiated the Treaty of Westphalia, which registered France's triumph over the Austrian Habsburgs, and the Treaty of the Pyrenees, which marked France's replacement of Spain as the dominant western European power. Furthermore Mazarin presided over the League of the Rhine, which safeguarded western Germany from Habsburg encroachment, and negotiated the Treaty of Oliva, which brought peace in the Baltic. Holland and England were already France's allies, so the country was at peace with its neighbours. Strategically Mazarin dealt Louis a strong hand.

But his achievements at home were mixed. Certainly France survived the Fronde. When king and cardinal subjugated Marseille, Louis insisted on entering though a specially created breach in the walls to indicate his triumph over rebellion. The Jansenists were humiliated. Condé abandoned the Spaniards and pleaded for his sovereign's pardon. Domestic reforms, however, were subordinated to the financial demands of Mazarin's foreign policy. The peasants were overtaxed and impoverished. Agriculture remained backward. Royal government was still handicapped by 45,000 office-holders. At Mazarin's death, the crown was 451 million livres in debt (Colbert's calculation). Mazarin's 'creatures', Le Tellier, Fouquet and Lionne, were able ministers, but they responded to events rather than controlled them. Louis exaggerated when he claimed in his memoirs that 'disorder reigned everywhere'. But France's recovery was slow and incomplete.

Louis must have been aware that to an increasing extent Mazarin was a liability. The French hated him especially for his greed. Whereas Richelieu's fortune had been considered excessive at 22 million livres, Mazarin's 39 million was obscene. A nobleman at the court of the Saxon king Ethelred the Unready had been nicknamed 'Styreona', the

'Accumulator'. It would have fitted Mazarin. Abbeys, offices, jewels, pictures, medals, cash – all were swept into his insatiable maw. He ordered the French representative at Whitehall, who was supposed to defend Charles I's interests during his trial, to look out for bargains when the royal collection of pictures came on the market, and he sold selections of the *Mazarinades*. On his deathbed Mazarin handed over his fortune to the king. Louis maliciously delayed the expected response for a whole day before returning the gift to its relieved donor. So the accumulator died a happy man.

While Treasure attributes Mazarin's greed to insecurity caused by his humble origins,[14] the French made no such concession. They could not forgive such a low-born foreigner for exploiting power so shamelessly. Maybe Mazarin benefited France in the long term, but in the short term the king risked unpopularity by tolerating the old scoundrel. Indeed, Mazarin's survival can be seen as a triumph for the crown in that its critics were defied by the retention of the chief minister. Furthermore, Mazarin infuriated those same critics by bringing his foreign policy to a successful conclusion. He could congratulate himself on his achievements at home and abroad, which he now bequeathed to his godson. One recalls the Kaiser's intention to let Bismarck 'snuffle on for a few months before I get rid of him'. Louis was not so callous or ungrateful, however popular the dismissal of Mazarin would have been. Perhaps he appreciated all that Mazarin had taught him.

In Treasure's words Louis was 'Mazarin's masterpiece'. For the last eight years of his life Mazarin coached Louis in statecraft. The master tutored his pupil in one-to-one sessions; he welcomed Louis to council meetings and the two travelled together to inspect the army or reduce recalcitrant centres of opposition. The relationship was based on mutual respect and affection, possibly homosexual on Mazarin's part.[15] Mazarin was proud of his pupil's progress: 'He is worth four kings and a man of integrity as well', he wrote to Marshal Gramont. And to Louis himself: 'It depends on you to become the most glorious king the world has ever seen, God having given you all the necessary qualities – including deceitfulness.' Mazarin encouraged his pupil to believe that men are actuated only by fear, pride and greed. He encouraged Louis to regard foreign affairs as the king's priority, while he commended to him Jean-Baptiste Colbert as the expert who would sort out the home front – or so Colbert alleged. Louis recorded his gratitude to Mazarin for advising him to employ a team under his own direction rather than appoint another chief minister.

Louis was obsessed with the danger of becoming an idle king, like the Merovingians. He had his own ideas, many of them the reverse of those of the two cardinals. Recent research stresses Louis' innovations. For instance, Mark Potter shows how Louis substituted a subtle policy of joint manipulation of the spoils with privileged elites in contrast to the confrontation provoked by Richelieu and Mazarin.[16] We know from Louis' memoirs how he longed for the day when he would rule alone, a prospect he regarded with understandable apprehension but also with excitement. 'Some years therefore having rolled by, the state of general peace, my marriage, my authority firmly established, and the death of Cardinal Mazarin constrained me no longer from putting into execution of the hopes and fears which I had entertained for so long.'[17]

One young, inexperienced princeling responsible for 20 million souls inhabiting the most powerful state in the world – it was enough to make one thoughtful. Still, Louis records how thrilled he was at last to have the opportunity of proving that he really was up to the job. The speed with which he acted almost before Mazarin's body was cold suggests how eagerly he had looked forward to putting his ideas into practice. Contemporaries and historians have been impressed by the way Louis slid over into the driving seat. Ian Dunlop argues that 'the apparent ease with which Louis took over the running of the state machine the day after Mazarin's death is the strongest evidence that he had already learnt a lot about it'.[18] This was partly his debt to Mazarin. But it was not the whole story. Louis XIV deserves credit for the way he had emerged from his testing apprenticeship during the Fronde and its aftermath.

If he was not quite in the same class as his cousin Condé, the great commander whose 'genius could dispense with experience' (Voltaire), he must be one of the most gifted, the most attractive, the most promising rulers in history at the moment of coming to power. Portrait painters depict a handsome young man of average height, with a slim figure, a complexion only slightly marred by smallpox, flowing hair and a cool, self-confident gaze. He possessed a swarthy masculinity, obviously very attractive to women, which became more Semitic with age, recalling his mother's Spanish descent from 'a beautiful Jewess'. He had a quick mind, an excellent memory, plenty of common sense, robust health, the capacity to be formidable when necessary, manifold artistic and sporting talents, plenty of self-confidence at a superficial level, charm in abundance and the capacity to learn from experience. He was a superb horseman. On the dance floor and in court ballets, he was a lovely mover. He was naturally courteous. He had an excellent grasp of spoken French, expressing himself concisely and wittily so that people treasured his bon mots.

With whom can one compare him? The young Henry VIII? François I from French history, Gustavus Adolphus from the seventeenth century? If you will forgive the anachronism, J.F. Kennedy or Tony Blair from more recent times? Harold Wilson – another possible candidate – remarked that a week in politics is a long time. Louis XIV's personal rule lasted fifty-four years – a very long time indeed in which to experience happiness and success, heartbreak and failure. In March 1661 it was all to play for. Time would tell if he was up to the job. But the omens were propitious. Like J.F.K. he was 'a hell of a candidate'.

3

THE KING AND HIS SUBJECTS

A MAGNIFICENT INHERITANCE

At Louis XIV's coronation in Reims cathedral on 7 June 1654, the bishop of Soissons placed a ring on the king's third finger. It was a very pretty ring, donated by the queen mother because the treasury could not afford so expensive a bauble. It was actually a rather important bauble, symbolising the marriage between Louis and his people. As in a marriage service, the two parties – monarch and subjects – entered into obligations. Louis XIV received the homage of France's temporal leaders. The emphasis on weapons, uniform and military virtues emphasised that this was a military occasion, when Louis accepted his duties as a warrior 'to drive out the enemy' and his nobles promised to support him in this task. The coronation was also a religious service in which 'The Most Christian King' undertook 'to extirpate heresy, to re-unite his subjects and to attach them to the steadfastness of the Catholic faith'; in other words, to terminate the Huguenot problem satisfactorily. As for his people's physical, moral and cultural welfare, Louis promised to keep the peace and dispense justice. He committed himself to the *soulagement* of his subjects; that is to say, the guaranteeing of their happiness, prosperity and lifestyle. They for their part accepted the duties of a wife to her husband, which in a male-dominated society meant obedience.

How effectively were these obligations fulfilled by king and subjects? This chapter establishes Louis' attitudes towards the French people and their needs, and their response to their monarch. What could they reasonably expect from him when his personal rule began? What could he expect of them? Only after studying Louis' foreign and religious policies and assessing the social and economic situation at the end of the reign (1 September 1715) shall we be in a position to answer fairly the crucial questions as to what was achieved by the Sun King. We shall then discover what sort of a husband Louis had been to his mystic bride, the people of France, and how they responded. How successful had Louis been during his long reign in achieving his subjects' *soulagement*? What reasons had Louis for being grateful for his people's loyalty and the French for being appreciative of their God-given king? Had basking in the Sun been an enjoyable and enriching experience?

A quick answer is that there was no reason why it should not have been. France is and was blessed with a benign climate. It was a fertile land, needing attention here and there, but basically one of the most productive in Europe. Corn, wine and oil abounded. There were plenty of fish in France's rivers, in the Mediterranean and in the Atlantic, lapping at her coasts. France's forests were adequate, only requiring disciplined management so that unhealthy trees could be uprooted and the most promising planted and nurtured. French oak, however, was average to poor in quality, which, combined with deficiencies in French ship-building methods, meant that France was at best on even terms with her Anglo-Dutch rivals. But there was never an absolute lack of timber. It was all to play for.

Louis XIV expressed appreciation of his good fortune when he succeeded Mazarin. The account which he wrote for his son is fascinatingly revealing. Anthony Levi writes: 'The *Mémoires* are patently sincere. What they chiefly show is Louis' need to justify himself to himself, and the extent of his self-deception.'[1] This is fair comment up to a point in that Louis clearly meant what he wrote. He was 'helped' by distinguished ghost-writers such as Paul Pelisson. But his memoirs do indeed ring true, not least because they are so naively self-satisfied and self-congratulatory. Because he knows it all, he is happy to instruct his son. That having been said, what emerges with regard to Louis' perception of his inheritance?

Louis famously wrote that 'all was confusion', when he succeeded the cardinal, his godfather and chief minister. But that was obviously not the whole story. Without any self-deception, he faithfully records the power vacuum in western Europe that was so much to France's interest.

He acknowledged his room for manoeuvre when it came to controlling his ministers. And he was well aware of the amounts of money to which the crown was entitled, but was not necessarily receiving. During his troubled teens Louis had travelled over the length and breadth of France, sometimes as a warrior-king, sometimes as a fugitive from his own rebellious subjects. So he knew France and was aware of its potential wealth and prosperity. And he knew his subjects – volatile, aggressive but fundamentally generous and loyal. All in all, he was aware that he had inherited a strong hand. He believed that God had given him all the necessary qualities in order to play it well – though there was indeed as much self-deception here as self-awareness.

WHO *WERE* THE FRENCH?

We cannot begin to answer questions about Louis' relationship with his people before establishing what we mean by 'the French'. This might seem an obvious question, but in truth Louis' problems, his successes and his failures cannot be assessed until the French people are identified. Confusion will occur if it is not appreciated that 'the French' were not a monolithic entity. They were divided geographically, politically and socially. These divisions radically affected the Sun King's priorities and attitudes towards his subjects.

First, there were a lot of them. The marriage contract between Louis and his people was, to say the least, between numerically uneven parties. There was only one king, whereas in 1661 there were probably around 18 million people living in what was then France. Clearly they would take some governing! This was far more than the populations of rival powers such as contemporary England. The total population of the British Isles perhaps reached 9 million at the end of the seventeenth century, Spain 6 million, Portugal 3 million, Holland 2.5 million. This French preponderance was highly significant in both military and economic terms. It meant a huge reservoir of military and naval recruitment, a vast source of strength for Louis' campaigns in an era of mass armies equipped with musket and bayonet, sword and pike, as opposed to bombs, torpedoes and tactical nuclear weapons. All those people were also the potential creators of wealth. In the seventeenth century's labour-intensive economy, endless reserves of ploughmen, grape pickers, weavers and sheep shearers guaranteed prosperity, provided that demand and supply could be satisfactorily related. If this was not achieved and the economy nose-dived for this or any other reason, it was a sobering thought that all those people had to be fed. In an agricultural economy, a recession did not necessarily lead to mass unemployment. Rather, the poor simply got poorer and more hungry. If they were not fed, they would lose their affection for their 'husband', the king. They might even rebel, forgetting their loyalty to 'France'.

Indeed, were these 18 million people *French* and what was their commitment to *France* and her glorious ruler? In an age of slowly developing nationalism, most dwellers in what is now present-day France, living and dying as they did within sound of their local church bells, felt loyalty first of all to their village, at the most to their local district (their *pays*). If the wider world intervened, they related to their nearest town – or conceivably to their province. Their lack of loyalty to the nation might become a live issue indeed if they were required to make sacrifices for their king or if they were involved in a protest movement against taxes imposed by the government in Paris, which could escalate into open revolt. In such cases they were far more aware of themselves as inhabitants of Normandy, Brittany, Languedoc or Quercy. Many outlying areas had only recently been incorporated into 'France', notably Burgundy and Brittany during the fifteenth century, and territories acquired as a result of the wars against the Habsburgs during the sixteenth and seventeenth centuries – for instance, in Flanders and on the Mediterranean seaboard. Furthermore, inevitably in an age when cartography was in its infancy, there was doubt as to the exact size of France. Once when Louis inspected some brand-new maps produced by the Academy of Science he was mortified to discover that his lands were not as great as he had thought, so that he was obliged to congratulate his cartographers on a triumph that had eluded his enemies.

National unity was challenged by local language, local tolls and local laws. Language was a crucial issue. Especially poorly educated peasants would speak their local tongue, incomprehensible to a Parisian or, for that matter, another peasant from a different locality. Bretan, Occitan, Provençal, Basque were all separate languages, spoken by at least 30 per cent of the king's subjects. Inevitably this made it hard for the king to explain his policies to the majority of his subjects and for church leaders to communicate with most of their parishioners. When the rebellion in

Brittany of 1675 was repressed, Mme de Sévigné heard the defeated peasants shouting 'mea culpa!' – 'the only French they knew'. Richelieu, the founder of the Académie Française, designed to reform and popularise the French language, knew what he was doing. As the supreme realist, he appreciated the role of language in uniting a country. Local tolls meant that there was no such thing as a national economy, simply a haphazard collection of local economies. The more remote and independent provinces, the *pays d'états*, were represented by their estates or by their parlements, both institutions dedicated to the defence of local laws and privileges, especially against the crown. Even the *pays d'election*, which were more open to direct control by the crown, needed careful handling. Local laws made a shambles of any attempt to create a national legal system. What possible steps could Louis take to redress this baffling and anomalous situation?

While the king had an immense mountain to climb if he was to be accepted as the leader of the nation by all his subjects, there was paradoxically a considerable groundswell of royalism to be exploited. The French – despite their various geographical divisions and differing interest groups – were a king-loving nation. They typified a pronounced and widespread early-modern inclination to blame ministers when disasters occurred and trust that only the king could save them. This was believed to have happened when, for example, the Valois kings drove out the English at the end of the Hundred Years War (1453). While approximately one-tenth of the population was Protestant, the Catholic majority accepted the claims of their kings to be uniquely favoured by God, anointed with the oil of Clovis and thereby enabled miraculously to cure sufferers from scrofula, known as the king's evil. Even the Protestants had been consistently loyal during the Fronde, fully believing St Paul's instruction's to obey the civil rulers even if they persecuted God's elect. The question therefore was, could Louis XIV effectively appeal to this latent goodwill towards the monarchy so as to win support for his unifying, proto-nationalistic policies, despite the geographical, cultural and historical forces defending local against national interests?

THE ESTATES

France was not only divided geographically but socially and economically. There were three estates – clergy, nobility and everyone else. It is historically accurate to separate the French into estates or orders rather than classes, in that money controlled people's positions in society less than in a classically Marxist context, where class based on cash is paramount. Nevertheless, money was essential if a nobleman was to thrive in the style that was expected of his exalted rank, while everyone else at least had to live. What were the relations between the king and his three orders – church, nobility and the rest? Were these orders a source of strength or weakness to the crown? Could the king play them off against each other, appealing to their greed for promotion, status, but above all cash?

Louis XIV's relationship with the first estate, the French church, is a complex story, addressed in Chapter 8. So far as the situation in 1661 was concerned, all that needs to be said here is that king and church were well aware of the support each could derive from the other, while at the same time remembering occasions in the past when they had been at cross purposes. During the Fronde, for example, the archbishop of Paris, Cardinal de Retz, had headed the opposition to the crown, while hundreds of his supporters among the Parisian clergy had mounted what was known as the Ecclesiastical Fronde. Louis XIV relied on money from the church, the *don gratuit*, which the clergy voluntarily offered on the unwritten assumption that it was more than they would have liked but less than they could afford. Here again there were opportunities for disagreements and hard bargaining.

Louis expected the ecclesiastical authorities to cooperate in the appointment to bishoprics of the king's aristocratic favourites. He relied on the church to celebrate his military victories and in general disseminate royal propaganda from the pulpit. The church expected the king to defend it from papal interference. The majority of clergy supported the king in his campaign against Jansenism, a heterodox movement within the Catholic church that Louis and the more conservative churchmen detested. But a significant minority of French clergy were Jansenist. There was more or less total agreement, however, with regard to the Huguenots. Any steps that the king took to reduce the influence and status of the Huguenots – the 'So-called Reformed Religion' – would be supported by virtually all French Catholics. On the face of it, the Most Christian King had little to fear and much to hope for from his ecclesiastical subjects, just as they admired and respected their pious and orthodox king. Rumours of his sexual peccadilloes might disturb the more prudish, but at least they were the uncomplicated, heterosexual sins committed by Louis' much-loved grandfather, Henri IV.

The second estate consisted of the nobility of the sword and of the robe. The sword, as its name implied, consisted of families who had distinguished themselves on the battlefield and had been ennobled as a reward. The more remote in time the ennoblement, the better – preferably going back to the fourteenth century. The robe consisted of families that had served the crown as administrators and lawyers. Many of these civil servants had earned the crown's gratitude over three or four generations, and had been ennobled as a result. On the other hand many 'robins' had bought their positions when the crown badly needed hard cash. In 1661 there were over 46,000 venal office-holders, far more than were really needed. These were headed by around 3,000 families of the robe nobility. There was ample opportunity for the king to play off robe against sword, as the latter resented the former's claim to be noble at all. An example of this resentment was the survival of duelling, officially outlawed but still prevalent as a way of settling quarrels, which the sword preferred to going to law, thus subordinating themselves to despised lawyer members of the robe. Physical courage, furthermore, was the unmistakable mark of the true aristocrat. To refuse a challenge was an admission of plebeian blood, just as it was ignoble to fight a notorious coward.

Louis XIV needed the loyalty of both kinds of nobles. His success in obtaining this is one of the major political triumphs of his reign. He never made the mistake that his mother and her chief minister Cardinal Mazarin had made when they provoked the Fronde by alienating the robins, and then the sword. As for the sword, Louis never forgot the disloyalty and irresponsible trouble-making of prominent aristocrats during his minority. He did not trust them. Hence his adamant refusal to tolerate members of the sword in his government, even if they were princes of the blood – a decision that caused resentment from such snobs as the duc de Saint-Simon.

But Louis was a snob too. He was himself a nobleman through and through, approving the rules against involvement in trade, and supporting the procedure known as *dérogeance* by which a breaker of the rule would lose his title. Louis shared his nobles' love of war. He set the tone for their belief in the importance of 'style'; that is to say, behaving like a gentleman in such matters as dress, expenditure on buildings and willingness to incur debt. This basic sympathy was partly responsible for Louis' success in retaining his nobles' support. In 1661, however, both sides studied each other with caution. Louis alarmed the nobles by backing his 'robin' minister Colbert when he launched a rigorous inquiry into genuine or bogus claims to noble status – a matter not just of prestige but of cash as genuine nobles were immune from taxation. Noblemen who survived this interrogation were gratified to see their order become even more exclusive. There was alarm too, however, when Louis empowered members of the Parlement of Paris to prosecute violent lawbreakers among the nobility of the Auvergne. By and large Louis got it right, avoiding the extremes of pandering to noble prejudices on the one hand and on the other offending them with gratuitously tough discipline. When he went to war in 1667 and again in 1672, many of his nobles loved him for it. He was their leader, never happier than when among his happy paladins.

The third estate was theoretically everybody else apart from the clergy and the nobility. To a considerable extent, however, it consisted of the bourgeoisie to the exclusion of the rural and urban poor who constituted about 80 per cent of the population and were wholly unrepresented politically, for example when the Estates-General met. The bourgeoisie had to justify their status by holding prestigious office or pursuing suitable trades. The majority lived and worked in the towns, making their fortunes out of management or trade, dominating the organs of government in the towns, building for themselves imposing town houses many of which can still be seen today. They were the most progressive and enterprising members of the state, spearheading the expansion of trade and industry. It is customary to compare the French manufacturing and mercantile establishments unfavourably with the English and Dutch. While there is something to be said for this contrast, nevertheless they achieved definite if limited success during Louis XIV's reign, especially in the great commercial centres such as Paris (population 550,000), Lyons (97,000), Marseille (75,000), Rouen (64,000), Lille (57,000) and Orleans (50,000). Prosperous ports and naval bases thrived on the Atlantic seaboard, though French merchants were consistently outsold by the ubiquitous Dutch.

There were several reasons for the relatively disappointing performance of French industrialists and merchants. Perhaps the most serious was the tendency for successful entrepreneurs to opt out by purchasing land, office or government bonds, rather than expand their business enterprises. Unfortunately there was an ineradicable prejudice in favour of the noble lifestyle, which contrasted with the bourgeois pursuit of trade. While this prejudice was not explicitly encouraged by the king, Louis was not especially interested in his country's economic development, provided that the cash arrived for his military expansion, buildings and diplomatic expenses.

In the early years of the personal rule, nevertheless, there was a serious government-led economic offensive, aimed at the establishment of an overseas empire, the regulation of manufacture and trade, and the exclusion of foreign competition. This campaign was the achievement of the controller-general, Jean-Baptiste Colbert, Mazarin's legacy to the Sun King. Colbert was a mercantilist; that is to say, a believer in the necessity of accumulating precious metals by boosting exports and restraining imports. He believed that the amount of money in circulation was limited, and that the sooner the French got hold of it all, the better. Historians are on the whole agreed that Colbert's *dirigiste* interference did more harm than good, though he was right to prefer peace to war. Furthermore, his success in prosecuting sloth and corruption in the royal financial administration was indisputable. Officially Louis backed his minister. Indeed many of Colbert's instructions and initiatives went out over Louis' signature. But the king's lack of interest was shown by his failure to visit factories and shipyards, or express interest in the development of the navy. Louis was a landsman, a soldier and a dynast. He wrecked Colbert's policies and ambitions by his aggressive foreign policy from the Dutch War onwards.

Louis XIV, however, was extremely interested in controlling the government and finance of urban oligarchies through patronage and the direct intervention of the intendants. Why? Because he wanted the towns to be sufficiently well administered to pay taxes promptly and because he was well aware of their trouble-making potential. An excellent example of Louis' determination to stand no nonsense from the towns was his treatment of Marseille in January 1660. During the past decade there had been consistent defiance of the king's first minister Cardinal Mazarin and of the royal intendants. So the king arrived with an army of 6,000 men. When the gates were eventually opened, Louis, as we noted in Chapter 2, ostentatiously entered through a breach in the walls, treating Marseille as a conquered city.

Louis' concern with the disruptive potential of the towns is further illustrated by his steps to discipline Paris. As will be explained in Chapter 5, Louis was glad to spend money embellishing his capital. His hatred and fear of Paris as a result of the Fronde have been exaggerated. Even so, he never forgot the potential menace of Paris's half a million undisciplined and disaffected inhabitants. As a countryman he loathed the stench and noise of the capital, nor did he like being jostled by crowds. So his gradual development of Versailles as his principal residence and centre of government, his steps to control the administration of Paris, and his creation of an efficient police force under de la Reynie were all of a piece. While Louis had little sympathy with the bourgeoisie, he had no intention of letting them get out of control. Nevertheless, when the banker Samuel Bernard was welcomed to Versailles in the hope that he would contribute to the cost of the war of the Spanish Succession, courtiers wondered whether the Sun King would know how to treat him. In the event Louis' charm and common sense prevailed, as he showed the banker round his gardens with typical courtesy.

Still less would Louis have known how to behave to the peasants and the urban riff-raff on whose not particularly broad and uncomplaining shoulders the *ancien régime* rested. He seems to have regarded the poor as barely human; in other words, as two-legged cattle. When Monsieur interceded on behalf of the suffering peasantry, the king replied: 'Brother, if four or five thousand of such *canaille* were to die, would France be diminished? They are not much use in the world. I pray you, do not meddle in matters which need not concern you.' Similarly Mme de Maintenon had her head bitten off and Vauban and Fénélon were disgraced for intervening on behalf of the poor. This might seem a far cry from Henri IV's intention that every peasant should have a chicken in his stew-pot every Sunday. But perhaps to blame Louis XIV for his hardness of heart is mere sentimentality. Was there much that Louis could do to redress the wretched conditions that the poor had to endure?

Could we be transported to France in 1661, perhaps the greatest shock would be the appearance of the country-folk and artisans. Humpbacked and stunted in stature, self-evidently tortured by goitre, dental decay and abscesses, their faces disfigured by smallpox, their poor, twisted bodies by rickets and malnutrition, the appearance of these people was indeed barely human. They were a dreadful illustration of the damage done by privilege and inequality in Louis XIV's France. For while there were a number of causes of poverty and hunger, one of the greatest was that those least able to pay tax paid the most. A thoughtful Blois doctor, writing in 1661 to the Marquis de Sourdis, not only confirms this generally depressing picture but suggests general causes and royal responsibility in particular:

> Monseigneur, I am quite sure that, in the 32 years that I have practised medicine in this province and in this town, I have seen nothing to compare with the desolation which there is, not only in Blois, where there are four thousand poor on account of the influx from neighbouring parishes and because of the poverty of the place itself, but in the whole country the dearth is so great, that the peasants, lacking bread throw themselves upon the crows, and as soon as a horse or some other animal dies, they eat it; and it is certain that in the parish of Cheverney, a man, his wife and child were found dead without any symptoms of a disease, and only hunger could be the cause. Malign fevers are beginning to break out, and when the hot weather comes on top of so much damp and rot, these poor people, who lack strength already, will die quickly enough; unless God works a miracle, we must expect a great *mortalité* [the contemporary term for widespread deaths]. People are so poor that there was even a little barley in a boat that was left unsold, for lack of money to buy it. Our artisans are dying of hunger, and the town bourgeoisie is deeply troubled, for though they are full of goodwill to help these poor wretches, the great numbers make them unable to satisfy Christian charity. I have just learned that they have found a child at Cheverney who had eaten one of his own hands. Such happenings make our hair stand on end. Wine normally provided a livelihood for the people of this country, but it is not selling, and there are no horses to transport it, because of the high taxes. A reduction by half in the *taille* is essential, and a delay in paying the other half until after the harvest, has been requested for the *élection* of Blois, Beaugency, the Sologne, Romorantin and Amboise. The king has promised the Queen his mother, a reduction for the aforesaid *élection*.[2]

Peasants and artisans had to pay tax to the local landlord, tax to the municipality to pay for bridges and roads, tithe to the church (which in theory funded the local priest but in practice often went to a fat abbey or cathedral), the compulsory tax on salt, excise tax on other commodities such as wine – and above all the *taille*. This was the equivalent of a poll tax in the *pays d'élection* and a rather less iniquitous property tax in the *pays d'état*. On average total taxation of an individual peasant's produce may have amounted to 20 per cent. This burden of taxation was crippling enough in times of plenty. During Louis' reign it was rendered all the more intolerable by poor harvests caused by bad weather and war. Louis, however, could hardly be blamed for the exceptionally severe weather that inexorably ruined the harvests in 1661–2, 1693–4 and 1708–9. The whole of Europe seems to have suffered from a mini ice age during the latter half of the seventeenth century.

When combined with the crippling taxation caused by war, harvest failure made conditions impossible for most peasants. They reacted by incurring debts to local profiteers – either quick-witted townsmen or wealthier villagers. Nothing could be less democratic or public-spirited than a French village. The reaction of villagers to hardship was to exploit the weak and the unlucky, or visit their frustrations on lonely old people by persecuting them as witches. Three-quarters of the population was illiterate. Even more were ignorant and superstitious, though Louis XIV shared with the Parlement of Paris a creditable scepticism on the subject of witches. But the majority of Louis' subjects had limited resources – physical and intellectual – if they encountered hard times. They usually reacted by staying where they were until they starved, or by taking to the roads as beggars, or by fleeing to the towns in the hope of shelter and municipal or ecclesiastical charity. In truth this was a sadly unrealistic hope. As a result of their disappointment, in their bewildered desperation men turned to crime, women to prostitution.

Because of the insanitary conditions in the towns, the death rate there was significantly higher than in the countryside. But truth to tell, death was everywhere. Expectation of life was barely thirty for a woman, late twenties for a man. Infant mortality cancelled out those who were fortunate or robust enough to live into their fifties. A quarter of live births ended in death before the age of one, another quarter did not reach twenty. Infant mortality was actually higher among the richer classes because of the unsound practice of wet-nursing, which the poor could not afford. Furthermore the poor were better off with midwives, rather than with doctors who rarely washed, were dominated by the latest ludicrous medical fad and would hack babies to pieces in their attempts to save a high-born mother's life.

The rich, on the other hand, were better fed and therefore capable of surviving the common cold and less liable to succumb to the diseases of malnutrition such as dysentery. Louis XIV represented his wealthy subjects by his gross gluttony. This caused constipation – tiresome no doubt but not usually a killer. Liselotte (Monsieur's second wife) witnessed the following royal meal: four bowls of different soups, a pheasant, a partridge, a dish of salad, two massive slices of ham, mutton with garlic gravy, pastries, fruit with hard-boiled eggs. Thus did Louis eat for 20 million. Nor did he share their living conditions. While he inflicted draughts on his shivering courtiers in his high-ceilinged palaces, the majority of his subjects huddled together with their animals or slept ten to a bed in their earth and timber village hovels or jerry-built sheds in the suburbs of towns wholly bereft of sanitation or clean water. Villages stank, but it was different from the stench of towns, especially Paris.

A major additional cause of rural poverty was the dire state of French agriculture. Too much of France was given over to the growth of cereals – simply because it was the cheapest and easiest form of husbandry, though worryingly vulnerable to adverse weather. At best primitive equipment guaranteed an indifferent crop – wooden ploughs dragged by men, wheat and oats garnered with sickles as opposed to scythes, the crop threshed with scourges. Because the only available fertiliser was manure, the rural economy was condemned to a disastrous downward spiral; too few animals meant too little manure, which meant poor crops, which meant too little fodder for animals. A wasteful medieval system of crop rotation condemned a third of the land to lying unproductively fallow. There was such a shortage of sheep that wool for weaving had to be imported. France's best specialist crop was the grape. But here again weather could destroy the vines – a sharp hailstorm in April, for instance, or a drought in June. Poor communications handicapped the internal circulation and the export of wine when the crop was good, and the distribution of corn and maize when the crops were bad. When harvests failed, as in 1662, country-folk ate dogs, cats and rats, acorns and roots – or they starved.

Was this sad state of affairs Louis' responsibility? Certainly his resort to wars, which he found it hard to limit in cost and duration, cancelled out the necessary reforms that Colbert had initiated during the relatively peaceful decade of 1662–72. On the other hand, Pierre Goubert blames Richelieu for initiating the policy of open-ended war against the Habsburgs, though whether Louis XIV was obliged to continue this disastrous policy is a good question. Like Richelieu, neither Louis nor Colbert did anything for agriculture, which was handicapped by excessive taxation and shortage of coin. Peasants suffered too when Louis

XIV legalised the purchase of communal land by nobles or bourgeois entrepreneurs. When the starving resorted to rebellion, the Sun King slapped them down with his troops and exacted a terrible revenge. In the Boulonnais in 1662, for instance, Louis was determined to show his hand: 3,000 rebels were arrested, 40 ringleaders executed and 400 sent to the galleys as slaves.

Neither king nor minister realised the importance of research and experiment if crops were to be improved and cattle to be reared more productively. There is a contrast here with Holland and England. Furthermore, in England innovative farming was often encouraged by aristocratic landowners who were free to cultivate their estates without the snobbish disapproval of society, as in contemporary France. Louis officially permitted nobles to invest in overseas trade, which was commended because it spread Christianity. But only in the later stages of his reign were the threats of *dérogeance* withdrawn from those who sullied their hands with manufacture or husbandry.

To be fair, Louis was only partly to blame. A sense of proportion is essential. Not all of France was hit by recession and starvation. Other parts of Europe were no better off. The Brandenburg Junkers still owned serfs. Irish peasants were starved by cruel, absentee English landlords. But contemporaries noted the contrast between beefy English and Dutch soldiers, and the crippled, emaciated skeletons who fought for the Sun King. In times of dearth Louis did what he could to encourage charity and move produce around from fortunate to unfortunate districts. But not even Colbert had been able to create a transport revolution, though he had some success in building roads and canals. Not even Colbert could rein in the four horsemen of the apocalypse – plague, famine, death and war – that galloped unchecked through the land.[3] Louis' favourite horse was war, which, alas, encouraged the other three. After the first peaceful decade of his reign, Louis' people to whom he had promised his best attempts at *soulagement* cursed him with good reason for his insensitivity, incompetence and fondness for war.

FREEDOM OF THOUGHT, SPEECH AND PUBLICATION

So could the French attack their government, or express views of which the establishment disapproved? Louis XIV, like the rest of us, did not take kindly to criticism. He was a natural authoritarian, and therefore a natural censor. After a brief flirtation with Molière, whom he defended against the *dévots* headed by his mother,[4] he remained rigidly orthodox in politics and religion. Assuredly he was no progressive. Not only did he have nightmares about the riots and rebellions of the Fronde, but he was well aware of the liberty of the press that had existed during those heady and halcyon days. Louis never forgot the grossly offensive *mazarinades* that insulted his mother and her chief minister (if indeed that was all he was), and even cast doubts on the Gift of God's paternity. Louis therefore exercised a rigorous censorship throughout his personal rule, keeping the total number of subversive pamphlets down to a mere 1,500 between 1661 and 1715, fewer than the *mazarinades* published in 1649 alone.[5] Here he followed the example of Cardinal Richelieu, who imprisoned disobedient journalists.

Like Richelieu, too, Louis patronised government propaganda, both in print and in the arts. It was only with the greatest reluctance that Louis permitted the talented but heterodox poet La Fontaine's entry to the Académie Française. The Abbé de La Chambre warned the poet: 'Understand that henceforth you are working under a prince who will be informed of the progress you make along the path to virtue, and who will have consideration for you only in so far as you aspire to advance in the right manner.'[6] 'He has promised to be good', Louis explained when he finally admitted La Fontaine in 1684. The French were told what to think and what not to think, about religion, about politics and, especially, about Louis the Great. How successful this campaign was, especially when things went wrong at the end of the reign, we shall see in due course. Louis, however, inherited a propaganda machine from the cardinals. Dramatist, poets and journalists all knew which side their bread was buttered on. The Sun King was especially enterprising in exploiting architecture. He soon demonstrated that he was not content simply to improve his predecessors' embellishments of Paris. Fouquet's beautiful chateau at Vaux-le-Vicomte indicated what might be achieved by his gifted team of Le Nôtre, Le Vaux and Le Brun. Louis disgraced the minister and appropriated his team, soon to be transplanted to Versailles, plus 12,000 orange trees. Versailles was eventually to emerge as a triumphalist statement of military grandeur to the glory of France and – it came to the same thing – of her magnificent Sun King.

While architecture was straightforward, unfortunately for Louis' attempts to impose an intellectual strait-jacket, the seventeenth century was a great period for the flourishing of heterodoxy and scepticism. Writing from the security of Holland the Jew Spinoza cast doubt on Christian tradition in the name of logical common sense. In this movement France played a distinguished role. Descartes was almost as bad as Spinoza, applying reason pure and simple to philosophical issues. No serious controversialist could ignore him. The Huguenot Pierre Bayle questioned the more absurd dogmas of the Catholic church. He castigated the employment of the text 'compel them to come in' as an alibi for forced conversions of his Huguenot brethren. Within the Catholic church the Oratorian priest Richard Simon caused panic among conservatives by demanding a critical approach to the Bible. No commentator, he maintained, deserved to be taken seriously if he had not mastered Hebrew, without which it was impossible to evaluate the reliability of the text. Simon accepted no excuse for unthinking and ignorant credulity. How could Moses, for instance, have written Deuteronomy when the last chapter describes his death?

A redoubtable champion entered the lists against Simon. Bossuet, the dauphin's tutor recently promoted to the diocese of Meaux as his reward for devotedly flogging his pupil and for creditable reasons, passionately defended scripture and the traditions of the church. To equip himself for the fight against Simon, at the age of fifty-five he taught himself Hebrew, having hitherto relied on Latin and Greek alone. He refuted Simon's scholarly if rather pedantic insistence that the text mattered more than theological tradition. What if Joshua or Samuel had discreetly added a footnote describing Moses' death to the patriarch's divinely inspired masterpiece? Simon exploded with laughter – 'So His Lordship of Meaux *does* admit that additions were made to Moses' writings! He is obviously a disciple of Spinoza.' Bossuet dismissed Simon's mockery: 'Right-minded people have little liking for jests of that kind.'[7]

Bossuet in fact personifies the strengths as well as the weaknesses of Louis XIV's regimented society. It is tempting to pigeonhole him as an unquestioning advocate of absolutism, as the thundering deliverer of obsequious platitudes from the royal chapel's pulpit. There is a dreadful portrait of him by Rigaud, suggesting what damage bishop's robes can do to a man. In truth, though, Bossuet was a brave and independent thinker who publicly rebuked Louis for his adultery, who attacked the rich for their indifference to the poor, and criticised wars of aggression. In his *Politics drawn from the very words of Scripture*, Bossuet contrasts the Old Testament's justification of war with the New Testament's instruction to love our enemies. Indeed, David was not allowed to build the temple because he had blood on his hands, and not just the blood of Uriah but of his foreign enemies as well. 'A Christian conqueror must spare blood, and the spirit of the Gospel on this point is quite different from the spirit of the Law.'[8]

It is to Louis' credit – and a corrective to the picture of him as an irredeemable persecuting conformist – that he promoted Bossuet to the bishopric of Meaux. Indeed, the dauphin had clearly forgiven those sadistic beatings when he backed his old tutor for the archbishopric of Paris. But Louis would not further promote such a plebeian. The job went to Noailles, who was much more aristocratic though he did not have Bossuet's brain. Perhaps, too, Bossuet was too much of a Gallican. Like his rival Fénelon he never visited Rome. Indeed he displayed more enthusiasm for visiting London, where he hoped to discuss reunion with his Anglican friends. Although Bossuet disliked the Jesuits, he was no Jansenist either, even though he much admired St Augustine (see Chapter 8). Certainly Louis would never have forgiven him if he had been a Jansenist. Though he supported the revocation of the Edict of Nantes, Bossuet had explored the possibilities of a compromise with the Huguenots. He had an independent mind to which Louis allowed him to give vent. It remained to be seen how long this royal tolerance would last.

THE OTHER HALF

What could the 50 per cent of the human race who happened to be female expect from the Sun King? Not a great deal, it would seem, either from him or from his male subjects. 'C'est une fille', spoken with disappointment and disgust, tended to be a baby girl's reception into the male-orientated society of seventeenth-century France. To a great extent Louis reflected and indeed encouraged this prejudice. Not that France was noticeably worse than contemporary England, although women there could succeed to the throne, and there was no French equivalent of the successful playwright Aphra Behn. In her book about women in seventeenth-century England, *The Weaker Vessel*, Antonia Fraser concludes that if anything the status of English women declined between 1600 and 1700, despite a temporary upsurge during the civil war.[9] So it would perhaps have been surprising if the situation had been markedly different in contemporary France, a conclusion implicitly reached by Wendy Gibson in her *Women in Seventeenth Century France*.[10] Actually, women were so anonymous, ignored, and for the most part illiterate that it is difficult to answer confidently questions about their status during Louis' reign. But it would be wrong to duck the question, unless one followed the French bishop who doubted if women were fully human.

As a matter of fact, Louis rather liked women and got on well with them. In his youth he was a total mummy's boy, and continued to be woken every morning by his old nurse. He was invariably polite to women, raising his hat to the most obscure chambermaid. Any foolish prejudice that men were inherently cleverer than women – as many contemporaries believed, and by no means all of them male – was knocked out of him by his second official mistress Athénaïs de Montespan, who was far more witty, malicious and perceptive than the king, and by his second wife Françoise de Maintenon who was more erudite. Then there was sex. Louis found women physically attractive, and ladies of the court queued up to have sex with him. Yet he was not just a sexual predator who enjoyed humiliating women. There is a description of the adolescent Philippe, Louis' homosexual brother, amusing himself by lifting court-ladies' skirts while Louis tipped them off their chairs, which everyone thought was a great joke until he was about to try it on the future Mme de Maintenon. Her glance made Louis draw back, exclaiming, 'No, not that one.' A somewhat eclectic respect as well as physical attraction influenced Louis' friendships with women. They for their part loved him for his charm and good looks.

Whether Louis was likely to do much for the cause of women's advancement was another matter. He was not exactly a feminist. He excluded his mother from any share in the government when his personal rule began in March 1661. Still less did he allow his first wife to mitigate his hostility to Spain, her beloved fatherland. Whereas English women had proved their ability as defenders and administrators of their family properties during the civil wars in their husbands' absence, French women behaved with culpable irresponsibility during the Fronde. Louis neither forgave nor forgot the antics of his cousin Mademoiselle, nor troublemakers like the Duchesse de Chevreuse. In 1670 Louis employed Philippe's first wife Henrietta to negotiate the secret Treaty of Dover with her brother Charles II. Otherwise women played little part in the reign's affairs of state, though Louis' second sister-in-law Liselotte and Mme de Sévigné wrote fascinating letters about what was going on. The one possible exception to this exclusion of the fair sex was Mme de Maintenon, whose role will be discussed in Chapter 10.

Meanwhile other women got on with their lives as best they could – as wives, nuns or whores. In village and town women supported their husbands and brought up their children. They got no help from the king, whose taxes escalated as the reign became more and more disfigured by war. In 1678 the English philosopher John Locke described the desperation of a poor peasant woman: 'The tax collector had not long ago seized all her cooking utensils, money not being ready.'[11] Under Tridentine rules nuns had to be cloistered. But women who joined the new religious orders that avoided vows looked after the poor and sick, though perhaps less so than in the first half of the century as Louis' government adopted a more aggressive approach to beggars and the unemployed. Whores plied their trade at every level of society, including the court. 'What a brothel!' exclaimed the duke of Palestrina when he arrived at Versailles. The declining moral tone of the court reached its nadir during the notorious poison affair that deeply disturbed the king.[12] So it should have done, as the court took its lead from the king's promiscuous and self-indulgent lifestyle. A real watershed, however, occurred when he married Mme de Maintenon in 1683. Overnight Louis changed from lechery to prudery, thus threatening his female subjects in a different way. His achievement as the moral director of the nation will be assessed in Chapter 10.

And then there was the army. Every European army in the mid-seventeenth century included a high proportion of women – how high varied according to time and place. The number carried around by the French army declined markedly during Louis XIV's reign. He inherited a tradition of soldiers' wives respectably meeting the needs of their husbands as cooks, seamstresses, laundry women and nurses. In addition, there were hundreds of camp followers – whores, in other words – with every regiment, whose presence was often defended because soldiers were less likely to rape and kidnap the wives and daughters of local civilians if their sexual needs were already met. Just as men frequently enlisted because civilian life was so grim, especially in time of famine, so women who were unfortunate at home tried their luck with the army. Calculations for provisioning the army had to take account of the swarm of women who invariably followed in the wake of their men – one reason in particular why Louis deliberately discouraged women's presence with his armies, which he made increasingly professional, disciplined and self-sufficient. Women were not welcome, though some remained throughout the reign.

WHAT SORT OF FRANCE?

While this chapter began by exploring the identity of the French, it concludes by looking at France herself. Clearly France would be affected by such a formidable, charismatic and intelligent ruler as Louis XIV. He had a great opportunity of moulding France. After all, his personal rule lasted for over half a century. France in 1715 was bound to be different from France in 1661. Consider the great extent to which England changed during the same period. Like France she had experienced social and political convulsions during the 1640s and 1650s. Now she survived an attempt at Stuart absolutism and became a mercantile oligarchy, united with Scotland. What was to be France's fate? If she was to be efficiently governed by an absolute monarch there was much to do. In particular, the young king had to impose his leadership on a nobility with a recent track record of disloyalty and defiance. France's role in Europe had to be defined. Many of her inhabitants lived on or below subsistence level, desperately needing help. What would be the religious complexion of a country with more than one established church? Would the French be encouraged to think for themselves? Would French *women* be allowed to express themselves more effectively and in general fulfil their potential? These issues, directly relating to the essential identity of France, will be explored in subsequent chapters.

Since the Revolution the real France has been an explosive issue. Napoleon, the revolutions of 1830 and 1848, the Second Empire, the Commune, Boulanger, Dreyfus, Stavisky, the Popular Front, Vichy, de Gaulle, Algérie française, such are the battle honours of a divided nation desperately seeking its soul. Was 1789 such a watershed that previous events had little effect on post-revolutionary France? Louis XIV's legacy to his immediate successors is clear enough. What contribution if any did he make to the more distant future? Perhaps the answer is not as negative as might be supposed. 'To know something of the great age of the monarchy is to know a surprising amount about modern France'[13] is Robin Briggs's comment on Louis XIV's reign. This is an intriguing issue that we should not ignore in our pursuit of more immediate matters such as the great king's ability to control and feed his subjects, and their response to his concern – or lack of it.

4

THE KING AT WORK

Had Louis XIV been asked to write his own job description he would have given priority to his leadership of the armed forces. War was what kings did. While Louis took his responsibilities for the French church and for the moral and intellectual welfare of his people seriously, domestic policies were primarily geared to preparation for war, raising taxes to fund war and recovery from the effects of war. Work for Louis XIV meant the government of France in the pursuit of these priorities. This chapter will explore his methods and his achievements. First, we shall see how the Sun King established his position as head of government after Cardinal Mazarin's death in March 1661. This entailed the disgrace of the man he saw as his chief rival, Nicolas Fouquet. What was Louis' relationship with his ministers, and with the country as a whole, once Fouquet had been dispatched? Can he be described as 'absolute'? Was he really the master or was it all make-believe? Louis' cultivation of his own image was certainly a crucial part of his professionalism, especially in the context of the court. Was this image based on reality, or was everything done with mirrors?

THE BOURBON REVOLUTION IN GOVERNMENT

On 10 March 1661, the morning after the cardinal died, Louis XIV, in the twenty-third year of his life, summoned his senior ministers, including the seventy-year-old chancellor Pierre Séguier, the experienced Hugues de Lionne who was in charge of foreign affairs, the veteran secretary of state for war Michel Le Tellier, and the brilliant *surintendant de finance* Nicholas Fouquet. These highly qualified old hands examined their new master with intrigued curiosity. Despite his frequent attendance at council meetings, he remained an unknown quantity. He always seemed very much under Mazarin's thumb: composed, self-controlled, undemonstrative, immaculately turned out, but a dark horse indeed. Whom would this unfathomable young man select to replace the cardinal as chief minister? Fouquet, who had the necessary all-round skills and experience and had worked hand-in-glove with Mazarin, was the obvious candidate – an opinion with which he concurred. Then came the royal bombshell:

> Monsieur the Chancellor, I have called you, together with my secretaries and ministers of state, to tell you that up to this moment I have been pleased to entrust the government of my affairs to the late cardinal. It is now time that I govern them myself. You will assist me with your counsels, when I ask for them. Outside the regular business of justice which I do not intend to change, Monsieur the Chancellor, I request and order you to seal no orders except by my command, or after having discussed them with me, or at least not unless a secretary brings them to you on my part. And you, Messieurs, my secretaries of state, I order you not to sign anything, not even a passport, without my command; to render account to me personally each day and to favour no one. And you, Monsieur the Superintendent, I have explained to you my wishes; I request you to use M. Colbert whom the late Cardinal has recommended to me. As for Lionne, he is assured of my affection. I am satisfied with his services.[1]

Thus Louis revealed his intentions to rule by himself. Compared to the virtual monopoly of business by the two cardinals since Richelieu came to power in 1624, it was indeed a revolution in the modern sense; in other words, radical, innovative change. Louis himself, however, would have accepted the term in its seventeenth-century sense; that is to say borrowed from astronomy to indicate a circular return to where matters had once stood. Louis saw himself reviving the personal monarchy of his dynamic grandfather Henri IV whom he admired much more than his strange, inhibited father. But was he serious? The general opinion, which Fouquet unwisely expressed, was that the young man would soon get bored with day-to-day affairs and would appoint another chief minister. Sign every passport? What a joke! The king would soon revert to his country pursuits: hunting, shooting and women.

But the cynics and the unbelievers were wrong. For there now began the most amazing marriage to the job in history. For the next fifty-four years Louis would be totally committed. Woe betide anyone who tried to bypass him. When Anne of Austria, who intensely resented no longer being a member of the *conseil d'en haut*, gave instructions to a secretary of state, she was instantly put in her place by her son: 'Madame, do not do that again without seeking my permission first.' Like any other workaholic Louis would occasionally go on holiday or, in his case, lead a military campaign in the Low Countries. But for the most part it was work, work, work: council meetings, interviews, writing of letters and reading of documents, every morning, every evening, every day. And Louis was not only head of state and his own chief minister, he also exercised direct control over the court, foreign affairs, the armed forces and the church. It was a grind that would have killed present-day politicians after a decade at most. Compare, for example, the two four-year terms that an American president would not normally exceed. Who compares with him in history? Elizabeth I of England (1558–1603)? The emperor Augustus (BC 29–AD 14)? Perhaps the closest comparison is with Louis' great-grandfather, Philip II of Spain (1556–98), whose conscientious professionalism he emulated. Louis' successor, his great-grandson Louis XV (1715–74), in theory ruled for fifty-nine years, though he was a minor for much of the time and was lazy and ineffectual. Irrespective of the quality of his rule, Louis XIV's long-lasting devotion to duty is awesome. In the stickability stakes he was supreme.

SHABBY DEAL: THE FALL OF FOUQUET

Nicholas Fouquet was the greatest financial wizard, the greatest arts patron, the greatest ladies' man of the time – and he knew it. His emblem was the squirrel, his motto, 'Whither shall I not climb?' Although his ambition, wealth and sexual exploits made enemies, on the whole he was popular and admired. He was a likeable scallywag. He was also a man of genuine Christian idealism, coming from a staunchly *dévot* family that produced two bishops and six nuns. His portrait shows a humorous, clever, tolerant, sensitive face. Many envied Fouquet his chateau at Vaux-le-Vicomte, a few miles south of Paris, where Le Vaux the architect, Le Brun the artist and Le Nôtre the gardener had produced a masterpiece. In Paris he was likened to Maecenas, the fabulous Roman patron of the arts.

But Fouquet forgot that Maecenas needed the emperor Augustus. He believed that *his* Augustus should be grateful to him for his undoubted loyalty and services to the crown during and since the Fronde. But Louis became convinced that Fouquet was a traitor and a crook. The Squirrel's greatest enemy was the Grass-snake – the emblem of the Colberts. Jean-Baptiste Colbert had been Mazarin's private intendant, responsible for building up his fortune. He was perfectly positioned to watch Fouquet and make detailed notes for the king. Fouquet was warned, for instance, by Louis' reference to Colbert at the famous meeting on 10 March. But Fouquet was not bothered. He thought Colbert dim whereas he was smart. He attempted to bribe the king's mistress, Louise de La Vallière, with the offer of 20,000 pistoles. Why? Fouquet's latest biographer cannot believe that the 46-year-old thought that he could replace the glamorous young king. More probably he just wanted to bring Louise on side, or perhaps he hoped to recover the favour of the queen-mother by persuading Louise to go. Anyway, when Louise told her lover, Louis was furious. Fouquet realised his mistake and grovelled. The king spoke graciously. Fouquet thought that he had been forgiven.

When Louis invited himself to Vaux in August 1661, Fouquet was determined that nothing should go wrong. No expense was spared to make the king comfortable and amused. Flowers, fireworks, banquets were in abundance. Molière and Lully produced ballets and comedies such as *Les Fâcheux*. But all the while Colbert whispered in Louis' ear that these sumptuous entertainments were paid for out of the crown's money. Far from feeling gratified, Louis felt like a poor relation, patronised and cheated. He had half a mind to arrest Fouquet in the middle of the festivities, in his own palace, but his mother persuaded him not to violate the obligations of a guest to his host. And in any case, two final details had to be settled. Fouquet had to keep his promise to pay the crown 30,000 écus and he had to fund this gift by selling his office of *procureur-général* of the Parlement of Paris – a post that would have entitled him to trial by his friends the Parisian magistrates.

So Fouquet was arrested a few days later on 5 September 1661 by D'Artagnan, the musketeer. Louis had travelled to Nantes to open the

Brittany Estates. Fouquet was Louis' twenty-third birthday present to himself. The *surintendant* was shattered. 'I thought His Majesty had a higher opinion of my worth', he remarked. And he then asked D'Artagnan to act discreetly, clearly failing to understand that Louis wanted as much publicity as possible. The king described the arrest in a self-satisfied though patently insecure letter to his mother, who had once been Fouquet's patron:

> You should have seen the difficulties I had in speaking to D'Artagnan, for I was burdened by a crowd of people, all of them alert, and they would have guessed my intentions at the slightest inclination. Nonetheless two days ago I ordered him to be ready. Finally this morning the *surintendant* came to work with me as usual. I occupied him in one way or another, pretending to look for papers until I saw D'Artagnan through the window in the courtyard. D'Artagnan caught up with him in the square and arrested him on my order at about noon. He demanded that he be allowed to keep the papers which he carried which, I am told, contain the truth about Belle-Isle. I have talked about the incident with the gentlemen around me and have told them that I will not appoint another *surintendant*. You will have no trouble in believing that these people are sheepish, but I am satisfied that they will see that I am not so much of a dupe as they thought, and that it would be wise to attach themselves to me.[2]

Fouquet's trial for treason lasted until December 1664. It was a shambolic travesty of justice. Fouquet proved too clever for the prosecution. With regard to the charge of misappropriating public funds, he successfully implicated both Mazarin and Colbert. He admitted that he had lent the crown money, but it was his own money honestly acquired through hard work and two shrewd marriages. Furthermore, it transpired that the *surintendant* was by now almost bankrupt. As for the charge of *lèse-majesté* (i.e. treason), he was clearly being accused of a crime that he had yet to commit. His fortification of Belle-Isle was naval and not military, directed at France's external enemies. When Chancellor Séguier took over the trial, Fouquet enjoyed reminding him of his disloyalty during the Fronde:

> At no period, Sir, even though at the hazard of my life, have I ever abandoned the King's person; and, at the time in question, you, Sir, were at the head of the Council of his enemies, and your relations gave free passage to the army against him.[3]

The vindictiveness with which the trial was conducted turned Fouquet from a swindler into a martyr. As a public relations exercise it was a disaster. Louis had admitted beforehand that if Fouquet was condemned to death, he would gladly allow the sentence to be carried out. Now, however, the judges voted 13–9 in favour of banishment. Colbert was furious. He ensured that their careers were ruined. Louis 'commuted' the sentence to life imprisonment in the remote fortress of Pinerolo. For years his conditions were harsh – solitary confinement, no fresh air or exercise, no books or writing paper. In the 1670s Louvois ordered an amelioration of Fouquet's imprisonment so as to spite Colbert, and there was even talk of his release just before he died in 1680.

What was the significance of the persecution of Fouquet? Historians admit that he was no choirboy. Petitfils, for instance, calls him 'a born seducer'. But his biographer Dessert fully demonstrates Colbert's malice and willingness to twist the evidence in order to save his own reputation. Fouquet clearly got a shabby deal. Were policy issues at stake? Colbert's admirers, such as Bluche and Treasure, have credited him with higher standards of state finance – in particular with the separation of private and public money. Fouquet would certainly have continued to protect his friends among the financiers when they were accused of peculation. After his fall, they were duly fined in a specially convened *court de justice*, to the financial profit of the crown.

Mark Fumaroli, on the other hand, has argued that Fouquet offered Louis XIV a real alternative to Colbert's reversion to aggressive royal authoritarianism, which had been put on hold since Richelieu's death; Fouquet personified compromise, synthesis, reconciliation.[4] This is perhaps a little too kind to Fouquet. Robin Briggs maintains that Fouquet's departure made little practical difference, though he believes 'that Fouquet was the victim of a frame-up by Colbert, who was far more guilty of peculation himself, as the principal manager of Mazarin's affairs, so to some extent it was a pre-emptive strike'.[5] What is indisputable is the light thrown on Louis' personality and values. He comes badly out of the affair, showing small-mindedness, ingratitude and cruelty. He stopped short of imposing the death sentence he had hoped for. But broadly speaking he got the result he wanted – a cowed political nation. Future ministers knew where they stood. Whether that justifies Louis' vindictive bending of the law is another matter.

A DELIGHTFUL BUSINESS: THE DAILY GRIND

Having disposed of Fouquet, Louis now had the team of ministers that he wanted. His government was conciliar. Various councils implemented the policies decided upon by the *conseil d'en haut*, so called because it always met at least twice a week on an upper floor (or because it was superior to other councils?). The membership of this council was crucial: Louis himself presided, plus Le Tellier (war), Lionne (foreign affairs) and Colbert, whose responsibilities included finance (he was made controller-general in 1665), the navy, royal buildings and the king's bastards. Louis also presided intermittently over the *conseil des dépêches*, which met once a week and executed policies affecting the internal affairs of France. Its membership included the chancellor and the four secretaries of state (army, navy, foreign policy and the 'so-called reformed religion'), each responsible for a quarter of the kingdom. Princes of the blood could attend this council if they wished. Louis usually headed the *conseil des finances*, of which Colbert was the key member. The *conseil de commerce* was set up by Colbert in 1664, lapsed in 1677 and was resuscitated in 1700. The *conseil des parties* drafted legislation and acted as a court of appeal. Louis left these last two councils to their own devices, but chaired the *conseil de conscience*, which met every Friday morning. Louis was joined here by the archbishop of Paris and by his confessor. Together they made the senior appointments in the church.

Louis was determined not to be an idle king like the Merovingians he had heard about in his boyhood:

> I made it a rule to work regularly twice a day for two or three hours at a time with various persons, aside from the hours that I worked alone or that I might devote to extraordinary affairs if they arose. I commanded the four secretaries of state to sign nothing in future without discussing it with me, and the same for the superintendent of finances, and for nothing to be transacted in the finances without it being registered in a little book that was to remain with me. I resolved to enter into details with each of the ministers when he would least expect it.[6]

Given that the *conseil d'en haut* sometimes met four or five times a week and the other councils two or three times, Louis spent much of his time presiding over ministerial discussions. He was a firm chairman, always well prepared and well informed. He listened carefully to his ministers, glaring angrily if they were inattentive or ignorant. He allegedly went to sleep during a council meeting only twice during the whole reign. He usually, but by no means invariably, accepted majority decisions.

Bear in mind the additional time taken in one-to-one discussions with ministers, ambassadors, foreign representatives, members of the royal family and higher aristocracy, plus the private study of documents, letters and dispatches. What a workload! How did he manage to do justice to it, plus the obligations of controlling the court and presiding over state occasions? And the man had to live, eat, hunt, make love, attend plays and concerts. How did he survive? Part of the explanation is that he was physically and mentally tough, and rarely ill despite his doctors. He was usually a sound sleeper. Nature gave him a retentive memory, the capacity to master a brief quickly, and abundant common sense. But the chief point is that Louis was in his element. While he brought to it a sense of duty to the state, he loved the work, describing it as 'a delightful business'.

He did not do it all himself. Pierre Goubert reckons that the ministers, administrators and secretaries who ran the royal machinery of government in the first part of the personal rule probably numbered about a thousand[7] – a small enough total compared to the civil service of a modern state. These included the thirty-two intendants and their assistants who represented the central government in the provinces and whose work we shall shortly review. The most important of the king's assistants were the members of the *conseil d'en haut*.

Here we have a strange story that tells us much about Louis' strengths and weaknesses. During the fifty-four years of Louis' personal rule there were only seventeen members of the *consel d'en haut*, of whom sixteen came from three families – the Colberts, the Le Telliers and the Phélypeaux. This is no exaggeration. The great Jean-Baptiste's brother Colbert de Croissy became foreign minister in 1679, his nephew Torcy succeeded him in that post, Colbert's son Seignelay succeeded him as the minister in charge of the navy, another nephew Desmarets became a member of the *conseil d'en haut*. Le Tellier's son Louvois succeeded him in the war ministry, to be followed by his son Barbezieux. Phélypeaux, his son Chateauneuf and his grandson Vrillière were secretaries of state for Protestant affairs, while another member of the family Pontchartrain was controller-general and then chancellor, while his son Jerome ran the navy. These men were able enough. But it would be absurd to suppose that they were necessarily the best that a nation of 20 million could produce. Louis was naturally loyal – an admirable trait. But he was also excessively conservative, preferring familiar faces. Although the ministers who succeeded the first generation of the Colbert/Louvois brigade were by no means the men of straw whom historians used to denigrate, the edge was undoubtedly missing towards the end of the reign when Louis had to take on more and more work himself. Clearly a flawed system.

Contemporaries criticised Louis for shutting out the aristocracy in favour of 'the vile bourgeoisie'. This was the complaint of Turenne and of that arch-snob Saint-Simon. But Louis was a snob too. The criticism is only part true. The three families were in fact scions of the robe nobility, involved in royal service for generations. But Louis was determined not to entrust the royal family, the ancient nobility and the clergy, with high office. He was not going to allow cardinals to exploit their right to address him as 'cousin'. He never forgot the Fronde when the ancient aristocracy had disgraced itself. He preferred men who were wholly beholden to him for wealth and promotion. As he said in his memoirs, written for the instruction of his son: 'To be perfectly honest with you, it was not in my interest to choose persons of greater eminence. It was above all necessary to establish my own reputation and make the public realise, by the very rank of those whom I selected, that it was not my intention to share my authority with them.' Louis was glad to promote his ministers. Three of Colbert's daughters married dukes, with Louis' financial assistance. Thanks to the king's support, his ministers were treated with respect by the highest nobility. The duc de Beaufort, for instance, wrote to Colbert: 'The honour of being in your good graces is more desirable to me than anything else.'[8]

Was Louis dominated by his ministers more than he liked to think? A recent biographer, Anthony Levi, reckons that Colbert in particular pulled the strings. One can only retort that Colbert was an extremely obsequious string-puller. Here he is congratulating the king on the capture of Besançon:

Caesar took the city and boasted of it in his works. The power of the entire House of Austria has been applied for seven years to making it impregnable and Your Majesty takes it in twenty-four hours. We must fall silent, Sire, in admiration, thanking God every day for bringing us to birth under the reign of such a king as Your Majesty.[9]

Louis was in fact paranoid about the dangers of being 'managed'. He insisted on 'all the details' whenever his ministers consulted him, writing his own comments in the margin. Even when he told Colbert, 'I order you to do whatever you think fit',[10] he had still been consulted. He forbade his ministers to meet on their own without him. At the end of the reign he vetoed one out of twenty majority decisions on principle – an absurd practice that cannot have made for good government. Ministers adjusted their advice when the king's wishes became known. Colbert, for instance, stopped opposing the Dutch War when Louis was obviously determined to go ahead. Torcy similarly swung round to acceptance of Carlos II's will when he realised that this was what the king wanted.

Louis prevented the emergence of a chief minister by encouraging rivalry between his assistants. Colbert and Louvois in particular frequently squared up to each other. They were well matched, both aggressive, self-propelling bruisers, both exuding massive anti-charm. Colbert's nickname was 'the north' in recognition of his bleak personality. Once a court lady, Mme de Cornuel, desperately trying to beg a favour, exploded in exasperation: 'Monseigneur, at least make some sign that you are listening to me!'[11] Louvois was if anything even less attractive. Overweight, sweating profusely, he compensated for his physical ugliness by making rudeness an art form. But Louis put up with him because of his loyalty, industry and ability. He sometimes found Colbert, the older statesman, patronising and far too prone to admire the cardinals. 'Colbert will now tell us what the great Cardinal Richelieu would have done', Louis would remark,[12] enjoying the opportunity to rile the touchy minister. Louvois, on the other hand, he regarded as his protégé. He was three years younger than the king whereas Colbert was twenty years older. One can almost speak of friendship between Louis and Louvois, a situation Colbert resented.

In the spring of 1671 Colbert was in a particularly grumpy mood. Louis had just awarded the desirable sinecure of *Chancelier des Ordres du Roi* to Louvois. At the next *conseil d'en haut* Colbert lost his temper with Louvois and was uncooperative and disrespectful, even to Louis himself. Two days later on 23 April 1671 he received the following letter from the king:

> I was master of myself the day before yesterday to conceal from you the sorrow I felt at hearing a man whom I have overwhelmed with benefits, as I have you, talk to me in the manner that you did. I have been very friendly

towards you, and this has appeared in what I have done. I still have such a feeling now, and I believe that I am giving you real proof of it by telling you that for a single moment I restrained myself for your sake. I did not wish to say to you myself what I am writing to you, nor to give you a further opportunity to displease me. It is the memory of the services that you have rendered me, and my friendship, which made me act as I did. Profit thereby, and do not risk vexing me again, because after I have heard your arguments and have given my opinion on all your claims, I do not wish to hear further talk about it, ever. I am telling you my thoughts so that you may know where you stand and make no further mistakes.[13]

Colbert's reactions to this masterly rebuke, on the face of it so restrained, so *nice*, yet at the same time silky with menace, can only be imagined. And to be fair to Louis he kept his promise to befriend Colbert. He constantly asked after his health, which deteriorated in the 1670s as the Dutch War wrecked the controller's plans. Colbert was understandably depressed when Louis compared Louvois' expanding fortresses with the lack of progress at Versailles for which Colbert was responsible. Despite the king's promotion of the whole clan, when Colbert died in 1683 the future clearly belonged to Louvois.

During such a long reign there were bound to be changes, both in personnel and in practice. Louvois exploited Colbert's death by appropriating many of his sources of power. He brought to bear an even sharper approach to laziness and incompetence. The propaganda campaign, based on paintings, statues and medals, became ever more shrill in its glorification of the Sun King. Rumour had it that Louvois' days were numbered when death suddenly relieved the king of his increasingly unpopular war minister. Louis once went for him with fire tongs, so exasperated was he by the way Louvois had made enemies abroad for France by his gratuitously offensive tactics. Yet the king 'could be seen pacing the terraces at Versailles, for once not meandering round his gardens and fountains'.[14] He loyally replaced Louvois as war minister with his son Barbézieux who drank, slept around and spent far too much time in Paris. When the king promulgated some promotions in the war minister's absence, he remarked with smug satisfaction: 'Barbézieux will read about these on his travels.' Louis, however, was sorry when the young man died: 'He was beginning to correct his failings well.' His undoubted abilities have been resurrected by Guy Rowlands.

Towards the end Louis became crotchety and impatient. Council meetings were held in Mme de Maintenon's bedroom, where the lady demurely bent her head over her embroidery behind a screen, supposedly to protect her from the gales blowing through the windows, which Louis insisted on opening. The screen was also meant to conceal female influence. Torcy, foreign minister from 1699, describes Louis' tendency to be tiresome:

> Louis became irate with those who pressed him on matters of state. His Majesty felt that his counsellors' excessive desires for peace had revealed to the enemy the fact that France would conclude a treaty at any price. His reproaches fell principally on M. de Beauvilliers, whom His Majesty singled out, but I too got my share of the blame for having urged upon His Majesty the necessity of reaching a decision in the matter of the ambassadors who were to be sent to the Low Countries. The King added ironically that he much admired my new-found zeal – I who was the slowest man in carrying out negotiations. I confess that I did not grasp the reasons for His Majesty's reproach, nor why I deserved it, for I had never delayed the execution of his orders; in fact I anticipated them. But since masters never believe themselves to be wrong, I held my tongue and tried to profit from this mortification.[15]

Torcy had a particularly difficult apprenticeship as he had to submit to advice not only from the king but also from his father, Croissy (until his death in 1696), and his father-in-law, Pomponne (until his death in 1699). Thereafter Torcy's main problem was interference by Chamillart who, not content with making a mess of both the war ministry and the treasury, saw fit to interfere in the conduct of foreign affairs. The wits attributed Chamillart's promotion to his ability to give the king a good game of billiards. Mme de Maintenon's favour kept him in office until 1709. After that Torcy was more or less unchallenged. The Peace of Utrecht was his triumph as much as the Peace of the Pyrenees had been Mazarin's. He was even able to counteract the king's influence by getting his ministerial colleagues to agree on a joint line of argument, despite Louis' prohibition of pre-meeting huddles. He also learnt to forge not only the king's signature but whole letters.

Equally typical of Louis' ministers in the long twilight of his reign were the Pontchartrains, father and son. Louis, the father, succeeded Le Peletier as controller-general in 1689, moving on to the chancellorship in 1699. He had the unenviable job of financing the Nine Years War. He brought to his task a meticulous concern for detail, preferring the official channels to the notorious *affaires extraordinaires* necessitated by the wars. His most famous remark indicates exasperation as well as cynicism: 'Every time Your Majesty creates a new office, God creates a fool to purchase it.' Pontchartrain's preference was for a new, rational, official tax, *le capitation* of 1695, which all sectors of society were supposed to pay, dependent on their wealth and status. It was not Pontchartrain's fault that the rich sidled out of their obligations, the clergy escaped scot-free and the peasants paid even more. Truth to tell, financing the Nine Years War was a horrible job. The late seventeenth-century French state was basically incapable of paying for the colossal army that, thanks to Louis XIV and Louvois, had mushroomed to almost 400,000 men (plus female camp followers). When Louis made Pontchartrain chancellor in 1699, that normally restrained and low-key professional clasped his monarch's knees and wept tears of gratitude and relief. He was far happier resuscitating the office of chancellor, though he finally resigned in disgust, disillusioned by the king's high-handed enforcement of the bull *Unigenitus*. He was the only chancellor of the reign not to die in office.

As for the son, Jerome, he certainly encountered problems as secretary of state for the navy. For instance, he battled unsuccessfully on behalf of his naval officer clients against the king, Mme de Maintenon and the comte de Toulouse, Louis' illegitimate son, who had been lord admiral since childhood. While both Pontchartrains exploited patronage, especially in Brittany where the navy was predominant, and manoeuvred determinedly among the various factions at court, the king's favour was decisive. For instance Louis XIV vetoed Jerome de Pontchartrain's promotion of one of his protégés: 'I see very well the patronage that you give the chevalier de Froulay who may well merit it, but there are those with seniority who are honest men too, and do not have a protector, and it is just and fair to them to choose the one with the most seniority to fill that post'.[16] Jerome not only had to get on with Toulouse but also to recognise that the old king missed nothing.

As his regard for his ministers declined, Louis himself took on more and more work. Indeed, there is a case for saying that the personal rule only really began after Louvois' death in 1691. Even so, for more than half a century Louis was the dynamo who powered the governmental machine at the political centre of France. For twenty-one years the court and the ministries moved between Paris, Saint Germaine, Fontainebleau, Versailles and the military front in Flanders. Then from 1682 the government was based more and more at Versailles, where Louis toiled night and day, winter and summer. Louis' professionalism and devotion to duty were an inspiration to all his colleagues and servants, even though disasters at home and abroad and his declining health must have made the daily grind less and less of a delightful business.

WHO REALLY RULED FRANCE BETWEEN 1661 AND 1715?

This would have seemed a stupid question until quite recently. For the obvious answer must surely be Louis XIV, with his obsequious bourgeois ministers, his scary intendants and his chief of police, de la Reynie. Together they were the personification of absolutism. His regime was characterised by authoritarian initiatives such as the persecution of the Huguenots and the Jansenists, the punishment of political dissenters such as Fouquet and Vauban, the raising of vast armies, the repression of representative bodies such as the parlements and the provincial estates, the reliance on the 'thirty tyrants' (that is to say, the intendants who imposed Louis' authority on the remotest parts of provincial France), the extraction of unlimited amounts of money from a starving population, the creation of a huge army of civil servants (justifying the title 'le roi bureaucrat'), and the imprisonment of the nobility at Versailles, itself a monument to the Sun King's pride and self-indulgence. The king's propagandists, such as Bishop Bossuet, bolstered practice with theory by preaching the Divine Right of Kings. 'You are gods', shouted Bishop Bossuet, who assured his audience 'that the whole of the state resides within the king'. If Louis XIV did not say 'L'état c'est moi', he should have done. Such used to be the consensus.

During the last thirty years or so, however, historians on both sides of the Channel – and the Atlantic – have largely demolished this picture. The very term 'absolutism' is now obsolete, so we are told. As has been frequently pointed out, 'absolutism' was never a seventeenth-century word. It was invented in the nineteenth century as a pejorative description of the tyrannies allegedly launched and imposed by the *ancien régime*, soon to be happily replaced by liberal democracy. Still more to the point, the limitations on the actual power wielded by the cardinals and by Louis XIV certainly invalidate the old-fashioned picture of 'absolutism' in France. For instance, the king treated his parlements with cautious respect, he attracted aristocrats to Versailles because he needed them, while his 'army' of civil servants were in fact 45,000 venal office-holders who could not be dismissed. The incompleteness of Louis' achievements have to be recognised as well. While the king and reformist ministers (Colbert being an example) tackled challenges such as different legal authorities, the multiplicity of internal tolls and the incidence of crime and lawlessness, France in 1715 was still a jumble of conflicting systems and authorities. Whatever the theory, in practice 'absolutism' makes no historical sense. One historian, Nicholas Henshall, has argued that 'absolutism' is just a myth and no longer any use as a historiographical concept. 'Kindly leave the stage!' should therefore be our correct response whenever it rears its absurd and discredited head.[17]

Historians such as Mettam, Beik, Bohanan and Kettering have proved that Louis XIV achieved his results, such as they were, through compromise and accommodation with the upper, propertied classes, especially in the *pays d'état*, notably Brittany, Burgundy, Provence, Dauphiné and Languedoc. No two provinces were the same. For instance, in Brittany the peasantry revolted against the aristocracy so that the social divisions in the province were horizontal; the crown cooperated with the higher nobility by suppressing the revolt of 1675 with 6,000 troops. In Languedoc Beik demonstrates the crucial role of patronage, whereby crown and aristocrats mutually benefited from the raising of taxation, of which only 40 per cent actually left the province. Louis XIV allied with sympathetic elites in building the Canal du Midi and the persecution of the Huguenots. Bohanan depicts the cooperation between higher nobility, estates and crown against the lesser nobles in Dauphiné and Provence. The picture that emerges is of the king sensitively playing off power groups against each other, awarding rich pickings of cash, office, rank, all this brokered by his representatives in the provinces in close touch with aristocrats at Versailles. The king had to make the best of a fluid and tricky situation. Throwing his weight about would do no good at all. He had to be realistic, attracting the key players to his side.

As for the intendants, the modern interpretation is that they were essentially there to find out the facts and convey them to the central government. In addition, where possible they were to act as troubleshooters on the crown's behalf. They were to solve the towns' financial worries. They were to sort out the problems involved in raising, billeting and funding troops. Often they found themselves acting as spokesmen for their *généralités* rather than pushing forward the crown's authority. They were there to cooperate with the local bigwigs, the bishop, the governor, the lieutenant-general, the parlement, the estates and the magistrates. On 23 December 1672 Colbert ordered M. de Creil, the intendant at Rouen, 'that you entertain with M. Pellot, the principal magistrate in your généralité, a close and perfect cooperation and that you listen favourably to the merchants every time they address you'.[18] The intendants' chief role was to keep the taxes flowing. Colbert, in a missive to all intendants dated 1 September 1670, wrote: 'You will look upon this work as the most important task of all those with which you are entrusted.' The ideal solution was to persuade taxpayers to pay up promptly, generously and cheerfully. A combination of firmness and tact was essential. 'If a peasant won't pay up, can I confiscate his cow?' Colbert was asked. 'Yes, but you must do your utmost to see that things don't get to such a pass', was the reply.

So who ruled France? The modern interpretation is to allow Louis XIV his success in creating a central machinery of government, staffed by his chosen ministers, that decided policy. But when it came to implementing policy he was at best the leading player in a team effort, the most important members being the higher nobility. They virtually monopolised the high command of the army, with few exceptions such as Vauban. Louis turned down Bossuet for the archbishopric of Paris because of his low birth, so that the aristocratic but less-gifted Noailles got the job. Aristocrats went as ambassadors to the monarchies, members of the robe nobility only to republics such as Holland and Venice. Louis himself was a nobleman through and through – witness his obsession with military matters and his lack of interest in trade. Though he had his reasons for excluding nobles from the *conseil d'en haut* (apart from Beauvilliers, who was a sword nobleman, but Colbert's son-in-law), he was happy to cooperate with the nobles in the provinces as well as in the church and the army. Indeed, there was no alternative, a truth that Louis the realist fully grasped. In Bohanan's words, 'the tentacles of central government that grasped at the periphery, were only as strong as the self-interest of the nobility on which they fed'.[19] Louis may have run Versailles, but in Brittany or Provence his writ was in the hands of the governor, the bishop and, above all, his aristocratic patronage broker, however skilfully he manipulated them.

The revisionist historians who have demolished 'absolutism' have based their arguments on meticulous research. Furthermore, one only has to drive from Paris to Languedoc to appreciate the physical handicaps against which an 'absolute' Bourbon worked. Even with today's motorways France is a big place, while Languedoc still impresses by its remote inaccessibility. Bear in mind too that 20 million Frenchmen took some controlling, especially if the government pursued unpopular policies such as high taxation. Colbert, acting on his master's behalf, had the greatest difficulty getting the French to cooperate with his schemes. One recalls Louis' contemporary Peter the Great, of whom it was said, 'The Tsar pulls uphill with the strength of twenty men, but thirty million Russians pull downhill.' The aristocrat feathering his own nest in remote Provence, the financier taking his cut of the king's revenue in Paris, the peasant beating up the tax collector in Brittany – in a sense they ruled France as much as the Sun King.

Or did they? Has revisionism gone too far? Clearly the revisionists have done us all a favour in demolishing an unsound structure. While 'absolutism' still has its use as shorthand for 'authoritarian, constitutionally unchecked royal government', no one is likely now to envisage it in its over-simplified, old-fashioned form. Maybe *sometimes* the sheer power of Louis XIV is played down too much, particularly in the context of the growth and development of the army, recently analysed by John Lynch and Guy Rowlands. Here Louis' remarkable achievement has to be acknowledged. To be fair Henshall, for one, does not deny this: 'I accept the counter-revisionist stress on Louis XIV's power. But neither I nor Mettam have ever denied this, or its relation to military capacity in particular. The issue is how the power was achieved – by force or negotiation?'[20] This is obviously fair comment, though the army – which we shall examine in Chapter 7 (pp. 122–42) – is not the only area where Louis flexed his muscles in a not particularly flexible manner. His sheer power can be recognised in his implementation of foreign policy and the persecution of religious deviants, or anyone else who defied him.

Louis' relations with the parlements is a case in point. His dragooning of the Parlement of Paris used to be quoted as a prime example of 'absolutism' in practice. We have noted in Chapter 2 his high-handed behaviour towards the Parlement when a beardless adolescent. From then on the key issue was whether Parlement could query or delay royal legislation. In 1667 he 'instructed the Parlement that acts of remonstrance (i.e. criticism) must be executed quickly and on one occasion only'.[21] In 1673 Louis went further by confining remonstrance to the period after legislation had been registered – which made a nonsense out of remonstrance. Revisionists have insisted that Louis saw this ruling as a temporary wartime measure only. They have also pointed out the difficulty Louis had in trying to force Parlement to register the papal bull *Unigenitus* in 1714. John Hurt, on the other hand, in what Mettam describes as 'an important though one-sided book',[22] has argued that 'we've pushed the revisionist thesis beyond its appropriate limits, possibly because we've given up looking for evidence which contradicts it'.[23] He shows how Louis consistently bullied Parlement. In August 1669, for example, Louis registered a *lit de justice* by entering Parlement with Swiss and French guards to the beating of drums. Furthermore, he ruthlessly exploited the parlementaires financially. A sensible compromise would be to stress Louis' domination of the parlements while at the same time noting his preference for negotiation. As he wrote in his *Memoires*: 'I know, my son, and can sincerely assure you that I feel no aversion or bitterness to my judicial officers. On the contrary, if age is venerable in men, it appears all the more so to me in these ancient bodies.'[24] Louis needed the parlements for the registering of laws and for such controversial measures as the legitimising of his bastards. It was therefore contrary to his interests to alienate them.

An instructive episode was the Grands Jours d'Auvergne in September 1665. Louis decided to send Denis Talon, the solicitor-general of the Paris Parlement, accompanied by several magistrates, to Clermont, the capital of the Auvergne, a mountainous region in the centre of France notorious for the criminal lawlessness of the local nobility. Their mission was to investigate and prosecute people who were guilty irrespective of their rank. Esprit Flécshier describes the arrival of the magistrates:

> Everyone from Clermont and Montferrand came out to watch as this troup of magistrates coming to render them justice passed by. All the corps of the city were assembled, spread out along the road in the open countryside, waiting for the opportunity to deliver their harangues. Saturday and Sunday were spent listening to a thousand compliments delivered by the principal officers from the local courts who had come to humiliate themselves in the presence

of the judges from Paris, and by various clerics who came in a group to cite Saint Paul and Saint Augustine and to compare the Grands Jours to the last judgement. The opening of the Grands Jours was held on Monday, with a nice speech from M. Talon.[25]

Clearly this product of Louis' cooperation with the Parlement of Paris created a stir, especially when eighty-seven nobles were condemned, twenty-three of whom were executed. Some ran off to their mountain strongholds, but had to submit to the disgrace of being executed in effigy. Why did such tough customers defer to royal authority? Some clearly did not, and lawlessness continued for the rest of the reign. But the Grands Jours made an impression, as is clear from Flécshier's account. King and magistrates took the initiative, backed by public opinion, which preferred royal authority to aristocratic violence. A commemorative medal was issued, which translates: 'the safety of the provincials achieved by the repression of the audacity of the over-mighty'.

During the two decades or so between Louis' assumption of power and the death of Colbert (1683), one gets the impression of a strong, self-confident regime, embarking on ambitious reforms. Louis was the boss, Colbert his man of dispatch. New codes of law were promulgated: laws for civil procedures (1667), rivers and forests (1669), the criminal code (1670), the commercial code (1673), the maritime code (1672), and then, after Colbert's death, the colonial code (1685), which made humane provisions for the treatment of slaves. Obviously legislation is not the same as enforcement. But some progress was made: witness the outrage when in 1664 Colbert launched a further assault on aristocratic presumption by investigating spurious claims to nobility. Again the magistrates cooperated with the crown in what in effect was the elimination of tax dodgers, genuine nobles being exempt. A clear example of successful, authoritarian reform was the assault on crime in Paris. Two lieutenants of the Parisian police, de la Reynie and then d'Argenson, vigorously and successfully pursued pickpockets, murderers, prostitutes and highway robbers. Attempts were made to remove rubbish, offal and excrement, which together made the city so uniquely malodorous. The streets were made safer at night by the erection of 6,000 vandal-proof lanterns.

If Louis' rule was certainly authoritarian at the centre, how effective was it in the peripheral provinces of that vast, sprawling geographical entity known as France? Perhaps it did indeed depend on the links between crown and provincial notables where patronage was intelligently dispensed by royal brokers, as the revisionists suggest. But Louis also resorted to force. Louvois, the war minister, was now the man, especially after Colbert's death in 1683. Because he possessed an increasingly large, loyal and disciplined army, Louis more or less had the necessary monopoly of violence to keep his regime out of trouble. These were Louis' instructions to Turenne:

> We find ourselves obliged for the conservation of the state as much as for its glory and its reputation, to maintain in peace as well as in war a great number of troops, both infantry and cavalry, which will always be in good condition to keep our people in the obedience and the respect that they owe, to insure the peace and tranquillity which we have won.[26]

No more Frondes! Judicious use of force suppressed the various revolts that disturbed provincial France: Boulonnais (1662), Gascony (1664), Roussillon (1666), the Vivarais (1670), Guyenne (1674), Brittany (1675), the Camisard revolt in the Cévennes (1704). According to Mme de Sévigné the royal troops who suppressed the revolt in Brittany 'behaved as though they were on the other side of the Rhine'.

Louis also depended on public opinion, which could be dazzled by the media offensive that we shall examine in the next chapter, impressed by the Grands Jours or sobered by the execution of the traitor Rohan (1674) who had planned to lead a revolt in Normandy, with Dutch support. The cutting of the first sod of the Canal du Midi, which illustrated the fruitful cooperation between the crown, the nobility in Languedoc and the church, was likewise an occasion for royal publicity. Louis' refusal to countenance defiance was flagged up by the fate of the unfortunate Fouquet when he was conveyed from Paris to his remote prison at Pinerolo in the Alps. Metaphorically his cage carried the placard, 'The disgraced Financier who got too big for his boots'. Everyone could get the message.

Actually money is the nub of the problem when the strength of Louis XIV's regime is analysed – the money needed to pay for Louis' wars. His domestic policy was nothing if not foreign policy led. And it was *his* foreign policy, which he arbitrarily imposed on the nation without consultation beyond the *conseil d'en haut*. While he certainly cared about the welfare of the church, or about his own authority in outlying provinces, or even about the happiness of his subjects (just a little, now and again), what really mattered to him was his *gloire* – that is to say, his reputation as a great warrior, a great statesman, a great dynast, or a great gentleman. In pursuit of *gloire* Louis bullied the king of Spain in 1661 and the pope in 1662 without going to war, because his victims backed down. But Louis neither expected nor desired this to last. Indeed *gloire* on the cheap, by peaceful means, did not really appeal, for instance, when Louis went to war in 1667–8 against his wife's relations – a quick, rather tame, easily afford-able affair. The Dutch War (1672–9) was different. The money Colbert had prudently accumulated was blown on this war. More and more cash had to be acquired for escalating warfare during the rest of the reign.

The quarter-century of war against virtually the rest of Europe (1688–1713) brought France to her financial knees. Because these wars were so horrendously expensive in blood and treasure, all Louis' plans for progress and reform were placed at risk. The *soulagement* (comforting, support, relief from burdens) of the people was put on hold. On the one hand, the magnificent monarchy of the earlier years was now reduced to a perpetually desperate scrimmage for cash. On the other hand, the money actually raised to fund the French army – nearly 400,000 men at the height of the wars – is a remarkable demonstration of power, in its way more impressive than anything achieved by Louis and Colbert in earlier, happier times. Taxes were ratcheted up to their realistic limit, especially indirect taxation. Sale of office was milked as far as it would go, though a limit was reached round about 1708 with the result that the percentage of war expenditure thus raised fell to below 10 per cent. Sale of government bonds, borrowing from financiers and the lucrative prosecution of those same financiers, devaluation of the currency – every measure was exploited by the king's financiers. Astonishingly there was remarkably little protest, either at the centre of government or in the provinces. Was France cowed by a resurgence of fiscal terrorism, or did public opinion support the king's wars, or was it all a great con-trick? Somehow it worked.

Arguably the period between Louvois' death in 1691 and the end of the reign in 1715 was the true period of absolutism. The revision-ists have tended to ignore this period, just as they have concentrated on the *pays d'état* where the local estates and the traditional leaders of soci-ety had a better chance of standing up to the crown. But the bulk of the taxation required by the wars was collected from the *pays d'élection*, supervised by the increasingly prominent intendants, now residing in their *généralités* for much longer periods than the originally designated three years, and supported by permanent assistants.[27] Absolutism, surely, though what's in a name? 'A great deal,' Henshall argues, 'it all depends on the reality.' But that is the point. Louis XIV's success in funding his wars *was* the reality, resulting from the exercise of power, flexibly negotiated but truly effective. What an achievement!

THE COURT

While Louis excelled in his control of government, church and armed forces, he was seen at his most impressive at court. In August 1715, he remarked that having lived in the midst of his courtiers all his life he was glad to die there. It was indeed appropriate that the last rays of the setting sun should illuminate the environment where, man and boy, Louis had lived and flourished. Everyone knows the myth, popularised by Dumas, of the mysterious prisoner in an iron mask who was Louis XIV's twin brother. In a very real though metaphorical sense, Louis was the man in the golden mask. At court he was perpetually on show, a professional frontman, presenting a dazzling mask to the world. It was part of the explanation for his success. Appearances were vital. And gold was his colour, the colour of the sun's rays.

Louis adopted the sun as his emblem, the Greek sun-god Apollo as his public persona. The sun's rays penetrated everywhere, bringing light and warmth. There was a Christian connotation too, the Sun of Righteousness bringing healing in its wings (mentioned in Malachi 4: 2). The unlimited nature of Louis XIV's golden sunrays was indicated by his motto, 'nec pluribus impar', which can roughly be translated as 'the sky's the limit' – 'a boastful reference to the way he had faced successfully a coalition against him formed by Austria, Spain and the Dutch republic'.[28] The sun is everywhere at Versailles, but was apparent too in paintings, medallions, pageants and statues before the court finally moved there in 1682.

Louis' self-presentation was part of his professionalism. Like his devotion to the routine of day-by-day administration, it was 'a delightful business'. Being permanently on show from morning *lever* to evening *coucher* was no penance for such a sociable man – and one might add such a vain man. Louis loved being the centre of attention and resented it when he was not. To be fair, he would have argued that it was his job. And again to be fair, there were inevitably occasions when his public appearances must have taxed him. Once when he was suffering excruciating toothache it was suggested to him that he might 'cut' that evening's reception with a clear conscience. 'No,' he replied, 'we owe ourselves to the public.' Similarly he insisted on his granddaughter-in-law, Adelaide, dancing with him in public, even though she was unwell. Even in his last illness Louis maintained the routine of public appearances.

The court shows the 'king at work' *par excellence*. The court was France's only national institution, apart from the monarchy. We have noted the political importance of the court as a centre of patronage and influence where the two-way relationship between monarch and aristocracy flourished (or did not as was later to be the case in the reigns of his successors). For the system to work Louis had to be accessible, but not too accessible. This explains the immense competition for apparently menial posts such as handing the king his shirt. The more intimate the occasion, the greater the honour, plus the opportunity for making requests, either on one's own behalf or on behalf of a client. This even included waiting on the king when he relieved himself on his *chaise percée* (where Henri III had been assassinated by a petitioner in 1589). Louis' technique was clever. He would listen patiently and courteously. Then, as often as not, he would make his favourite reply: 'We shall see.' Although a cautious man, Louis was not a procrastinator. With his prodigious memory, he did attend to petitions – otherwise people would have given up approaching him. But it was not easy: 'Every time I do someone a favour, I make ninety-nine enemies – and the hundredth betrays me.'

Because Louis could not allow himself to be mobbed, the court was dominated by protocol. Louis – and his half-pint lookalike brother – led the courtiers in the imposition of precedence, hierarchy, ritual and formality. These detailed rules and regulations were directly linked to power. 'People who think that courtly rituals are merely ceremonial affairs are seriously mistaken', Louis warned his son. In few other contexts is the problem of *mentalité* so apparent. In other words, it takes imaginative effort for members of an informal, egalitarian society in the twenty-first century to get inside the attitudes and aspirations of such a rank-conscious environment. Saint-Simon, for instance, can hardly control his fury when Louis' bastards were promoted above dukes such as himself. He describes the embarrassment when he and the duc de Chevreuse found the duc de Rochefoucauld playing chess *with his valet*. Everything was ordered by protocol. Even in the royal chapel, in the presence of the God who died for all, the worshippers were graded according to rank, devoutly facing the king rather than the altar. In processions or at official receptions, precedence was sometimes settled only by duels. At meals people sat where they were entitled to sit − or did not sit at all. And the various types of furniture were of profound significance: chairs with or without arms, stools, benches, and so forth. 'Who was allowed to sit in the presence of whom and on what?' sums it up. Hence the popularity of the game-table, where rules of precedence were waived for obvious reasons. The only thing that mattered was whether you could pay when you lost.

Louis dominated the court by his charm and good sense. 'The evidence suggests to me that he was often rather good at handling people, he had a real grasp of psychology and usually behaved very decently in human terms', writes Robin Briggs.[29] The recorded occasions when he behaved badly are few. He rarely lost his temper. On one occasion he assaulted a footman for stealing a biscuit when the real cause of his wrath was the discovery that his favourite bastard the duc de Maine had proved himself a coward in battle. Normally, however, he remained affable, approachable, urbane and aware of what was going on. Saint-Simon tells how, when his father died, acquisitive courtiers scrambled for his post at court. 'Has he not a son?' demanded the king, before ensuring that Saint-Simon was duly rewarded.

The only crime for a courtier to commit was not to be there. 'We never see him' was Louis' invariable sentence of social death on an absent nobleman. The king's gaze missed nothing, penetrating everywhere like the rays of the sun. Attendance was essential at court functions, not merely the official entertainments (*appartements*) but at concerts, tours round the gardens and at chapel. There was no excuse for absence. Everyone knew the king's programme. As Saint-Simon remarked, 'with a watch and an almanac, one could know exactly what the king was doing, even if one was a hundred leagues away'. Once a malicious courtier circulated a rumour that the king would not be attending mass that day. Great was Louis' indignation when he arrived as usual to find an empty chapel.

Louis also achieved domination by his omniscience. He constantly listened to his valets and his guards who were encouraged to tell all they had seen. Courtiers' mail was frequently intercepted and passed to the king − a poisonous practice that presumably he would have justified on professional grounds. He needed to know what was going on. Yet there is an undoubted element of malice at work here. Compare the occasion when he forced his illegitimate daughter to read out an injudicious letter she had written. Or there was the time when Mme de Maintenon read out Liselotte's letter to the electress of Hanover in which she criticised the king and his second wife. Liselotte was Orleans' widow, a high-ranking German princess who might have been expected to have exploded – 'how dare you read my letters?' But no, she wept with shame and remorse. Malice, too, was self-evident when Louis and his mistress de Montespan used to lean over a strategically chosen balcony and amuse each other at the expense of passers-by. Courtiers used to make long detours to avoid such pitiless scrutiny. More seriously the court shuddered when Louis had his adolescent bastard son Vermandois stripped and beaten in his presence because he had been initiated into homosexuality. Nevertheless, Louis was liked and respected by his court. There was a human side to the golden mask, and a sense of the ridiculous too, as when Louis passed a rotten pear to a notoriously obsequious courtier who pronounced it delicious. Again, though, there is the malice – though which of us in such a position would not show malice occasionally?

To a sadly increasing extent, there was not much to laugh at from 1688 onwards. David Ogg described Versailles as 'a cross between Monte Carlo and Whitehall'. Now it resembled a military hospital, peopled by walking wounded and their grieving relatives – perhaps an aristocratic version of the Invalides. But it was also the headquarters of the armed forces. Perhaps not so very much changed. Louis had always been the first nobleman of the state, personifying the military virtues of the sword. His greatest alibi against the charge of making war too much is that it was what his nobility expected and desired. Perhaps his position resembled the elector of Brandenburg-Prussia's partnership with his junkers: 'We put our fate in our monarch's hand, As long as he does what we demand.' Well, up to a point.

In Chapters 7 and 9 Louis' control over the army will be explored. Recent research has demonstrated that he dominated the conduct of war as much as the making of foreign policy. Suffice here to say that towards the end of the reign Louis laboured even more than in earlier decades on diplomacy and war. Some freedom of manoeuvre had to be allowed to diplomats, generals and admirals. But Louis interfered to an increasing and disastrous extent. As he saw it, he was doing his job. Generals and diplomats had to report to the king at Versailles, both the centre of the court and the administration. The Dutch historian Jeroen Duindam has questioned the reality of Louis XIV's power as exercised both at court and throughout Europe:

> As an instrument of power, the myth Louis XIV helped to create was just as important as the standing army he greatly expanded at the same time. The myth, however, retained its effectiveness much longer, for down to the present day Louis' power continues to be overestimated.[30]

My comment is that if Louis' self-promotion was really even more effective than his control of the army, it must have been some myth. Duindam, however, can point to the catastrophic defeats in the War of the Spanish Succession (1701–14), which destroyed the reality of the predominance of Louis' beloved army. The partial recovery that Louis master-minded was arguably his finest hour.

What the king did not do until it was too late was help his perplexed finance ministers find the money to pay for both court and armed forces. That was their job. As a mercantilist, Colbert believed that the amount of cash in circulation was limited, the trick being to rob your neighbour of his share. But Louis was not a mercantilist. He believed that there was no limit to the money available. 'Have another look at those figures', he told Colbert, 'and if you cannot produce the money, I will find someone else who can.' Occasionally he would make gestures such as donating his golden furniture to be melted down or showing the plebeian banker Samuel Bernard round the gardens at Versailles in order to flatter him into organising loans for the war effort. To his credit Louis supported the new taxes introduced by Colbert's successors: Pontchartrain's *capitation* (1695) and Desmaretz's *dixième* (1710). But there is little evidence that he shared Pontchartrain's concern for the impoverished peasants. The Sun King's legacy was basically *gloire* – and bankruptcy.

In the meantime it was study work: reports, dispatches, correspondence, and interviews with prospective generals to one of whom Louis gave a quick eye test as he was reputedly short-sighted. The king was basically a kind man and was at his best consoling defeated commanders. He greeted Villeroy after he had lost the battle of Ramillies with the fatuous, though well-meant, observation that 'at our age, M. le Marshal, we cannot expect to be lucky'. Mme de Maintenon remarked darkly that

'God was in wrath', which really meant that she was in wrath with her husband's obsession with war. But he had little choice except to labour night and day to dig France out of the mire.

Amazingly court life went on. It was not the gay, permissive court life of the 1660s and 1670s. Now all was sober and proper under the beady eyes of Mme de Maintenon and her reformed husband. Sexual licence and drunkenness occurred, if at all, behind closed doors or in faraway Paris. But services were still sumptuously performed in the palace chapel, recently built out of stone rather than marble – an economy that still did not reconcile Mme de Maintenon to the expense. Huge meals were still consumed by the king, waited on by his courtiers while the rest of France starved. Concerts, receptions, parades were uninterrupted despite the war. It was Louis' job to keep the royal show on the road as much as it was his job to administer the war and prepare for the peace. In the same way when peace came to the king's armed forces, ecclesiastical warfare raged. The king remained at work up until his last illness, misdirecting the campaign against the Jansenists that concluded with the disastrous *Unigenitus* affair: as it was in the beginning, 'one king, one law, one faith' remained the goal.

Indeed Louis' priorities looked increasingly old-fashioned and irrelevant. As the king aged, the court divided into factions, jostling for what really mattered – the succession. Women came to play an increasingly prominent role – the duchess of Burgundy, Mme Choin, the dauphin's morganatic wife, and above all Mme de Maintenon. No better illustration could be found of Louis' backward-looking conservatism as he glowered at these warring court factions. Some progress had been made in the creation of a national system of law and government. But not a great deal. Louis *backed* into the eighteenth century, his gaze fixed on the past. National politics, determining the future of France, were smothered by dynastic in-fighting between the king's legitimate and illegitimate relatives, so memorably described by the duc de Saint-Simon and interpreted (see Figure 4) by Le Roi Ladurie.[31] Monseigneur's group operated from Meudun, Burgundy attracted the reformers, de Maintenon battled for her favourite the duc de Maine. All the while the old king exercised his ultimate control. Court and government lived side by side. Courtiers and politicians competed with each other, all none too cosily housed in that huge mausoleum that was the Sun King's bequest to his suffering people. It was his life's work.

5

CULTURE WITH A PURPOSE

What did Louis XIV get up to when he was not chained to his desk? Although council meetings sometimes continued into the afternoon, the king's normal daily routine usually included a period for relaxation between lunch and his evening commitments. As soon as possible, Louis would escape into the fresh air. A countryman through and through, he loved exercise out of doors, almost in any weather. Even if it was raining heavily, he would still sally forth, expecting his courtiers and attendants to show the same indifference that he invariably brought to bear on all climatic conditions. Only very rarely would Louis relent and stay indoors, perhaps to play billiards or spend time *chez les dames* – the contemporary euphemism for 'one afternoon stands' (Antonia Fraser). Otherwise Louis would be outside, walking in his park, conducting visitors round his gardens or enjoying a 'naval' expedition on the Versailles canal. He loved riding, for he was an excellent horseman. When gout incapacitated him, he would still enjoy the fresh air by driving a barouche or a carriage. Here again his rapport with horses was outstanding. In old age he impressed bystanders by taking control of a team of panicking horses and bringing them to a halt.

Louis' favourite outdoor pursuit was hunting. Whereas his son Monseigneur the dauphin had a mission to rid the countryside round Paris of wolves, his father's quarries were game birds, wild boar and, above all, deer. The hunt was often a magnificent, stylised affair with musicians and court ladies in attendance. The huntsman would identify a suitable stag, having traced it to its lair. The unfortunate beast would then be driven towards its executioners, who would direct its massacre by hunting dogs in the presence of the king and court. Louis once displayed his lack of sympathy with dumb animals in a rather nasty poem about an amorous stag that was so exhausted by its rutting that it could not escape the hunt. Perhaps it took one to know one.

> Making love is a dangerous thing
> A happy stag who's had his way
> And passed the night in amorous fling
> Thinks he can sleep the following day.
> But when the pack of baying hounds
> And the horn's relentless sounds
> Drive him out into the plain,
> He feels his breath is on the wane,
> He has no more strength to spare
> And by too much pleasure filled,
> By the hunter he gets killed.[1]

Louis was also a crack shot. Shortly before he died he is reputed to have brought down thirty-four partridges with thirty-six shots. An astonishing feat, even given the improved accuracy of the fowling pieces of the time.

What else apart from government, war and exercise? This chapter will explore Louis XIV's outstanding contribution to the cultural achievement of his reign, while Chapter 6 will examine his private life from which we can learn about his values and personality.

L'HONNÊTE HOMME

In the Introduction we noted Chateaubriand's favourable comparison of Louis XIV with Napoleon in the context of cultural achievement. Napoleon allegedly created nothing, whereas Louis was a profoundly successful initiator of French culture. Louis XIV was certainly a remarkable enabler of intellectual and artistic achievement. In particular, the first twenty years of his personal rule constituted a golden age. Colbert cooperated with the king in recruiting gifted writers, artists and musicians, and encouraged them to give of their best.

Louis is sometimes represented as second-rate in his appreciation of the arts and the products of the mind. Admittedly he never read anything except state papers. But he was one of the greatest cultural all-rounders in history. He was a competent and knowledgeable musician, playing the lute and singing in tune. He was fascinated by architecture, constantly demanding details of the progress of his building projects. Louvois once insisted that a new building should be disfigured by a faulty angle so that Louis could have the pleasure of spotting it. The king played a major part in directing and participating in court ballets, masques and operas. He was a discerning critic of drama. Perhaps his greatest claim to real erudition was his knowledge of landscape gardening and horticulture. Who else among rulers can rival him? Prince Albert was cleverer, though his interests were not so broad; Charles I was a more discerning art connoisseur; and Frederick the Great a better musician. But Louis would never have joined George V in calling *Hamlet* 'sad stuff', nor equalled Elizabeth II in showing only polite, clearly forced interest in anything except horses. Above all Louis excelled in his capacity for enjoyment and in his ability to communicate this to others.

Louis master-minded the cultural life of the court. For instance, he imposed his own interests and priorities on such potential troublemakers as the formidable Condé. The way that Louis brought Condé into line was an impressive demonstration of man management. While the king remained a soldier throughout his life, he established the *honnête homme* as the ideal to be emulated as opposed to the hero of mud and blood formerly personified by Condé. '*Honnête homme*' is untranslatable into concise English; something like 'man of honour, culture and erudition, self-controlled and well-mannered' sums it up. Such was Louis XIV. So after Condé had been welcomed back to court and formally forgiven in 1661, the great general 'had to take his place in a new world in which he rejoined the mass of his fellow men and looked up to a monarch who had gathered all the heroic qualities into himself'.[2] Condé had the sense to see where his bread was buttered. Given Louis' outstanding success in quickly establishing his own cultural and social hegemony, there was clearly no future now in subversive disloyalty. So Condé accepted that his only claim to fame was his Bourbon blood and buckled down to the life of an obedient courtier, following his sovereign's lead and becoming as *honnête* a man as the Sun King.

Louis was a different kind of hero, updated and civilised. When the Sun King instituted a triumphal entry into Paris after the birth of the dauphin (December 1661), he dominated the *carrousel*; that is to say, a grand procession combined with a tournament, laid on to impress the citizens. He starred as the leader of the Romans, with his brother as the king of the Persians; Condé had to be content with being the king of the Turks. Soon Condé was rowing ladies round the lake at Versailles. When he received an independent command in the Dutch War, it was entirely on Louis' terms. All the *gloire* went to the king. While Condé established an independent court at Chantilly in the early decades of the reign, it was a loyal imitation of Versailles, not a rival. Although he welcomed Huguenots and free-thinkers, only receiving communion himself just before his death in 1686, Condé finally acknowledged the victory of faith over reason, meekly following his sovereign's lead.

Public displays show Louis' creativity. It has been suggested that the only innovation introduced by the Sun King was the sheer scale of his buildings and entertainments. This is not entirely fair. While Richelieu and Mazarin anticipated several of Louis' measures, such events as the *carrousel* were the results of Louis' deliberate innovations, directly linked with his self-promotion as the Sun King. For the benefit of his son, he explained his intentions:

> The *carrousel*, which has furnished me the subject of these reflections, had only been conceived at first as a light amusement; but, little by little, we were carried away, and it became a spectacle that was fairly grand and magnificent, both in the number of exercises and by the number of the costumes and the variety of the heraldic devices. It was then that I began to employ the one which I have always kept since. For the device they chose the sun which, according to the rules of this art, is the most noble of all, and which, by its quality of being unique, by the brilliance which surrounds it, by the light which it communicates to the other stars ... is the most striking and beautiful image of a great monarch. Those who saw me governing with a good deal of ease and without being confused by anything, persuaded me to add the earth's globe and for motto, *nec pluribus impar* (not unequal to more), by which they meant something that flattered the aspirations of a young king, namely that, being sufficient to so many things, I would doubtless be capable of governing other empires, just as the sun was capable of lighting up other worlds if they were exposed to its rays.[3]

Louis' genius for inventive innovation was best illustrated in May 1664 by 'The Pleasures of the Enchanted Isle', a series of ballets, plays and displays supposedly in honour of the queen mother Anne of Austria and Louis' queen Marie Thérèse. In fact it was Louis' gesture of adoration for his mistress Louise de La Vallière. It was a tour de force, which those present never forgot. Ballets, fireworks, banquets and plays culminated with Molière's *Tartuffe* – a brilliant satire on religious hypocrisy, which infuriated the *dévots* headed by the queen-mother. To his credit Louis – who found the play hilarious – defended Molière. 'Why do people get upset by *Tartuffe* and not by blasphemous plays like *Scaramouche?*' Louis asked Condé. 'Because nobody minds God being attacked, whereas in *Tartuffe* they themselves are ridiculed', was the reply. *Tartuffe* reads well today. It is a masterpiece, representing the French genius that Louis so effectively mobilised. But it is not difficult to see why it offended the godly and the self-righteous. For instance, Tartuffe has just rebuked a serving-girl for her low-cut dress, prompting the retort, 'you must be mighty susceptible'; he then immediately attempts to seduce a married woman:

> Ah, but I'm not less a man for being devout! Confronted by your celestial beauty one can but let love have its way and make no demur. I realise that such a declaration coming from me may well seem strange, but, after all, madam, I'm not an angel. If you condemn this declaration of mine, you must lay the blame on your own enchanting loveliness. Moreover your honour runs no risk with me. These courtly gallants that women are so fond of noise their deeds abroad. But men of our sort burn with discreeter fires. Our concern for our own reputation is a safeguard for those we love, and to those who trust us we offer love without scandal, satisfaction without fear.[4]

Ballets, masques, operas and musical entertainments were regularly performed until the 1680s when more formal concerts replaced them. Louis himself stopped ballet dancing in 1669 when it was suggested to him that he was demeaning himself – though he continued to dance beautifully at formal court functions until extreme old age. He was always a naturally graceful mover. By his own example he gave the necessary lead. He showed his priorities by befriending Molière. When courtiers objected to eating with such a commoner, Louis ostentatiously put them to shame by inviting Molière to join him for a midnight feast.

THE PATRON OF MUSIC

Louis also befriended Lully, his chief court musician, whose music he rated highly. Lully was widely feared, obsequious to the great and tyrannical to his subordinates, a homosexual paedophile who deliberately feathered his own nest at the expense of rival musicians such as Charpentier. While one notes *en passant* how selectively inconsistent Louis' homophobia was, our concern here is with his musical judgement. Though David Sturdy refers to Lully's 'outstanding talent and versatility', Donald Jay Grout is not impressed: 'Page upon page of music void of imagination, pale in colour, thin in harmony, monotonous in invention, stereotyped in rhythm, limited in melody, barren of contrapuntal resources and so cut into little sections by perpetually recurring cadences that all sense of movement seems lost in a desert of clichés, relieved all too rarely by oases of real beauty'. James Gaines contrasts the courts of Louis XIV and Frederick the Great where J.S. Bach's genius was recognised. The second-rate Lully on the other hand, 'fiercely disliked and openly opposed by many, hung on, getting richer and richer, until finally he made them all happy by impaling himself on the foot with his baton and dying of gangrene'.[5] Gaines accuses Lully of writing his music purely to flatter the king and keep the nobles amused. Certainly Lully wrote with these ends in mind. But he was a genuine innovator. His music is tuneful, though repetitive and unmemorable. He relies on contrasts between bombastic noise and orchestral gimmicks to maintain his audience's interest. Basically he writes programme music, designed to support the visual arts and incapable of standing on its own merits. While no one can lift a candle to Bach, Lully compares badly with Purcell, his English contemporary, to say nothing of Charpentier.[6]

But Lully suited Louis. He fitted in well with the campaign to enhance the reputation of France and the Sun King's *gloire*. This campaign was masterminded by Colbert, who applied his favourite mercantilist doctrines to the arts. Whereas under the cardinals France had imported foreign talent, now she was to develop her own home-grown musicians, artists, craftsmen and architects in order to astonish the world. France would thus become an exporter rather than an importer. The campaign was centrally directed through the creation of state-sponsored academies, such as the Académie Royale de Danse (March 1661). Louis, who as we have seen danced beautifully, wished to impose the necessary skills on the court. He explained his thinking in the academy's letters patent: 'The art of the dance has always been recognised as one of the most respectable and necessary to train the body. It is one of the most advantageous and useful to our nobility and to others who have the honour of approaching us, not just in war times and in our armies but even in times of peace, in the *divertissement* of our ballets.'

Lully supervised the training of dancers at the academy. He also controlled the Académie Royale de Musique. Thanks to Louis' support in his frequent rows with jealous rivals, including Molière, Lully became 'unquestionably the most powerful musician of modern times',[7] while the success of his operas made him 'probably the wealthiest composer in history'. Lully repaid the king by writing, producing and conducting the concerts that were such a feature of the court *divertissements*. Furthermore, the operas that entertained the court were also shown to the French people. 'Both court and citizenry were treated to the spectacle of the opulence and grandeur that were the hallmark of the royal absolutism under Louis XIV.'[8] The theme on such occasions, and also in the operas, was invariably the grandeur of the Sun King. Music was everywhere – when the king ate his meals, when he led *promenades* round the park, when he entertained at the evening *appartements*, when he hunted deer. When he conducted parties round his gardens, musicians sprang up from behind bushes and hedges. All was masterminded by Lully to the glory of his appreciative master.

In Louis' later years, when the court became a more sober, less rumbustious place, music still dominated the scene, with chamber music concerts replacing Lully's ballets and operas. Louis personally interviewed candidates for the post of chapel organist at Versailles. He appointed the genius of chamber music François Couperin – and one would think he got it right. Louis also appointed a harpsichord teacher for Adelaide, Burgundy's child bride. There was nothing that Louis enjoyed more than a sing-song with his granddaughter-in-law at the keyboard. He would raise the roof with a drinking song, relaxing in his armchair while Mme de Maintenon frowned her disapproval and concentrated on her embroidery.

THE VISUAL ARTS

If the ears of Louis XIV's public were perpetually bashed, their eyes were dazzled by the Sun King's media specialists. Coins, medals, statues, flowers, plaques, triumphal arches, and – above all – buildings testified to the greatness of France and of her magnificent monarch. Colbert, who masterminded this campaign until his death in 1683, once told Louis that nothing, absolutely nothing, mattered more than the king's *gloire*. It used to be thought that Colbert was opposed to so much building on the grounds of expense, but the truth is that it was not so much the cost that troubled Colbert but the way the money was spent. In particular he was against the construction of a vast palace at Versailles, preferring the Louvre in Paris as the king's chief residence.

It used to be thought that Louis was opposed to spending money on his capital. This is not true. The magnificent colonnade designed by Le Vau at the Louvre and the chapel at the Invalides are examples of Louis' determination to beautify Paris. Both are gorgeous, both in their way illustrations of the French artistic genius set to work at the behest of the Sun King. So as to get the best possible design, Louis had the great Bernini summoned from Rome to compete with French architects in updating the Louvre. Bernini's plans were turned down, though he did not return home empty-handed, being well paid for a magnificent bust of the Sun King. Nevertheless, it was a significant triumph for French culture when Perrault's design for the Louvre was preferred. Bernini was outraged.

Henceforward, *French* architects would beautify Paris. For instance, the golden dome of the Invalides chapel still dominates the rest of the city. Designed by Mansart, the hospital is a tribute to Louis' concern for the physical health of his wounded soldiers, while the chapel reflects his insistence that their spiritual welfare should be in the hands of the Counter-Reformation. Mansart designed a separate entrance to a gallery where Louis could look down on his convalescent soldiers without rubbing shoulders with them. Paris as a city was modernised and improved during the Sun King's reign. 'Beginning in 1662, a coherent plan of urban renewal and administration took shape that lifted Paris out of its medieval past and into early modernity.'[9] As well as the construction of the Invalides and the improvements to the Louvre, which was finally beautified by Le Vau, the Tuileries was given a face-lift, while the Place des Victoires, the Place Royale, the Place Louis-le-Grand, the Porte Saint-Martin and the Port Saint-Denis all reminded Parisians how privileged they were to inhabit the Sun King's capital.

But Louis' real enthusiasm was for Versailles, about which he sent Colbert innumerable instructions. By contrast his relatively cavalier attitude to Paris is apparent from this hastily written note (1670) informing the great minister of his whistle-stop programme:

> I will leave Versailles on Tuesday at nine, and will be at the Triumphal Arch at eleven at the latest. I shall go from there to the Observatory, and then dine at my brother's. After the baptism which will be early, I will go to the Louvre, and from there proceed to the Tuileries whence I will leave to return here. I'm letting you know my plans early so you can take appropriate measures.[10]

Colbert was not alone in his preference for Paris and his reservations about Versailles. Bossuet called it 'the city of the rich'. Courtiers referred to it as 'the undeserving favourite'. Saint-Simon damned the place for not having woods, water or views. 'The violence done to nature everywhere repels and disgusts. The abundance of water, forced up and channelled from all directions, is made green, thick and muddy; it spreads an unhealthy and perceptible humidity and an odour which is worse.'[11] Even Voltaire, who admired the Sun King, admitted that 'the nation would rather that Louis XIV had preferred his Louvre and his capital to the palace of Versailles'.

But Louis was adamant. If only because he had to overcome both nature and the disapproval of his advisers, Versailles was Louis' supreme statement to his contemporaries and to posterity: 'Versailles, c'est moi!' he might well have exclaimed. Work proceeded during the 1670s despite the frequent presence of the court. About 35,000 men laboured there, including soldiers who toiled in vain to build a canal to bring water through fetid marshes and across lofty aqueducts from the river at Maintenon 40 miles away. Other sources, including the diverted river Eure, brought more water to Versailles than to Paris. Over 5,000 soldiers, employed in the construction of Versailles and its waterworks, died from disease and exhaustion. Their corpses were removed at night so as not to lower morale. Louis hoped to bring the court back from its autumnal 'voyage' to Fontainebleau to a completed palace in the autumn of 1682. Louvois, however, warned him that atrocious weather had slowed everything down. Louis contented himself with an instruction to 'pay more attention to my bedroom than the rest'. In the event much of the palace, including the Hall of Mirrors, was ready for the courtiers' admiration, though work was to continue well into the eighteenth century – on the chapel, for example, which was built from stone instead of marble to save costs.

The scale of Versailles is awesome. It covers 25 acres and is 700 yards long. It has 2,143 windows and 1,252 fireplaces. It was designed to accommodate the royal family, including the king's mistresses, in splendour. Madame de Montespan, for instance, had a gigantic marble bathroom built for her, perhaps a hint from her royal lover that she was not especially clean, even by the low standards of the age. The palace accommodated something like 5,000 courtiers and their servants in varying splendour and comfort, while another 5,000 lived in the town. Many of the thousands of rooms, however, were pokey and cold, and sanitation left much to be desired, so that the palace stank in high summer. Versailles was also a military depot for the king's elite regiments (*le maison du roi*). The stables alone were vast. Versailles was the centre of government as well. Ministers no longer had to chase round the various governmental departments in Paris – a great improvement. Visitors were welcome if they were equipped with a ceremonial sword. Louis would have approved of the swarms of Japanese, Americans and other races, now armed with cameras, who marvel today at the Hall of Mirrors (238 by 35 feet), the various salons and the gardens.

Everywhere there were homages to Louis XIV's successes. Le Brun, for instance, painted enormous, pompous canvases for the Hall of Mirrors celebrating Louis' victories over the Dutch, while the ambassadors, mounting their special staircase, were reminded of Louis' crossing of the Rhine, his conquest of Franche-Comté and his humiliation of Spain. No palace had ever been so dedicated to the glorification of an individual. Even God was relegated to a chapel outside the Cour Royal – as the central court yard was known – and there is little Christian imagery in the palace's decorations. Magnificent carpets and tapestries covered the walls and the floors. The newly invented parquet tiles prevented water seeping through when the floors were cleaned. Versailles was French wherever possible, an advertisement for French craftsmanship and artistic taste. It was expensive, costing over 81 million livres between 1664 and 1690, though many of Louis' admirers claim that it was not *that* expensive. On an average this worked out at about 6.5 per cent of the king's total revenue. So far as Louis was concerned it was worth it.

Versailles, however, poses the crucial question about the whole of Louis' cultural achievement: was it more than a gigantic propaganda exercise, ramming Louis XIV's glory down everyone's throat? Versailles is big. It contains amazing craftsmanship. It has suffered from the 'improvements' of later generations, in that Louis XV removed the famous ambassadors' staircase, Louis Philippe introduced the horrors of nineteenth-century refined taste and the Germans desecrated it in 1871. While it is still impressive, its merits are a matter of personal choice. The expertise of Bluche, Dunlop, Mitford and many other enthusiasts should be respected. Others of us, however, may wonder if it is not about power rather than art. Would Fouquet have presided over a more spontaneous and creative achievement? Indeed, can the unending combustion of incense on Louis XIV's altars be justified?

To some extent Louis can defend himself by arguing that such exercises in self-glorification as Versailles were all part of a calculated campaign. Peter Burke has analysed this 'fabrication' of Louis XIV in its various manifestations; that is to say, the projection of his public image. Was it not part of Louis' job? Chandra Mukerji has demonstrated how Versailles was an integral part of Louis' campaign to strengthen France militarily. Versailles, she argues, should be linked with Vauban's frontier fortresses, constructed in the interests of what she calls 'territoriality', meaning the rational pursuit of power by war and building in defence of French security. It was logical that Versailles should be constructed by soldiers, already used to building military earthworks. Mukerji maintains that Louis was impressed by the military potential of the terraced gardens at Vaux – hence his suspicion of Fouquet and his appropriation of the team that had worked there. Everything had to serve France, personified by the Sun King. Louis Marin has explored the sophisticated techniques employed, such as the use of the unexpected, so carefully used in the court masques, ballets and *divertissements*, in promulgating the Sun King's image. He quotes one of Louis' publicity hacks, the author André Félibien, who has this to say about a portrait of the king:

> It is true that having to speak about the greatest king in the world is a subject so much beyond my power that my endeavour can be accused of temerity, if the subject itself did not serve as an excuse for this endeavour, since I cannot better fulfil my duty than by using all my power to speak about those great qualities that the whole earth admires in your august person and that are painted so mysteriously in the picture that I want to describe.

Contrast La Fontaine's fable of the Fox and the Crow – a funny and perceptive depiction of flattery where the fox persuades 'Sir of the

Crow' to drop the cheese in its beak by persuading him to sing. No wonder Louis disliked La Fontaine, and not just because he defended and admired Fouquet.[12] On the other hand, Molière transferred his allegiance from Fouquet to Louis. With due recognition of the danger of anachronism – it was after all a deferential age – it is a disagreeable shock to find such a sharp, witty, perceptive send-up of hypocrisy as *Tartuffe* end with gross flattery. Tartuffe has just displayed his true colours by betraying his friend for alleged treason. But a policeman arrives to put matters right:

> Calm your fears, sir. We live under a prince inimical to fraud, a monarch who can read men's hearts, whom no impostor's art deceives. The keen discernment of that lofty mind at all times sees things in their true perspective; nothing can disturb the firm constancy of his judgement or lead him into error. On men of worth he confers immortal glory but his favour is not shown indiscriminately; his love for good men and true does not preclude a proper detestation of those who are false.[13]

How could Molière thus demean himself? Yet Louis once rebuked Racine: 'I would praise you more if you flattered me less', while he had too much common sense and indeed a sense of the ridiculous to be taken in by flattery. He was amused when the smooth cleric Polignac claimed that 'the rain at Marly is never wet', and there was the courtier who replied to Louis' question as to when his wife expected to give birth: 'Sire, whenever Your Majesty pleases.' Yet Louis never tired of praise, and resented criticism. So do we all, but Louis could never have enough recognition of his *gloire*. Ultimately he must accept responsibility for permitting the never-ending glorification of himself – for example, the preacher who compared the king with John the Baptist whom Christ pronounced greater than any man who had ever lived.

As well as creating Versailles and smartening up his chateaux at Chambord and Fontainebleau, Louis built palaces in the vicinity of Versailles. Trianon and Clagny were specially designed to please Mme de Montespan. Marly was specially built to please Louis XIV. It was ironic that Louis built Versailles to escape from Paris and then had to build Marly to escape from Versailles. Marly had a central banqueting hall, where the company could be entertained before everyone dispersed to the little pleasure houses that circled the main building. The whole complex was supposed to represent the sun and its satellites; to us, though, it might seem more like a glorified motel. Etiquette was more relaxed at Marly. No wonder the courtiers would besiege Louis with 'Marly, Sire?' It was the ultimate privilege to be invited there by the king.

And then there were the gardens. Here Louis' hands-on approach can be seen to perfection. His expertise was second only to that of his gardening expert, André Le Nôtre. This gifted specialist came as close as anyone outside the king's extended family to a genuine friendship with Louis, with the possible exception of the portly Alexandre Bontemps, the king's long-serving valet. Louis and Le Nôtre would greet each other with bear hugs. They were united by their love of gardening. Louis was an expert on the cultivation of vegetables. So visitors to Versailles had to admire the vegetable garden as well as the more glamorous flower beds. Colbert, who approved of flowers because they were cheap, imposed a mercantilist strategy. Instead of being imported from Holland, tulips and hyacinths were grown in Provence and shipped en masse from Toulon.

Even the flowers were recruited as flatterers. In 1688 Donneau de Visé, who successfully applied to be an official court historian, imagined the flowers addressing the king:

> We assemble today to work on the history of a monarch who should be praised by all that the Earth produces, since all the Earth is indebted to him. Although we may have come from different countries, we are all French by inclination, or rather we are all devoted to you and we are all in accord in praising you.[14]

Sunflowers were especially welcome because of their built-in tendency to face the sun. There were flowers everywhere, especially at Marly and Trianon, where special rooms were designed for the enjoyment of their scent.[15] In addition the canals, the fountains and the statues repeated the same unveiled message. Impressive groups of statues show the sun-god Apollo driving the chariot of state. A quaint depiction of the frogs who persecuted Persephone being turned to stone reflects Anne of Austria's triumph over the Parisians during the Fronde.

Louis encouraged other visual arts such as sculpture and painting. Not everyone warms to Le Brun's bombastic landscapes, though his sketch of the poisoner Marquise de Brinvilliers is truly haunting and his masterly portrait of Chancellor Séguier is a brilliant depiction of cynical ruthlessness. Was Séguier pleased with it? Louis' favourite portrait of himself was painted in middle age by Rigaud. There is no concealment of the tired expression or of the caved-in jaw ruined by clumsy dentists. The artist, however, flatters Louis by giving him a young man's body, the athletic legs positioned for dancing. There is a marvellous portrait of the young king by Testalin at the establishment of the Académie des Sciences – no less impressive when one recalls that Louis did not visit the academy until many years after its foundation. There he sits in all his arrogant finery, coolly weighing up the artist. Louis was not pleased with Bernini's equestrian statue, which made him look too amiable and barely in control of the horse, or with the celebrated bust: 'Do I really look like that?' he wanted to know. One wonders if Louis liked the revealing profile of him painted on wax by Antoine Benoist, a study of arrogant ruthlessness. The portraits of Mme de Maintenon by Ferdinand Elle and Mignard are interesting attempts to reveal that elusive prude. Mignard did a lovely job on Mme de Montespan as well, but the best portrait of her is by an unknown artist. She is shown reclining on her sofa at Clagny, a nipple coyly peeping out from her chemise, her shoes sluttishly discarded, every inch the high-class whore, insolently and provocatively attractive.

THE WRITTEN WORD

French literature blossomed, much of it, though by no means all, thanks to Louis' patronage. Racine doubled as a dramatist and a royal historian. Corneille was an outstanding tragedian. 'Which of our dramatists will be remembered for his genius?' Louis asked Boileau, the critic and theologian. 'Molière!' 'Really? That buffoon? You do surprise me. But you know more about these things than I do.' A number of rather ordinary court poets, such as Perrault, pleased the king, but he only reluctantly allowed the brilliant La Fontaine into the Académie Française. Louis could not forgive his friendship with Fouquet whom he had courageously defended. Fénelon was to bring vituperation to a fine art as a propagandist. Bossuet was renowned for his preaching and for his theology. Bourdaloue's sermons were celebrated for their profundity and also for their length. In fact they were so long that court ladies secreted portable chamber pots under their dresses, these pots being known as 'bourdalous'. Pascal too excelled as a religious thinker, as well as being a satirist of genius and the inventor of the computer.[16]

Dangeau, Visconti and Torcy wrote impressive memoirs, with Louis himself not far behind, though he was 'helped' by Colbert, Périgny and Pelisson. Mme de Sévigné, Liselotte and Mme de Maintenon shone as letter writers, the only literary activity permitted to women apart from novels and fairy tales. Saint-Simon was the prince of memorialists, though whether Louis can claim any credit is a good question, given the baleful survey of the Sun King and of his court by the little duke. It is also open to question whether Saint-Simon can be trusted. Not surprisingly, François Bluche thinks not. On the other hand Saint-Simon was there, he is presumably a reliable indicator of the prejudices and preferences of his class, however warped – and he is such fun. Historians who distrust him still cannot resist quoting him. Saint-Simon's use of anecdote is unforgettable – and sometimes barely credible. There was the story about Luxembourg's potential brother-in-law who was so stupid that he had to become a priest lest he sire legitimate heirs. Or take his flair for detail – for instance, the high and mighty Marshal Villeroy 'who used to sniff loudly in all directions, sounding for all the world like a pneumatic pump'. Here is his pen-portrait of Monseigneur, the Grand Dauphin, Louis' only legitimate child, perpetually bored and perpetually boring, never reading anything except the obituary notices:

> Monseigneur was without vice and without virtue, without enlightenment or knowledge of any kind, radically incapable of acquiring them, very lazy, unimaginative and unproductive, without taste, without selectiveness, without discernment, born for boredom, which he communicated to others, born to be a ball rolling randomly at the impetus of other people, stubborn and petty in everything to the point of excess, with an incredible proclivity toward believing everything that people claimed to have seen, falling into the most pernicious hands, incapable of getting away from them or of realizing it, consumed by his fat and his gloominess and who, though he had no will to do evil, would have been a pernicious king.[17]

ART OR PROPAGANDA?

Peter Burke impressively argues that there was a deliberate media campaign to 'fabricate' Louis XIV. Art, architecture, music, literature, sculpture, medals, statues – all were regimented to the glory of the Sun King. Hence the lack of spontaneity in much of the artistic achievement of the reign. Hence the basically fraudulent nature of the whole exercise, so wittily satirised by Thackeray. The whole boiling match was so deliberately orchestrated by Louis himself that one hesitates to suggest that he was really at leisure. It was all part of his job, so to speak. A possible comparison might be with a headmaster, anxiously attending – and overseeing – his school play, which is theoretically supposed to entertain and delight one and all, but at the same time reflects the competence of his staff and the ability of his pupils. One recalls Evelyn Waugh's headmaster in *Decline and Fall* gloomily predicting yet another disastrous sports day. Or perhaps a cathedral organist is a better parallel, masterminding choral evensong to the glory of God – and of himself. Louis XIV similarly scrutinised the buildings, the gardens, the ballets, the plays and the concerts with a critical eye. They had better not be disasters, but worthy of France; that is to say, of the Sun King.

To dismiss the cultural and artistic achievements of Louis XIV's reign as mere propaganda – all done with mirrors, so to speak – would be absurd. It was a golden age, in which the French genius flourished, both spontaneously and thanks to the king's encouragement. Europe paid the most genuine compliment possible by slavish imitation. Louis' role as an enabler is entirely to his credit. Above all he backed Colbert in his foundation of the academies and encouragement of education and enlightenment. After Colbert's death, Louvois, despite being a self-confessed philistine, continued to encourage all that was best in French art and literature. Although censorship of subversive material was deemed politically necessary, Louis and his ministers demonstrated their awareness that they were inhabiting a new age. If culture had a purpose, the spirit of artistic, intellectual and scientific innovation that uniquely flourished in France could only do so in a relatively free environment. To a great extent this was guaranteed under the warm rays of the Sun King.

6

RELATIONS AND FRIENDS

Louis XIV was an intelligent and sociable man who enjoyed the company of clever and witty people. He got bored more easily than his legitimate son, whom Saint-Simon so memorably demolished. This, plus his sexual appetite, explains his pursuit of extramarital company when he had had enough of his uninspiring nearest and dearest. Nevertheless, he was too much of a dynast totally to ignore his family who always meant much to him.

He was devastated when his mother died in January 1666. Her death from breast cancer was gruesomely distressing, her doctors excelling themselves with tortures such as boring holes in her affected parts. Anne was especially demoralised by her own stench, for she had always been a meticulously clean person. Louis watched by her bedside during her death agony. She deserved his loyalty. Anne had defended the crown on behalf of her God-given son since her husband's death in 1643. In his memoirs Louis pays tribute to Anne with a condescending reference to 'this excellent princess'. But she had always been there for him, both personally and politically. She profoundly influenced his values and priorities.

Unfortunately his wife could not fill the void. Poor Marie Thérèse was as stupid as she looked and pathetically lacking in self-confidence. Just occasionally the king and the queen were happy together, for instance when their four-year-old son delighted his parents by marching at the head of his troops at a military parade. But Marie Thérèse failed to get close to her disloyal and promiscuous husband. She bored him with her cloying devotion and disapproval of his infidelities. She never learnt to speak French properly, or to dance. Hence she lacked the necessary accomplishments to shine at court. Indeed, there was some excuse for Louis' promotion of his mistress Madame de Montespan as she was brilliant as his partner on public occasions, justifying her biographer's description of her as 'the real queen of France'. So poor Marie Thérèse was sidetracked, only appearing at the gaming table where her stupidity and her wealth made her a popular participator. Everyone enjoyed gambling with her as she frequently had not worked out which game they were playing. Louis good-humouredly settled her debts. Most of the time she withdrew into her own suffocatingly devout household, peopled by priests, dwarves and little dogs.

Apart from her entourage, Marie Thérèse's consolations were her religion and Spanish chocolate. At first she was too unperceptive and naive to be aware of her husband's infidelities until kind friends enlightened her. Her angry attempts to remonstrate with Louis were disastrous. She may even have reacted by having a fling with her negro slave and producing a baby girl who became a nun. Louis, so the story goes, preferred not to know, being in no position to criticise his wife's conduct. When Louis and his wife did have sex, her gratitude was touchingly apparent. Next morning she would beam at everybody and rub her fat little hands. Just occasionally her opinions mattered, as with the proposed *mésalliance* between Mademoiselle and Lauzun (see pp. 109–10), though she was unable to prevent her husband invading her family's territory on her behalf. Louis treated her abominably by requiring her to tour the territories that had once belonged to her family in the company of his two mistresses. On one occasion her prudish objections were overruled when they all slept side by side in a stable; Louis kept a light shining so that the queen could satisfy herself that no hanky-panky was occurring. Marie Thérèse was a truly tragic figure. When she died in 1683, Louis was gracious enough to admit that this was the first time that she had inconvenienced him. Even that inconvenience did not last long. Louis soon discarded the violet mourning suit that he considered appropriate.

Marie Thérèse bore Louis six children, all of whom died in infancy except the dauphin. Was this high mortality due to Habsburg/Bourbon inbreeding or to the gonorrhoea that Louis had contracted as a teenager? It is perhaps relevant that several of Louis' bastards were deformed. Louis the grand dauphin, always known as Monseigneur, resembled his mother in appearance and intelligence; that is to say, he was not overly bright. Louis XIV, who always regretted his own ignorance of Latin, imposed a ferociously intense education on his son, nominating the brilliant Jacques-Bénigne Bossuet as his tutor. Seldom has such worthy erudition been wasted on such unpromising material. Despite the textbooks specially written for him and the thrashings devotedly administered, the dauphin knew a thousand Latin words at ten and none at twenty. The education that Bossuet provided for the dauphin was, like the butter in the Mad Hatter's watch, 'the best', and he was deservedly made a bishop. Meanwhile the dauphin's only reading was the obituary column in the *Gazette*. He is supposed to have spent a whole afternoon tapping the floor with his cane.

Saint-Simon was not wholly fair to Monseigneur, who was courageous enough to defy his father by setting up a rival establishment at Meudun. He was popular in the army due to his bravery in the field and for his concern for his soldiers' welfare. He was well liked in Paris. His unprepossessing German wife produced three sons before her untimely death: the dukes of Burgundy, Anjou and Berry. Monseigneur then copied his father by morganatically marrying his mistress, Mme Choin, memorably summed up by Saint-Simon: 'a large, short, witty brunette, who became exceedingly fat and stank as she grew old, but was modest, honest and disinterested'. She had enormous breasts, which the dauphin enjoyed beating as though they were kettle drums. Who knows what sort of a king this amiable nonentity would have made? In the event smallpox and his doctors killed him before his good intentions were given the opportunity of compensating for his laziness and stupidity.

The other significant Bourbon for the first forty years of the personal rule was Monsieur, Louis' brother Philippe. In appearance he looked like a scaled-down imitation of his brother, a half-pint Louis XIV: the same Semitic nose, protruding belly, immense wig. He too walked on high heels to conceal his lack of stature. Perfumed, berouged, beribboned, superficially he never ceased to be the effeminate doll whom his mother had created in his childhood so as not to rival his masculine brother. But Philippe was not to be despised. He proved himself a brave and resourceful commander in the field, provoking Louis' jealousy by winning the battle of Cassal in 1676. Louis treated Philippe badly, never giving him a command again or admitting him to the *conseil d'en haut*: 'Brother, go and amuse yourself, we're going to take counsel.'

Philippe was relegated to the position of supreme authority on etiquette and precedence. But he had qualities. He was loyal and intelligent. He skilfully built up his own fortune, based on an unrivalled collection of jewellery and medals. While he behaved badly to Minette, his first wife, who did not exactly commend herself to her husband by philandering with the king, he managed to beget children with both Minette and with his second wife, Liselotte of the Palatinate, who was nevertheless enraged by her husband's extravagant gifts to his boyfriends. Philippe was the only person who could have a shouting match with Louis le Grand. For instance, when Louis reprimanded him for his affairs with his boyfriends, Philippe retorted, 'You're a fine one to talk!' Louis' smug, homophobic reply was only too predictable: 'My affairs are with women, your affairs are the results of abominable vices.' Actually Louis was not too displeased by Philippe's overt homosexuality, which enhanced his own masculinity. Philippe's final row with his brother in 1701, about Louis' lack of generosity to Philippe's son, the duc de Chartres, was to his credit. He turned purple with rage. Having had a huge meal he went home to die from apoplexy. Louis was justifiably covered with remorse.

So what about Louis' wider 'family'? The reviewer of a recent book on Louis XIV ironically complimented the author, David Sturdy, on making only one reference to Mme de Montespan. Academics do indeed tend to regard Louis' sex life as no fit subject for a serious historian. Yet while there is obviously a danger in sensationalism, Louis' mistresses and illegitimate brood played a significant role. His relationships with them throw revealing light on his personality. Louis certainly took them seriously, whatever modern historians prefer to think. There is no need to be shocked by Louis' and his courtiers' supposed sins and wickednesses. Most contemporary rulers had mistresses, the assumption being that a king married for reasons of state, and was justified in sleeping around for self-gratification. As Le Roy Ladurie remarks: 'As recently as a generation or two ago tales of such escapades could still arouse virtuous indignation, but today such a reaction would seem quaint. Our era has no licence to give moral instruction to the past, nor do we like to think of ourselves as lesson-givers.'[1]

Yes indeed, yet without wishing to play God and speculate on Louis' ultimate destination, one can pinpoint the light that the Sun King's extramarital *affaires* throw on his character, especially his quite extraordinary chauvinistic selfishness. For one thing there were so many of them. Who had more mistresses? Certainly not Henry VIII nor even Charles II. Possibly Augustus the Strong of Poland. Possibly Louis' decadent great-grandson Louis XV. Just as he was a glutton for food, buildings and war, so Louis' sexual appetite was voracious. Furthermore, the *way* he treated his women, especially the queen, was indicative of an astonishing insensitivity. Basically they were there to gratify him. Just as his dynastic attitudes enabled him to squander the money that Colbert raised from his 'estate' (that is to say, by taxing the French), so Louis exercised a kind of nationwide *ius primae noctis* by helping himself to his female subjects' bodies as though they were his property. If Louis' sex life is ignored, one misses a thought-provoking and crucial aspect of his values and personality. Equally enlightening was his drastic conversion to monogamy after his marriage to Mme de Maintenon, when he came to resemble a reformed alcoholic who will not have a bottle in the house.

Louis' attitude to his illegitimate children is also revealing and, by contemporary standards, unusual. On the whole people of all classes were ashamed of their extramarital liaisons and their products. In the same way bastards were believed to be automatically lacking in the more admirable qualities. They were supposed to be deceitful and cowardly. It was assumed that they could not inherit their parents' finer qualities any more than their wealth. But not by Louis XIV. Actually royal bastards often achieved political and social respectability – the Vendômes in France for instance or Monmouth in England. In his turn Louis maintained that his bastards were 'children of France'; that is to say, possessors of the royal blood of the Bourbons because they were *his* offspring, whoever their mothers may have been.

This had important consequences when at the end of his life a spate of royal deaths persuaded Louis not only to legitimise his bastards but even to have them pronounced heirs to the throne. This policy was unpopular, especially as Louis' eldest and favourite illegitimate son, the duc de Maine, was a deceitful, cowardly young man – in fact, contemporaries would say, 'a typical bastard'. While his younger brother the comte de Toulouse was preferable – modest, sensible, brave and a great success in the navy – Louis further defied convention by promoting his female bastards, who were frivolous and dissolute. When Mlle de Blois – his daughter by Montespan – married the duc de Chartres in February 1692, her dowry funded by the taxpayer came to 6 million livres, and the happy couple glittered with diamonds, reflecting Louis' determination that girls too could be 'children of France'. This episode encapsulates Louis' shameless arrogance. How did he get away with it?

The Sun King resembled his grandfather Henri IV in being oversexed, although, as one of Louis' casual conquests, the sexually experienced princess of Monaco remarked, 'his sceptre was not great'. Unlike his grandfather, however, who had a bulbous nose and stank, so that all his women had to be bought, Louis was attractive to women. This was partly because he was the king. But he was also charming and handsome, at any rate between 1655 when he first had sex and 1683 when he married. For nearly thirty years he was irresistible and had no hesitation in exploiting his good fortune. While Louis acknowledged three official mistresses – Louise de La Vallière (1661–8), Athénaïs de Montespan (1668–82) and Françoise de Maintenon (1682–1715) whom he married morganatically – he had numerous other mistresses, some for a few weeks, others for a few moments. Louis sired thirteen bastards at least, and there may well have been more. Once Mme de Maintenon visited a nun in order to assure her that she was *not* Louis' daughter. 'Madame,' said the nun, 'the fact that you have come all this way to tell me this convinces me that I am indeed the king's daughter.' Each of Louis' official mistresses had worked for and was older than her predecessor. All three were aristocratic. But Louis slept with plenty of women who were not so well born. 'Hope of capturing the king's affections was open to any woman since he democratically slept with the very humblest, as well as the most exalted, of his subjects.'[2] When Marie Thérèse died, the duc de Noailles predicted that Louis would marry the first chambermaid who fell into bed with him – an incorrect guess that nevertheless reflected contemporary opinion.

The Sun King's great-grandson Louis XV would entertain contemporary gossips by sleeping with four sisters, one after the other. What fidelity! The Sun King too displayed a measure of fidelity, provided one forgets his long-suffering queen. While he cast his net far and wide, he acknowledged three mistresses *en titre* in the meantime. By allowing them to sit next to him in church, he flagged up their 'official' status. These three women, in their different ways, symbolised the moods and ambiences of the personal rule. It is not too much to think of them as personifying the seasons of the reign.

SPRING (1661–8): LOUISE DE LA VALLIÈRE

Louis' first official mistress was the unintended result of an affair with his sister-in-law Henrietta ('Minette'), Charles I's daughter, who had married Monsieur in 1660. The marriage was doomed. Minette was an adorable flirt; Monsieur contrived to be both a raving homosexual and a jealous husband. Louis had first met Minette when she was a gawky teenager. He had cruelly nicknamed her 'the Bones of the Holy Innocents' – a cemetery in suburban Paris. Now she had filled out physically and mentally. She was great fun. While Louis may or may not have slept with her, the relationship infuriated her husband, his mother and his wife. Louis had to clamber across the roof to spend time with her. Then they had a better idea. Louis would pretend to be attracted to one of Minette's ladies-in-waiting so that he could ostentatiously visit her while stealing time with Minette. Louis' first choice offended the girl's father who withdrew her from court. So Louis settled on the colourless, harmless Louise de La Vallière who was not very bright and limped. Given that the idea was to shield Minette from the wrath of her husband, the scheme worked a treat, for Louis and Louise promptly fell in love with each other.

Historians have been kind to Louise, some downright sentimental. She was only seventeen. She was shy and diffident. She reluctantly surrendered her virginity, crying out at the top of her voice, 'have pity on my weakness' while the king raped her. Thereafter she never ceased to be ashamed of her own sin, especially when rebuked from the pulpit by Bishop Bossuet: 'Hanc mulierem videte!', he stormed, 'Look at this woman!' According to Mme de Sévigné, she was 'a reluctant violet, blushing unseen'. She did however show persistence in obtaining rewards for her relations. Courtiers were puzzled as to what Louis saw in her. One of her fellow ladies in waiting, Athénaïs de Montespan, wrote this catty jingle:

> Be limping, fifteen, witless,
> Ill-born, brainless, titless.
> Have your children
> In a back room.
> Believe me, you'll have the best of lovers.
> La Vallière proves me right.[3]

As a matter of fact, her portrait suggests that she was pretty enough and she was touchingly devoted to her royal lover. Furthermore, she was an outdoor girl, which chimed in with Louis' preferences. Not only was she an excellent shot, but she rode superbly, which enabled the two lovers to outdistance the more sedate court and enjoy time together on their own. Their most virulent critic was the queen-mother. Her voice became falsetto with rage when Louis confessed that he knew that he was sinning, but just could not control himself. 'At least you admit that you're doing wrong!' she spat at him.[4] As for Marie Thérèse, she was the last to know. 'That girl with the jewelled ear-rings, she's the one the king loves',[5] she sadly admitted to one of her ladies. After Anne of Austria's death in January 1666, Louis revived a custom of Charles VII's reign (1422–61) by making Louise *mistresse en titre*, an honour which entitled her to sit next to him at mass. When Louise produced a baby girl, he defied conservative prejudices by making the young mother duchesse de Vaujours: 'I thought it just to ensure that this child enjoyed the honour of its birth.' So the baby was not to be seen as the illegitimate result of adultery but as a princess of the most glorious blood in France.

We have seen how Louis presented 'The Pleasures of the Enchanted Isle' at Versailles in May 1664, supposedly as a compliment to Marie Thérèse, though in reality to Louise. It was the springtime of the reign. In a ballet commemorating the seasons, Louis himself danced as Spring. The two young lovers symbolised love, productivity, a glorious future. But poor Louise was not happy in her role. She lacked the wit and self-confidence to be respected by the courtiers, while she was understandably envied by the queen. After one of her five pregnancies Louise was expected to attend a court function immediately after being delivered. She looked ghastly. 'Unwell, Mademoiselle?' asked Marie Thérèse spitefully.

Most worrying of all, Louis was clearly becoming bored with his official mistress. She had lost her looks. She had no conversation. So Louise brought in the cleverest of her ladies to amuse the king, the recently married Athénaïs de Montespan. Initially Louis was unimpressed. 'She does what she can, but I am not interested', her remarked to his brother. But soon he was fascinated – 'You know, I like clever, amusing people.' He certainly liked this one and was soon calling on her behind Louise's back. Things went from bad to worse when Louise disobeyed her lover by driving her carriage across open country in order to be the first to congratulate him on his latest military exploit. Louis was furious with her for reaching him before the queen. Montespan smugly remarked: 'Heaven defend me from becoming the king's mistress, but were such a misfortune to befall me, I should certainly not have the audacity to appear before the queen arrived.'[6]

In July 1668 Louis launched another fete at Versailles that was clearly in Montespan's honour. Louise was now retained purely as a blind for Louis' love-making with her rival. In despair Louise ran away to a convent. Colbert was sent to bring her back. Did this indicate Louis' affection for her? If so it was not for long. Louis treated Louise with calculated cruelty. He enjoyed 'running' more than one mistress at a time – perhaps it appealed to his vanity. So Louise's rooms opened into Montespan's. Once Louis, sauntering past Louise on his way to see her rival, chucked a little dog at her: 'Here you are, madame, you will enjoy its company!'[7] In 1674 Louise ran away again and became a Carmelite nun. 'Let her go', was the king's reaction. But Montespan did her best to dissuade her, anxious that her cover would now be blown. Furthermore she was worried that, when the king tired of her, she too would be required to become a Carmelite and spend her days in solitary silence. Before she departed, Louise knelt before the queen to ask for her forgiveness. Louis was now completely indifferent to Louise, and never forgave her for preferring her God to her king. As we have seen in Chapter 4, he had no compunction in having their son Vermandois thrashed in his presence for being involved in a homosexual affair, nor was he upset when the young man died in the army aged fifteen. When Louise heard of his death, she exclaimed: 'It is too much to weep for the death of a son for whose birth I have not wept enough.'[8] When Louise completed her vows after a year as a novice, Marie Thérèse attended the ceremony – but not the king. Louis' comment on Sister Louise de la Miséricorde's death in 1710 was that he had not given her another thought since the day that she left his presence.

SUMMER (1668–82): ATHÉNAÏS DE MONTESPAN

During the years when Athénaïs de Montespan was Louis XIV's official mistress, between 1668 and 1682, the Sun King shone brightly. It was high noon. These were the years in which Versailles was planned and built, when the French army invaded Holland, when the court flourished in all its splendour. It was summer time. The king was passionately in love, despite – or because of – his mistress's malice and her other faults. According to the duchess of Orleans:

> La Montespan had a whiter complexion than La Vallière: she had a beautiful mouth and fine teeth, but her expression was always insolent. One had only to look at her to see that she was scheming something. She had beautiful blonde hair and lovely hands and arms, which La Vallière did not have, but at least La Vallière was clean in her person, whereas La Montespan was filthy.[9]

Easy on the eye if not the nose, extremely clever, devastatingly witty, Madame de Montespan radiated her unique brand of infectious gaiety. Under her influence, the court hummed with laughter. She was great fun.

According to her successor's biographer, Charlotte Haldene, Madame de Montespan was a bitch. The king and his new mistress used to mutter humorous comments to each other, mocking other people's weaknesses. Even so, if Athénaïs was malicious, she was basically good-natured, and unlike her successor did not bear grudges. The poor queen, however, looked back with regret to the days of nice, harmless Louise de La Vallière. She feared and loathed Athénaïs de Montespan. 'That whore will be the death of me',[10] she would say. Whore she may have been, though Athénaïs displayed the arrogance of the Mortemarts, one of France's oldest families. Typically she maintained that her relationship with Louis de Bourbon was a *mésalliance*.

Athénaïs, however, came with baggage. For one thing she was married and a mother. This meant that she and her lover committed double adultery, as opposed to Louis' affairs with single women such as La Vallière on which the church looked relatively indulgently. After all, Louis' confessor, Père la Chaise, was alleged to have a mistress. But there was the additional problem that the duc de Montespan was by no means a compliant husband. On the whole he was exceptional in this matter. For several husbands deliberately ignored their wives' infidelities with the king who gratefully rewarded them with cash or promotion. Both Montespan's own father and his father-in-law were delighted and rubbed their hands: 'God be praised, at last our fortunes are made!'[11] But Montespan was not like that. He would play the jealous husband! For several months the lovers hid behind Louise. But then disaster struck. Athénaïs became pregnant. Louis in disguise assisted at the secret birth of his child, having to prepare a snack for the doctor and being rebuked for his dilatoriness – a new experience for Louis, one fancies. Montespan was furious when he discovered not only that his wife had been unfaithful but that he had been duped.

Montespan was a silly, nasty man who forfeited sympathy by kidnapping a servant girl for whom he lusted – and then beating up the bailiff who came to recover her. He had long ago destroyed his wife's affection by his gambling debts. His attempts to pursue a military career were farcical. Now he ranted and raged, embarrassing both his wife and her royal lover. He vowed that he would resort to the seediest brothels in Paris in order to pass on syphilis to the king. When Louis finally lost patience and exiled Montespan to his chateau in Gascony, he distressed Athénaïs by taking their children with him. Then he made a great show of demolishing the gateway to his chateau because it was too restricted to accommodate his cuckold's horns. He publicly buried an effigy of his wife. He continued to cause trouble until the marriage was annulled. Athénaïs was so scared of her husband's violence – and he had hit her and threatened to remove her by force – that Louis had to give her a body-guard. The greatest damage that Montespan did was to quote 2 Samuel 11, publicly comparing himself with Uriah whom David had killed in battle so that he could slake his lust for Bathsheba. Nobody had much sympathy for Montespan, though he represents a group of men who are seldom mentioned – the devastated husbands and lovers of women to whom the king helped himself. When Montespan died in 1701, his will – in which he left his considerable fortune to his wife – testified to the thirty-five years of anguish that her adultery had caused him.

In the immediate aftermath the church sided with Montespan, however absurd and inadequate a husband he may have been. The clergy upset Athénaïs by refusing her communion, on the grounds of her adultery. She was surprisingly devout, retorting to a friend's amused surprise, 'Just because I commit one sin, it does not mean that I have to commit the lot.'[12] Bishop Bossuet publicly rebuked the king from the pulpit and privately urged him to mend his ways. During Lent 1676 Louis went off to the front. When he returned on leave it was agreed that he and Athénaïs would only meet in company. But alas for good intentions. The lovers withdrew into an alcove, conversed passionately – and bowing to the company withdrew. Bossuet and his colleagues were furious. So was the widow Scarron, whom Athénaïs had recruited as governess for her and Louis' bastards. This redoubtable do-gooder had resolved to make the king's salvation her life's work. Now she was baffled.

Other clouds drifted across the sun, also involving marriage. One of Louis' favourite courtiers was the absurd, irascible little soldier of fortune, comte de Lauzun. In the autumn of 1670 he attracted the affection of the king's cousin, la Grande Mademoiselle, Gaston's daughter who had turned the guns on Louis during the Fronde. Well connected, immensely wealthy, usually amiable, she had nevertheless failed to find a husband. Now aged forty-three, she saw Lauzon as her last chance of marital bliss. So they asked Louis for his consent – very necessary as the proposed marriage was clearly a *mésalliance*. Louis was amused by the incongruous pair. 'Cousin, you're old enough to know your own mind. I do not recommend the marriage, but I give my consent.' Friends advised the couple to marry at once. It was good advice. Not only did the news astonish the court, Mme de Sévigné calling it 'miraculous, triumphant, baffling, unheard of, brilliant'. But also several heavyweights moved in to stop such an inappropriate match that would demean the royal family. Monsieur and the queen told the king to go back on his word. Mme de Montespan – whom Lauzun regarded as an ally – secretly advised Louis against the marriage, for she had her eyes on Mademoiselle's wealth, which she pencilled in for her favourite bastard the duc du Maine. The upshot was that Louis had the couple summoned and told them that he had regretfully realised that their marriage could not happen. Lauzun was stunned, Mademoiselle dissolved in tears. Louis was embarrassed, and rightly so.

The story had an even more discreditable sequel. Lauzun petitioned the king for the prestigious post of Grand Master of the Artillery. He asked his friend Athénaïs to plead his case, to which she agreed. But Lauzun was beginning to doubt his 'friend'. So he persuaded her chambermaid – whom he had bribed and probably seduced – to hide him under the bed when the king was due. After sex, while Louis and his paramour chatted together, as one does, the Master of the Artillery issue was part of their post-coital agenda. But neither king nor mistress favoured Lauzun's candidature. Later that evening Lauzun asked Athénaïs how his cause had progressed. 'Oh, I did support you, and the king is thinking about it.' 'You liar, you whore, you fat bitch!'[13] shouted Lauzun – and the last insult was especially wounding as Athénaïs had been trying to slim. Lauzun then recounted word for word what was really said. Athénaïs fainted. When Louis heard from her what had passed, he was so angry that he broke his stick in two and flung it out of the window in case he should be tempted to strike Lauzun, a gentleman, and dispatched him to join Fouquet at Pinerolo. There Lauzun stayed for ten years. He was promised release when Mademoiselle was persuaded to make the duc du Maine the heir to much of her property on condition that she could marry Lauzun, and that he would be restored to favour. In the event they never appeared in public as a married couple. Neither Louis nor Athénaïs emerged with credit from this shabby affair.

Far worse was to follow. Whenever an apparently healthy person died suddenly in Louis XIV's France, poison was suspected. Sometimes suspicion was justified. The marquise de Brinvilliers, for example, poisoned her father and two brothers and was executed in 1676. The first Madame however, Minette, who died from an exceedingly painful stomach in 1670, was probably not poisoned by Monsieur even though he treated her abominably. But a veritable poison industry came to the notice of the superintendent of police in Paris, Nicholas de La Reynie, as a result of the arrest for witchcraft of Madame La Voisin, a dodgy fortune-teller and manufacturer of spells, much consulted by court ladies. It was the involvement of the court that disturbed Louvois when La Reynie instructed him. Both believed that the king should know. Louis was touchy about the reputation of his court. As he doubted whether the lawyers of the Parlement would be rigorous enough, he instructed La Reynie to set up a special Commission de l'Arsenal, popularly known as the Chambre Ardente. Between April 1679 and July 1681 it arrested 367 people, sentenced thirty-four to death and exiled twenty-three more. Many who appeared before the court were aristocrats – for instance, France's most accomplished general, the duc de Luxembourg, whom Louis envied and disliked. He consulted the king as to whether he should escape before La Reynie caught up with him. 'If you're innocent, you've nothing to fear', Louis replied. Luxembourg was wrong to trust his king. Though he was innocent, he nevertheless suffered several months of uncomfortable imprisonment.

The poison scandal was badly handled. Undoubtedly sinister and foolish people were at work. But Louis overreacted, La Reynie was a fussy and officious prosecutor, and much unnecessary panic was caused. What really distressed Louis was that several witnesses implicated Mme de Montespan. What had Athénaïs got up to? She had a problem. She was losing the affection of the king. Like Louis she was a big eater. Like him she ran to fat. Visconti happened to see her thigh when she alighted from her carriage; he reckoned it was as large as his own body. For one reason and another – notably Louis' dalliances with other, prettier women – there were ugly scenes. Athénaïs shouted at Louis. Desperate for her survival, she may well have administered love potions to the king. Lurid rumours hinted at black masses performed across Athénaïs' naked belly. It was suggested that she poisoned her rivals, and even contemplated poisoning the king. Louis realised that much of this was nonsense. Why on earth should his mistress want to poison her benefactor? Probably rightly, Louis did not think Athénaïs capable of poisoning anyone, nor of indulging in black masses. But around this time he certainly suffered excruciatingly painful stomach cramps that were probably caused by love potions administered by his desperate mistress. Louis was worried enough about her reputation to tell La Reynie to keep her name out of court and to close down proceedings as soon as possible. Years later Louis sent for the documents implicating his mistress, and destroyed them himself – though copies survived in the police files.

Meanwhile, those who cared both about the king's body and his soul were discomfited by Louis' love affair with a lay canon, Madame de Ludres, who presented Louis with the future cardinal de Rohan, and the arrival at court of Mme Marie-Angélique de Fontanges, a rather dim eighteen-year-old stunner with whom Louis was soon infatuated. Athénaïs had pointed her out to the king, hoping to distract him from his increasing interest in the intellectual conversation of the widow Scarron. Athénaïs was all the more incredulous that Louis fell for Marie-Angélique, even though she was 'stupid as a basket'. He was clearly embarrassed every time she opened her mouth. How could he enjoy the company of such a nitwit? But it was not her nonexistent wits that interested the king, though some thought that he should have known better than to be car-nally minded at his age, for he had turned forty. Primi Visconti was amused by the two rivals trying to impress the king with their piety, sitting side by side at Mass, rolling their eyes like plaster saints. Poor Fontanges was never the same again after miscarrying with a little sun-beam. Shortly afterwards she vomited pus and died. Was she poisoned, or was she a warrior 'fatally wounded in the service of the king', as the court wits heartlessly put it?

Fontanges was not quite the last of the king's mistresses. Mlle Doré caused distress to Madame de Montespan's concern for the king's body and the widow Scarron's concern for his soul – until shortly afterwards the latter nobly replaced Mlle Doré in the king's bed to prevent the arrival of less virtuous successors. The 'holy whore' was to qualify for the distinction of being the king's last mistress, before Louis made an honest woman of her, and then put his galloping days behind him.

This seems a sensible moment at which to speculate about Louis XIV's lust. Did he damage the women he slept with? Judging by the inexhaustible supply of nubile candidates for his bed, it would seem that the women of the court, high and low, did not expect to be harmed. Indeed, Antonia Fraser reckons that Louis' women more than met him half way. Several found the wages of sin quite advantageous. Several enjoyed the prestige of being the king's lover. Several no doubt experienced physical satisfaction from the embraces of such a sophisticated fornicator. On the other hand there were the casualties such as La Vallière who was raped and shamed and Fontanges who died as a result of sex with the king, to say nothing of heartbroken lovers when the king, for one reason or another, terminated the relationship: Mancini, La Vallière, Montespan spring to mind. Then there are the 'one afternoon stands' about whom little is known. There is the story of a girl whom the obese and sweaty Louvois commandeered and who fainted when she saw him naked. While Louvois naked could make anybody faint, did *every* lady's maid and serving wench whom the king pushed into an anteroom necessarily want to be impregnated with the royal seed? Did they have a choice? All we know is that Louis frequently amused himself with *les dames*.

Did Louis harm himself? Although various forms of contraception were in use, my guess is that the Sun King would have been affronted by the suggestion that he should offer protected sex. So he was lucky not to catch the dreaded pox – an important achievement before penicillin was invented. Liselotte tells how she once dined with her son and eight other young men, seven of whom had syphilis. While there is no reason to doubt that Louis had a great time satisfying his carnal desires, did he worry about his spiritual health? Yes he did, as we shall see in Chapter 8. Did he damage the reputation of the monarchy? This is not a straightforward issue. Historians talk about the desacrilisation of the monarchy – a topic to which we shall return. In this particular context, Louis seems to have come midway between his grandfather Henri IV, whose sexual exploits endeared him to his public, and Louis' paedophile great-grandson Louis XV, whose brothel in the park inhabited by little girls did him no good at all. His horrible death from smallpox, caught from raping a gardener's daughter, seemed just desserts. Furthermore, Louis the God-given at least avoided Louis the Well-beloved's gaffe in appointing plebeian chief mistresses – Pompadour's bourgeois maiden name was Fish, while Barry's origins were lower still. But when Louis XIV's German mercenaries excitedly pointed to Athénaïs as 'Koenig's Hure, Hure!' ('the king's whore'), one suspects that he demeaned himself just a little.

AUTUMN (1682–1708): FRANÇOISE DE MAINTENON

Louis' last mistress and his second wife, Mme de Maintenon, was an autumnal figure. Not for her the dazzling sights and sounds of summer that Athénaïs so loved. She was sober, often dressed in black, with her ample figure and double chin justifying Louis' nickname for her: 'votre solidité'. But she had a colourful past. Françoise d'Aubigné was born close to Niort prison in 1635 where her spendthrift father was doing time for espionage and debt. She came from a mildly aristocratic Huguenot background. As a child she went to Martinique where her father tried in vain to recoup his fortune. Back home she was known as the Indian (from the West Indies) and was adopted by an aunt who converted her to Catholicism. The aunt was as poor as her father, so that Françoise had to muck in and mind the turkeys. At seventeen Françoise, with only her wit, her charm and her good looks to commend her, sensibly accepted a proposal of marriage from Paul Scarron, a middle-aged poet. His work was often scurrilous – he had written several *mazarinades*. Horribly deformed, he joked that he was Z-shaped. Though he was aware of his pretty young wife's sex appeal, he could only paw her in a rather degrading way. But Scarron gave Françoise his name and a little security. When he died in 1660, the widow Scarron was acceptable in high society, making herself useful and agreeable to her posh friends. Mme de Montespan snapped her up as her bastards' governess. She thought she had made a smart choice.

And so in a way she had. The widow Scarron was brilliant, imparting her own erudition to her charges and winning their affection and respect. She was resourceful in struggling to procure the best treatment for the crippled duc du Maine. She comforted the unfortunate child when the 'cures' prescribed by the doctors were especially painful, and accompanied him through the length and breadth of the realm in search of healing waters. She soon came to the notice of the king. Initially Louis detested her. She was too clever. He hated being shown up by brighter people than himself, especially if they were female. But her conversation was delightful, her personality alluring. 'It must be wonderful to be loved by someone like that',[14] he remarked wistfully. La Scarron was less frivolous than Montespan and much more soothing. And she was in her infuriatingly demure way sexually attractive. Athénaïs and Françoise had a love-hate relationship. As intelligent and witty people, they enjoyed each other's company, but squared up to each other in private. Friction arose due to the children's embarrassingly clear preference for their governess rather than their mother. And it got worse. The king spent more and more time with the widow Scarron. He was fascinated by her. He was clearly in love with her – or as the lady remarked with typical smugness, 'in so far as he was capable of loving anyone.' It is not clear exactly when (or even if) she became the king's mistress, but Françoise was certainly having trouble in the confessional in 1681.

Athénaïs was beside herself with rage, especially as it was all her own fault. What had possessed her to appoint the woman? But then, what on earth did Louis see in this wretched parvenue who was older than both of them and looked it? When Louis made an estate to the south of Paris over to Françoise, which entitled her to be the Marquise de Maintenon, Athénaïs shouted at Louis: 'How am I to address this goose-girl, this arse-wiper?'[15] Louis had now had enough of Athénaïs. She had lost her looks and her manners. Her latest biographer, Lisa Hilton, thinks that Athénaïs had virtually been queen of France until poor Marie Thérèse's death in July 1683. But the shadows cast by the poisons affair ruled her out, apart from her other defects. Her unwise attempts to hold on to her position hastened her departure.

The queen died quite suddenly from a tumour in her armpit, which the doctors exacerbated with purges and bleedings. Prompted by Françoise, Louis made the queen's last hours happy. It was he who perceived how near the end was, and rushed to bring the Holy Sacrament to her bedside. The queen died in Françoise's arms. As we have seen, Louis the supreme egotist famously remarked that it was the only trouble she had ever caused him, and was soon displaying a tasteful mourning suit of brilliant violet. When Mme de Maintenon wore deepest black and wept profusely, Louis laughed at her for being such a hypocrite. 'Don't leave the king now, when he needs you more than ever',[16] the duc de Rochefoucauld whispered to her. A few weeks later, in the presence of Louvois, Pére La Chaise and Bontemps the valet, Louis and Françoise were married by the archbishop of Paris.

Louis did not throw Montespan out at once; indeed, she lingered on at court until 1691 when her proposal to retire was snapped up by the king. He promptly awarded her suite to her devoted son du Maine – who threw her furniture out of the window to prevent her changing her mind. Athénaïs followed Louise's example and founded her own convent (she avoided the Carmelites), proving the truth of the adage that in France only three roles were available for a woman – wife, whore or nun. For the rest of her life she devoted herself to good works. When she died in 1706, Françoise had a good weep in her privy. After all, Athénaïs had been her best friend. Louis, however, was unmoved by the death of his most enthusiastic lover: 'When she retired, I thought never to see her again, so from then on she was dead to me.'

The court now settled down to a sober regime where vice was driven behind closed doors or exiled to Paris. The only scandal was provided by Maintenon's brother who was a great frequenter of brothels, to his sister's horrified disgust. He sponged off her outrageously, hinting at the trouble he could cause 'm'brother-in-law' and entertaining the courtiers with witty accounts of his sister's love life in her youth. According to her brother, she had been quite versatile. She was mortified that her hypocrisy should be thus exposed. Otherwise the court's lifestyle was dull, though not exactly Spartan. There were still the concerts and receptions, the *appartements* and the gambling tables, the hunting parties and the gargantuan meals – Visconti, for instance, watched Louis demolish four plates of soup, two partridges, a pheasant, several slices of mutton and vegetables. The king wolfed his food virtually unchewed as his upper jaw had been removed by a clumsy dentist. The noise of his eating could be heard in the next room, nor did he bother with the knives and forks that refined people were beginning to use. When he died, his autopsy revealed a belly and entrails twice the normal size.

Louis' health deteriorated. Not surprisingly he suffered from indigestion, diarrhoea, constipation and worms. His doctors prescribed endless emetics and scrupulously monitored his bowel movements, their detailed notes providing Louis with bedtime reading. Louis' mobility was frequently handicapped by gout so that sometimes he had to be wheeled round his palace and conveyed to the hunt in a specially fitted barouche. When he could, he rode. But in 1686 sitting on a horse became agony due to a growing anal fistula. After several treatments had been tried in vain, surgery was the only remaining option. D'Aquin, the royal surgeon, had practised on several other sufferers, some of whom died under his knife. The operation was a humiliating and agonising experience for the Sun King – spreadeagled face down on a bed, a pillow under his stomach, two doctors forcing his legs apart, Louvois holding his hand. Louis endured the hour-long operation without a groan – his detractors pointing out that he never did feel pain of any sort. The operation was basically successful, though subsequent tidying up was necessary before Louis was able to ride again. Scurrilous rhymes circulated throughout Europe on the subject of the Sun King's anal ordeal. His orchestra soothed him with a march by Lully, the words of which eventually became, more or less, the English national anthem. D'Aquin got a huge pension from his grateful sovereign.

While Louis' working day was taken up with religious disputes, an aggressive foreign policy and eventually a European war that lasted twenty-five years, his private life was cheered and enlivened by a little girl. A marriage treaty was negotiated with Savoy between the Grand Dauphin's son, Louis the duke of Burgundy, and Marie-Adelaide, the duke of Savoy's daughter. Louis went to meet her and reported his delight to Mme de Maintenon. His only criticism was that she did not know how to curtsey. When he introduced her at court, Saint-Simon remarked that she was so tiny that she seemed to be in the king's pocket. The wedding took place in December 1697. But Adelaide was not yet ten, so there was no question of her living with her fourteen-year-old husband. So Louis XIV and Mme de Maintenon adopted the child. She immediately became the light of their lives. Marie-Adelaide was a tomboy who cultivated the old couple. She called Maintenon 'auntie' and deferred to her discipline when it was expedient. She showed intuition in the way that she treated the king, astonishing the courtiers with the liberties she got away with. She would climb onto his knee and adjust his wig. She would skip around his office, reading the papers on his desk. She would interrupt council meetings and, taking Louis by the hand, would lead him away while he raised his eyes to heaven in a mock grimace to his ministers. The king and the little scallywag loved to go hunting together or for rides in the country. She really was extremely cute.

This wholly innocent and delightful relationship brought laughter and joy to the court and to the ageing couple. Inevitably it could not last. Soon Adelaide and Burgundy had to forge their own marital relationship. A solemn, idealistic, good young man, he loved her devotedly. She initially found him dull. But in due course she became fond of him and supported him in his misfortunes, though she continued to sit on the king's knee. Since Adelaide gambled and drank, Mme de Maintenon worried about her refusal to take care of herself. But the king never ceased to love her,[17] though Saint-Simon describes his unbelievable callousness when she miscarried: 'God be praised, I can now do what I want without having to defer to a woman's condition.'[18] The courtiers studied their feet in their embarrassment while Louis, realising that he had gone too far, tried to divert people's attention to some carp in the royal pond.

Another diversion for the royal couple was the school for impoverished noblemen's daughters that Mme de Maintenon founded at Saint-Cyr. Recalling her own childhood, she identified with the pupils. She was a natural school-marm and was in her element bossing the girls and the nuns who taught there. She laid down the rules and the uniform. Maintenon liked the children and they liked her. They also liked the king, who was in his element being made a fuss of by the girls. Maintenon often went there alone, as she found the court increasingly unappetising, being too old for fun and games and disapproving of her husband's involvement in warfare. So she would leave Versailles at six in the morning and drive to Saint-Cyr for peace and relaxation in enjoyable company, returning to court mid-morning.

An extraordinary woman, La Maintenon. She has to plead guilty to hypocrisy – witness her constant moaning about her exalted position at court, which she had intrigued ruthlessly to obtain; witness her apparently austere clothing, concealing expensive underwear and barely revealing a cross round her neck, embossed with priceless jewels. She has had the misfortune to be denigrated by two of the most gifted character assassins of all time, Liselotte and Saint-Simon. Liselotte could not stand her, as a fellow convert suspecting the sincerity of her demonstrative piety and blaming 'the old turd' for prejudicing the king against her. In particular, Liselotte held her responsible for the promotion of the bastards, especially the duc du Maine who was indeed Maintenon's pet. Saint-Simon likewise loathed 'the old trollop', whom he despised as a parvenue. They were not the only people who disliked her. She had the unpleasant characteristic of turning against people for no apparent reason. But there was no doubt that Louis loved her, finding her more and more indispensable, both for company and sex. In her seventies, she asked her confessor if she really had to allow the king his conjugal rights twice a night. She was without doubt influential, both with regard to appointments and the adoption of policies. Saint-Simon gives an unforgettable picture of Louis conducting a military review at Compiègne in 1699 during the truce between the two great wars, and all the time consulting and informing a mysterious figure in a nearby coach with its blinds drawn. Council meetings were held in her bedroom. Ironically, Louis had warned his heir to avoid female influence.

Liselotte and Saint-Simon were at one in deploring the influence of the bastards – their golden age according to Saint-Simon. Louis formally legitimised his bastards, in his arrogance believing that they possessed the royal blood of France. A chauvinist to his fingertips, he believed that it was the father and not the mother who mattered. The bastards married into the highest aristocracy. For instance, his daughter Françoise-Marie (Mademoiselle de Blois) married Philippe, duc de Chartres, later the regent Orléans, the son of Monsieur and Liselotte. Liselotte's anger can be imagined when the match was proposed. She hit her son for agreeing to it. She described the bastards as 'mouse-droppings' – as opposed to pepper, which was the genuine article. The most important was 'the limping bastard' – Liselotte's description, needless to say – the duc du Maine. He was the only one of Louis' children who was not afraid of him. He had his mother's wit and charm, though he betrayed her by taking Maintenon's side when they quarrelled. His gift as a mimic delighted his father. Maine would enter unannounced and unaffectedly enjoy the company of the king and his devoted ex-governess. Together they plotted his replacement of Orléans as the real ruler of France.

WINTER (1708–15): SUNT LACRIMAE RERUM

Virgil's wonderful aphorism (literally: 'these are the tears of things') perfectly sums up the last phase of the Sun King's reign. The winter of 1708–9 serves as an appropriate introduction. It was exceptionally severe. Writing to her friend Mme des Ursins at the Spanish court, Mme de Maintenon claimed that the glass had sunk to fifteen degrees below zero and that they were having to survive on eggs during Lent as there were no vegetables – and that was at the privileged and pampered court. The country experienced cannibalism, starvation and death. Rivers froze and so did the wine on the king's table – which proves both the severity of the weather and the inefficiency of the heating at Versailles. When the spring crop began to peep through as a result of a thaw, nature played a cruel joke, for the iron grip of winter suddenly returned and destroyed the shoots. Coming on top of six disastrous years of war, the winter reduced morale to zero – or should one say below zero. These were indeed tragedies that prompted tears.

And then the medical profession took a hand. Nancy Mitford memorably observed that in former times doctors wore black coats and bonnets and bled their patients, now they wear white and pump blood into them.[19] But her implication – that there is little to choose between them – will not do. Early modern doctors and dentists were horrendously incompetent. They had occasional triumphs, such as Louis XIV's fistula, and they had worked out that quinine cured malaria. But they got pretty well everything else wrong. The worst of the lot was Guy Crescent Fagon whom Mme de Maintenon succeeded in imposing on the court. Actually Saint-Simon depicts him as a cultivated and likeable scholar. So he may have been. But his track record was abysmal. His specialism was to turn a curable ailment into a killer. In 1711 the Grand Dauphin was the first to go, admittedly from smallpox. Louis had never been close to his son, but was nevertheless devastated. The combination of measles and Fagon now dispatched Burgundy and his wife, the irrepressible Adelaide. Louis gave up all pretence at self-control and wept in public. Burgundy's brother Berry and two of his little sons followed. By 1712 one feeble infant stood between the Orléans branch, the bastards and the throne. Louis and his wife hated and feared Orléans and therefore bullied Parlement into ruling that the bastards, long legitimised, could succeed to the throne if the direct line died out. As it happened, the infant's governess, the marquise de Ventadour, who danced beautifully at the age of ninety and was obviously herself a talented survivor, refused to allow any doctor near her charge. He lived until 1774 as King Louis XV, the Well-Beloved.

Although France's luck at last turned in the war – if the bloody drawn battle of Malplaquet can be called luck – and the peace party achieved power in London, Louis' last months were dark and wintry. His wife and his confessor badgered him with threats of eternal hellfire if he did not confess the right sins. They bullied him into another joust with the Jansenists – though truth to tell the old bigot did not need much bullying. The result was the utterly disastrous *Unigenitus* episode.[20] Soon the winter Sun would set for the last time, in tears of bitterness, frustration and defeat.

DID LOUIS XIV'S WOMEN MAKE A DIFFERENCE?

In the conclusion to this book, Louis XIV's personality will be discussed, including the light thrown on it by his dealings with relations and friends. Here it is worth examining the difference made in political and social terms by the story covered in this chapter. In particular, how successful was Louis in preventing his lady friends from influencing policy, the danger of which he warned the dauphin in his memoirs?

Until Mme de Maintenon came along, Louis only permitted petticoat influence on his own terms. The most striking example was Minette's embassy to England in the summer of 1670 when she brokered the secret Treaty of Dover between her brother and brother-in-law. He also dispatched his niece to represent French interests at Madrid when the unfortunate Marie-Louise was forced to marry the repulsive Carlos II – a living death sentence as she rightly predicted. With equal ruthlessness Louis cooperated with Charles II's lust for Louise de Kerouailles who, as the duchess of Portsmouth, became a French mole at Whitehall. He listened to, but frequently rejected, the advice of the princess Des Ursins, his unofficial representative at the court of Philip V. Louis cheerfully ignored the tears of Marie Thérèse and Liselotte when their respective homelands were ravaged by the French army.

But La Maintenon was different. Indeed, Louis completely broke his own guidelines, not simply by holding council meetings in her presence but by taking her advice on specific occasions. She has been wrongly blamed for the revocation of the Edict of Nantes and for accepting Carlos II's will – though both decisions undoubtedly received her approval. But she undoubtedly persuaded Louis to support the Jacobite cause from 1688 to 1690 due to her fanatical belief in the divine right of kings, while her admiration for James II and his wife Mary Beatrice impelled the king to acknowledge 'James III' when his father died in December

1700 – a disastrous decision opposed by Louis' ministers for excellent political reasons. Maintenon encouraged Louis to regard the promiscuous and inept James II as a saint – a truly comical state of affairs. The court's verdict on James was, 'when you speak to him, you realise why he's here'. Maintenon also allowed her love for Maine and her hatred of Orléans to persuade Louis to include the bastards in the succession to the throne. Her myopic prejudice against Jansenism drove Louis down the fateful road to *Unigenitus*. On the other hand, she could not make a pacifist of the old warlord when he defied her preferences for peace during the 25-year-war at the end of the reign, though she influenced his choice of generals and diplomats.

There remains the economic cost of Louis XIV's 'family'. He has been praised, for instance by Antonia Fraser, for being such a generous lover, both to his *maîtresses en titre* and to more transient girlfriends. Certainly La Vallière was able to pass on benefits to her relations and her children. Montespan was treated with lavish munificence, while her children by the king were fabulously wealthy. 'Madame de Montespan's tastes must be gratified',[21] Louis instructed Colbert. Maintenon typically boasted that she gave away all the money that came to her from the king, though there was the little matter of her estate at Maintenon, to say nothing of the expensive lingerie for which her confessor rebuked her. Other paramours received jewels, pensions and promotions for their relatives in church and state. Like Louis' allegedly extravagant building programme – or for that matter his gluttony while his people starved – did all this amount to much compared to the soaring cost of war? Maybe not, in relative terms. But Louis' subjects struggling to subsidise the Sun King's *gloire* can hardly have enthused over the public enrichment of the king's high-class whores.

7

THE WORLD AT HIS FEET

FOREIGN POLICY, 1661–84

UNAVOIDABLE QUESTIONS

France was at war for fifty out of the seventy-two years of Louis XIV's reign, and for thirty-two out of the fifty-four years of his personal rule. To a great extent therefore, when we talk about his foreign policy, we mean his preoccupation with war: occasional attempts to avoid war but more often preparations for war, the conduct of war, the exploitation of victory or the mitigation of defeat. Furthermore, because Louis' domestic policy was foreign-policy-led, it too was dominated by war: raising taxation to fund war, recruiting men to fight war, helping civilians to survive the economic hardship of war, enabling France to recover from war. Unfortunately, while Louis XIV, like many other aggressive rulers in history such as Edward III or Henry V, hoped to benefit from quick and easy victories, by and large these eluded him so that the results of his wars were damaging, both at home and abroad. Although significant territorial additions were made to France between 1643 and 1715, which can be quoted as justifications for Louis' aggression, literally millions suffered and died during the course of the wars over which he presided, to say nothing of the material costs – towns ravaged, crops ruined, trade interrupted. So even if Louis XIV was no Genghis Khan or Hitler, there are still unavoidable questions to be answered. Were his wars, entailing so much human misery, really necessary? Could they have been avoided?

The consensus among historians is that Louis XIV was not a war criminal. Seventeenth-century people must be judged by their own and not by twenty-first-century standards — if they have to be judged at all. All seventeenth-century rulers pursued their dynastic ambitions by marriage and by going to war. Far from deploring this, most of them agreed with their aristocratic subjects in welcoming war as a bracing and glorious experience. Louis XIV in particular mirrored the values of his sword nobility. War was the only fit pastime for gentlemen, while many of their wives and mistresses found warfare an aphrodisiac. Arguably, Louis would have forfeited popularity and the respect of the French political nation if he had *not* gone to war. The question therefore was not whether but when and against whom France would be involved in war. So there was no expression of shame or guilt on Louis' part when, for instance, he attacked the Dutch in 1672: 'I shall not attempt to justify myself. Ambition and gloire are always pardonable in a prince, and especially in a young prince so well treated by fortune as I was.'[1] Lynn argues that 'given the mentalité of the young Louis XIV, the War of Devolution and the Dutch War were all but inevitable'.[2] Even Louis' Dutch victim, Jan de Witt, predicted that Louis would need 'an extraordinary and almost miraculous moderation if he did not try to extend his frontiers'. That could be achieved most quickly by war.

And yet ... There *were* contemporaries who advocated peace. La Fontaine wrote a fable about two goats fighting for precedence on a plank stretching over a ravine. The goats were Philip IV of Spain and Louis XIV. In the end both fell in. La Fontaine's friend and patron was Nicholas Fouquet. Marc Fumaroli argues that Fouquet offered Louis a real alternative to Colbert's aggressive nationalism, both at home and abroad. Fouquet stood for compromise, low key informality, friendship.[3] In the European context that meant negotiation rather than aggression. Louis' uncle Charles I had been tried and executed for causing unnecessary wars. Though the English were condemned throughout Europe as wildly eccentric and misguided, the way of peace was advocated by Christian idealists such as Bossuet and Fénelon. While Louis' preference for the aristocratic warrior code ensured that 'Christian virtue fell victim to Roman *virtus*', even the Romans had established 'pax Romana'. On his deathbed Louis told his great-grandson that he had fought too many wars.

Louis may well have changed his mind and his values during the course of a very long reign. Furthermore, no two wars are the same; some are more reprehensible than others. So we must examine each of Louis' wars to see why he resorted to force on each occasion. Did he always know what he was doing? Did he sometimes hope for such a quick triumph that neither friend nor foe would suffer too much? Perhaps the horrors that he inflicted were due to miscalculations rather than insensitivity to suffering. Yet his experience of the Fronde should have shown him the true nature of warfare. He had no excuse for not realising what the consequences of aggression would be. The Fronde convinced Louis that an authoritarian monarchy was the only way forward. But if that was the only lesson he learnt, he took the wrong cue. When due allowance is made for the aristocratic *mentalité* of the time, Louis has a case to answer.

A STRONG HAND

'It can be said that never did France enjoy such near-perfect security on its frontiers as in the last years of Mazarin's life.'[4] Louis showed in his *Mémoires* that he appreciated his good fortune:

> There was peace with my neighbours for as long as I would want it myself, owing to the circumstances in which they found themselves ... England was barely reviving from her past troubles and sought only to consolidate the government of a newly restored king whose inclinations, moreover, drew him towards France. The entire policy of the Dutch and of those who governed them aimed at only two things: to maintain their commerce and humble the house of Orange. Sweden needed me for her true and lasting interests.[5]

The threat from the Habsburgs was cancelled for the time being by the Peace of the Pyrenees, and by the emperor's problems in Hungary and with the Turks. France patronised the League of the Rhine. When Cardinal Mazarin died, not only did France have no enemies, no threats with which to contend, but she also had the largest armed forces in Europe. While the war minister Le Tellier compared the army to a Swiss republic with the generals resembling the independent cantons, the troops, the equipment and the experienced officer corps were all there, waiting to be led. Richelieu had created a navy that could quickly be revived. The diplomatic corps had achieved a relative professionalism under its experienced and capable foreign minister Hugh de Lionne.

And supporting the frontmen were 20 million French people, a rich and thriving economy and a governing class united behind its glamorous leader. What would Louis do with all these top cards? The answer came quickly: he would play them.

The Sun King's style was established in November 1661 when a fracas broke out in London between the staffs of the French and Spanish embassies. Shots were fired, three of the French ambassador's horses were killed. The issue was precedence between the representatives of France and Spain, or, in the terminology of the time, between the Most Christian King and the Catholic King. Louis threw his weight about, sacking his ambassador in London for being feeble, expelling the Spanish ambassador from France, and demanding from his uncle and father-in-law a complete apology and recognition of French superiority over Spain. As Louis cynically observed in his *Mémoires*: 'Their King was old, in doubtful health, he had only one son who was very young and rather sickly, he and his minister were afraid of war.'[6] So why not exploit their weakness? Louis behaved outrageously, for there was no precedence that justified his arrogance. The only opposition came from Marie Thérèse, who with uncharacteristic indignation berated Louis for humiliating her father. Louis took no notice. Philip backed down and apologised. Louis was cock-a-hoop, congratulating himself in his *Mémoires* on this brilliant display, which justified his motto of *nec pluribus impar* (literally 'not unequal to more' or 'the sky's the limit'). Clearly Louis' sensitivity to his *gloire* meant that no hint of an insult would go unnoticed. By the same token he took on his spiritual father when the French ambassador was allegedly insulted by the pope's Corsican guards. Louis sent troops into the papal territory of Avignon. The pope apologised and erected a monument outside the guards' barracks, recording their shameful behaviour. Louis bullied his own ministers too – for instance, overruling them when he tried to procure Lorraine by the Treaty of Montmartre (February 1662).[7]

If that was the Sun King's style, what was the substance of his foreign policy? Did he have consistent aims? Perhaps a clue was given by Louis XIV's first resort to a full-scale shooting war that occurred in summer 1667. He had more or less kept out of the Anglo-Dutch war, which had raged between 1664 and 1667. Louis was embarrassed by this conflict between his Dutch allies and his English friends, who had allowed him to buy back Dunkirk (April 1662). His preferred enemy was Spain whose weakness he had already exploited. Now she was weaker still, due to the death in 1665 of Philip IV. His widow Mariana ruled as regent on behalf of her infant son Carlos II (1661–1700). This pathetic product of Habsburg inbreeding, 'Carlos the Sufferer' as he was called, was to defy medical science by living to the age of forty. When his father died, he was not expected to get beyond four. So the destiny of the Spanish inheritance, which was to engage European diplomacy for the next forty years, already beckoned. In the wrong hands, the immense wealth of the Spanish Empire could spell trouble for France, reviving threats of invasion and internal subversion. Therefore Louis responded to what was perhaps the chief priority of his foreign policy. His critics have argued that Louis aimed at universal monarchy or, less ambitiously, at such natural frontiers as the Rhine. This is certainly an exaggeration. But Louis was understandably concerned about the security of France's frontiers. Furthermore, as a dynast, he was determined that his family should receive its rights. These were his primary preoccupations throughout his personal rule.

The Sun King staked an immediate claim on behalf of his wife, who was Philip IV's elder daughter by his first marriage. The marriage clauses of the Treaty of the Pyrenees had been cleverly devised by Mazarin to give France maximum advantage. Marie Thérèse renounced her claims to the Spanish inheritance only on condition that her dowry of 500,000 ecus was paid within two years. The fact that it had not been paid enabled Louis to quote an obscure Brabantine law which entitled Marie Thérèse to the parts of the Spanish Netherlands that were adjudged to have devolved on her. Hence the name given to the war that Louis fought on her behalf – the War of Devolution. He sent a highly slanted summary of his legal case to Madrid, explaining that he was motivated solely by the desire to obtain justice for his wife and child, nor did he wish to use force but to enter as a beneficent sun whose loving rays would spread prosperity and peace.

Actually Louis' justification for war was claptrap, as the queen-regent pointed out. For the Brabantine law applied only to private inheritance, not to the rival claims of states. Confident that she had right on her side, the queen-regent cast aside her late husband's feebleness and chose to fight. Before Louis invaded, he circulated to the European powers a tendentious summary of his wife's case, blaming the queen of Spain for provoking war by her 'formal and positive refusal' to negotiate:

Yet the Most Christian King, instead of executing his rights, was willing to suspend for some time the design of pursuing them in the belief he had, that the Queen of Spain would take care to be better informed about them, but at last perceiving that a longer patience might prejudice the interests of the Queen his wife, Spain having already taken advantage of it, in exacting a new oath from these Estates that were fallen to him, he is resolved to march and take possession of them.[8]

This was by no means the last example of 'in your face' French propaganda that insulted the reader's intelligence. But Louis was right to be concerned about European reactions to his assault on the Spanish Netherlands.

As it turned out, the French military juggernaut functioned with alarming efficiency. It was a promenade rather than a war. The Spanish commander had 20,000 troops as against Louis' 55,000. But French quality was even more impressive. The Spaniards allowed themselves to be cooped up in fortresses, which quickly fell victim to the artillery directed by Vauban. Louvois masterminded the supplies needed by the field armies. Louis himself played a prominent role, showing that he was not afraid of enemy fire by joining his men in the front line. He enjoyed himself immensely, sleeping rough, losing weight and twirling his moustache every morning. He personally directed the sieges of such vital fortresses as Lille. He brought his queen with him – it was her territory after all that he was securing. Louise de La Vallière and Athénaïs de Montespan came too, presumably as camp followers to whom Louis could show off, a bizarre touch that cannot have pleased Marie Thérèse any more than Louis' generals appreciated Louvois' bossiness. But Louis would not permit long faces when everything was going so well. Thanks to the war minister's brilliant organisation, the French army had enough ammunition, food and fodder not only to dominate Flanders but also to invade Franche-Comté in mid-winter (1667–8). This was a remarkable campaign logistically as seventeenth-century armies were usually confined to barracks in winter due to the absence of fodder. But Louvois had prepared the necessary provisions and supply lines. Franche-Comté proved a useful bargaining counter when peace was made.

Louis complacently congratulated himself in his *Mémoires* on his statesmanlike generosity at the end of the war. By the terms of the Treaty of Aix-la-Chapelle France returned Franche-Comté to Spain, but kept most of the towns in Flanders that had been captured, for instance

Armentières, Oudenarde and Lille. Ironically some of the towns were in Walloon Flanders where the law of devolution did not apply. Vauban got to work incorporating France's new acquisitions into a complex system of defences known as the *pré carré*. This was a duelling term meaning a defensible, enclosed field, and very suitable given the prevailing ethos of insult and response.

These gains were welcome though hardly substantial enough on their own to justify war. But Louis was willing to settle because he had in the meantime negotiated a secret treaty with Emperor Leopold. In the event of Carlos II's eagerly awaited death, it was agreed that the Habsburgs would keep Spain and the overseas empire while France would get the whole of the Spanish Low Countries, Franche-Comté, Naples, Sicily and Navarre. This was a remarkable diplomatic achievement, reflecting the skill of Louis' secretary of state for foreign affairs, Hugues de Lionne, and Leopold's awareness of his own military shortcomings. It throws interesting light on the arguments of Louis' defenders that conflict with the Habsburgs was inevitable. It was clearly no such thing. Further warfare was now no longer necessary.

The War of Devolution has often been seen as a textbook exercise in controlled aggression, conducted expeditiously with limited war aims and minimum loss of life, and concluded with statesmanlike moderation. But this is too kind. Louis' justification for the war was tendentious. The suffering inflicted on civilians who got in the way was substantial: they certainly had a raw deal, however much Louis enjoyed the war. By his irresponsible aggression he had blown sky-high Mazarin's system of alliances that had so signally benefited France. The League of the Rhine had disintegrated, alarmed by French aggression. France's erstwhile allies Holland and England had hastily concluded their own war and had been joined by Sweden in forming a triple alliance, committed to opposing further French aggression. For Louis' bullying and dishonest diplomacy was highly alarming, especially when backed up by French military might. An English diplomat spoke for the rest of Europe when he expressed his concern at the emergence of this 'great comet that is risen of late, the French King, who expects not only to be gazed at but adored by the whole world'. Those who could not accept the Sun King at his own valuation were free to conclude that a mad dog was loose in Europe – and that it would almost certainly bite again.

INGRATITUDE PUNISHED: THE DUTCH WAR (1672–9)

While the Sun King had his reasons for the War of Devolution and a strategy for bringing it to a satisfactory conclusion, the war against Holland is harder to justify. Indeed, some contemporaries and most historians have maintained that this is where he went wrong. Peter Robert Campbell claims that 'the war seems to have been the most serious mistake of his reign'.[9] Archbishop Fénelon, writing to Louis in 1694, had this to say:

> So many terrible troubles that have been devastating all of Europe for more than twenty years, so much blood spilt, so many outrages committed, so many provinces pillaged, so many towns and villages reduced to ashes, are the disastrous consequences of that war of 1672, started for your *gloire* and so as to humiliate those makers of gazettes and medals in Holland. That war is still the true source of all the evils that France is suffering from. Since that war you have always wanted to grant peace as a master, and impose the terms, instead of offering them with justice and moderation. That is why peace could not last.[10]

Fénelon sent the letter to Mme de Maintenon who may or may not have shown it to Louis, though she almost certainly gave him the gist of it. The historian Paul Sonnino has argued that while there may have been strategic and economic considerations in the king's mind, fundamentally he was motivated by enjoyment of war and resentment against the Dutch for initiating the Triple Alliance. Louis despised the Dutch for their Protestantism, their republicanism and their efficiency as merchants. 'The maggots', he called them, or 'the herring curers'. He found them irritating and tedious. Had he not been their ally against England! What monstrous ingratitude to turn against him! A Dutch medallion had compared van Beuningen, their ambassador to Paris, to Joshua who had stopped the sun in its tracks (see Joshua 10: 12). This intolerable insolence must be punished. In so far as he had rational motives, Louis probably saw a swift, punitive campaign as a shot across Dutch bows, deterring them from further interference with his acquisition of the rest of Spanish Flanders. He obviously had such a strategy in mind when he bought Charles II's cooperation by the secret Treaty of Dover (May 1670), negotiated by Minette, Charles's favourite sister and Louis' favourite sister-in-law, and when he secured his eastern frontiers by occupying Lorraine and squaring the archbishop of Cologne and the bishop of Munster whose lands would be ideal for an invasion of Holland.

As always Louis listened to his advisers, though he did not always follow them. Louvois and Turenne were the most prominent hawks assuring Louis that swift victory would be his, while Colbert and Lionne were the doves, urging caution. When Colbert saw which way Louis' mind was moving, he too supported war. Maybe war was the only way of defeating the infuriating Dutchmen whose mercantile practices were seemingly invincible. Lionne favoured diplomacy. When he died in 1671, Louis condescendingly dismissed him as 'a capable man though not without faults'. He was replaced by another dove, Arnauld de Pomponne, whose influence was limited by his lack of ministerial experience and his Jansenist connections. Pomponne had sympathy with the Dutch appeasers, headed by his friend Jan de Witt. But when the foreign minister de Groot presented a letter outlining his government's concessions, Pomponne could not save him from humiliation at Versailles. Tortured with gout, he had to be carried upstairs, and was then obliged to run a gauntlet of threatening generals before being confronted by Louis XIV. The king was barely civil, assuring de Groot that he would follow the interests of France in his own time and in his own way. After de Groot had left, Louis circulated his letter for laughs. Louis thanked Pomponne for his views, but took the final decision himself. It was to be war.[11]

In his sympathetic biography of Louis, François Bluche provocatively calls the Dutch War 'the inevitable conflict'. He argues that the war was a *kulturkampf*, a clash of civilisations so different in religion, politics and economics that war was bound to come. Apart from the fact that no war is inevitable, France's friendly relations with the Dutch Republic for half a century confutes Bluche. On the other hand, there is no reason to sentimentalise over the resistance of 'gallant little Holland', which was in fact a wealthy, grasping and formidable great power, widely detested by her neighbours and rivals. It is similarly perverse to blame Louis as a warmonger when England fought no less than three wars against the Dutch between 1651 and 1674. The case against Louis relates to his competence as a statesman and a strategist. In October 1671 Louis envisaged measures 'to keep the Spaniards from joining the Dutch and then to make them join'. In other words, the Spaniards were the real enemy. So why attack the Dutch? In his *Precise History of the Campaigns of Louis the Great* [*sic*] Racine, tragedian of genius turned hack historian, comes to the rescue: 'Leagued with the enemies of France, the United Netherlands prided itself on limiting the conquests of the King ... The King, tired of these insolences, resolved to punish them. The vigour of his campaign astonished them.'[12] However obsequious, Racine was basically correct in perceiving that Louis the Great's motivation was irrational, childish resentment. It was all the more essential therefore that such an unnecessary and pointless war should be concluded as quickly as possible. Louis' strategy should have involved not only a vigorous prosecution of the war but as speedy a victory as that so triumphantly achieved in 1667–8.

Unfortunately the campaign, which Louis launched in April 1672 without even bothering to declare war, had no strategy. This was because Louis had initiated the wrong war against the wrong enemy. While he was glad to teach the Dutch a lesson, he did not want their land, which compared to the Spanish Netherlands was of no real use to him. When Condé proposed a cavalry raid on Amsterdam to kidnap the Estates and decommission the sluice gates, Louis agreed with Turenne that this was too risky. He was not interested in Amsterdam. Louis personally led a ponderous invasion of Dutch territory, allowing his vast army of 130,000 men to provision itself from the dumps of stores so thoughtfully prepared by Louvois, crossing the Rhine with maximum publicity, in the presence of his wife and his mistresses. Dutch forces initially numbered a mere 27,000. They were swept aside. In July Dutch plenipotentiaries grovelled before the king, who insisted on humiliating terms: he was to keep the towns he had already taken, preferential tariffs in France's favour were to be conceded, plus full toleration for Catholics, an annual submission to Louis XIV and 24 million livres. The Dutch rejected these terms and opened the dykes at Muiden; Amsterdam became an island. 'Keep advancing, and they will eventually concede even more', was Louvois' advice. 'Splendid', agreed Louis, when he sent the Dutchmen packing. Everything was going so well – and it soon got better. In August a proletarian mob urged on by fanatical preachers erupted in downtown Amsterdam and lynched the de Witt brothers. Their bourgeois supporters were swept aside in favour of William of Orange, the people's hero, who became Stadtholder, the office traditionally held in reserve for a national crisis. Louis was cheered by this slaughter of the contemptible oligarchs and the promotion of his diminutive relation, whom he had always patronised and regarded as a client.

But William was not to be underestimated. Though this asthmatic, round-shouldered midget had not been treated kindly by nature, he had a good mind and a great heart. He proved a resourceful politician and a persistent rather than an inspired soldier – indeed he must be the most frequently defeated general of all time. Although he admired Louis XIV, once opining that he was the greatest man in the world, he had already flagged up his defiance by rejecting Louis' offer of one of his illegitimate daughters as a bride. 'Members of my House marry the daughters of kings, not their bastards', retorted the little Dutchman. Louis was sufficiently cheered by the news from Amsterdam to leave the front in favour of the hunting at Fontainebleau and Versailles where he was greeted by a different army of 22,000 men and 650 horses at work on the fabulous alterations designed to please Mme de Montespan. In the meantime he was amazed to learn that William of Orange was still fighting and that the war was not yet over. In his *Mémoires* Louis wondered if he should have tried harder to get a quick settlement: 'Posterity may blame me for my ambition and my desire to avenge the injuries which I had received from the Dutch.'[13] Louis should indeed have addressed his failure to get the quick result his country needed. So far as William was concerned, his own crusade against Louis had only just begun.

This particular war lasted until 1679. There was no result in 1673, despite the brilliance of Condé and Turenne. The rising star was the hunch-backed duc de Luxembourg who risked an attack on Amsterdam across the ice until a sudden thaw nearly drowned his army. William of Orange now acquired allies – the rulers of Spain, the Empire and Brandenburg, worried by the increasing power and arrogance of the Sun King. 'I am in for a long war', Louis grimly observed. He led his men in several successful sieges, notably the capture of Maastricht. His generals occupied Franche-Comté – again – while his admirals distinguished themselves in the Mediterranean. But Turenne was killed by a stray musket ball and Condé retired to his estate, offended by Louvois' interference. Louis' allies deserted him – Munster and Cologne in 1673, England in 1674. Meanwhile, increasing taxation provoked rebellions in Roussillon (1674) and Brittany (1675), where 15,000 peasants took up arms. Bishop Bossuet pleaded for peace. Negotiations began in 1676 at Nijmegen.

If Louis willed the Dutch War for his own particular motives, what part did he play in its conduct? The answer is, immense. Moltke, the victor of the Franco-Prussian War of 1870–1, used to divide officers into four categories: stupid and lazy (they can be used if kicked hard enough), clever and hardworking (ideal staff officers), clever and lazy (the stuff from which great commanders are made), stupid and hardworking (a menace, to be dismissed at the first opportunity). Louis XIV was undoubtedly a first-rate staff officer, very intelligent and very industrious. Possibly he lacked the overall inspiration to be a great commander – and he certainly lacked Moltke's idleness.[14] Louis was at his best supervising the preparations for a campaign. No detail escaped him. He loved parades, inspecting his troops' turnout and casting a critical eye over their drill. He was interested and knowledgeable about military matters, where his quick mind and excellent memory stood him in good stead. He was a supportive boss, awarding medals and promotion for bravery and taking the trouble to write letters of congratulation when they were deserved. He was kind to soldiers who were down on their luck, and his foundation of the Invalides in Paris was only one of the measures he adopted for their welfare. If artillery and siege trains were revolutionised under Louis XIV, so were the medical services.

Actually Louis was not a bad field commander, though he preferred sieges as they were more predictable than pitched battles. His forte was meticulous planning rather than inspiration. He began the war by directing the sieges of four fortresses, and his capture of Maastricht was a masterpiece where Louis deserved credit for backing the expertise of another rising star, Sébastian Le Prestre, seigneur de Vauban. Louis had his moments on the battlefield, especially during the 1678 campaign when he softened up the Dutch in preparation for peace. Perhaps he lacked the flexibility that Condé displayed during the bewildering chaos of a seventeenth-century 'field', and the gambler's instinct when a sudden opportunity arose. He never forgave himself for passing up an opportunity at Heurtebise in 1676 for attacking William of Orange when he had caught him off balance. Unwillingly he deferred to his generals – 'You know more about these things than I do'[15] – but he used to wake up in the night in later years still seething with rage. Nor was his temper improved when in the following year Monsieur – with a little help from Luxembourg – defeated the Dutch at Cassel. Louis never gave his brother a command again, and appointed Boileau and Racine as official historians to put the record straight. These unlikely warriors of the pen could be seen plopping around in the Flanders mud, ensuring that not even the king's loyal brother should outshine the Sun.

Louis' greatest claim to originality was his cooperation with Louvois in supplying a modern army. This was new. It was largely a matter of size. The armies of the first half of the seventeenth century, for instance during the Thirty Years War, seldom numbered more than 30,000. The record during the English Civil War was Parliament's 22,000 at Marston Moor. Louis invaded Holland with 130,000 men – and his armies and those of his enemies were to approach 400,000 before the century ended. David Parrott has researched the unbelievable chaos of military administration under Richelieu and Mazarin – a combination of corruption, improvisation and loot. How on earth was an army twenty times the size to be fed? Louis' answer was Louvois. 'This horrible man', as Nancy Mitford called him, personified loyalty to his master, ruthlessness and ability. He was an organisational genius. He pioneered the methods later adopted by Marlborough and Wellington. Supplies had to be ordered from the manufacturers, financed and delivered to the right place, at the right time. Campaigns had to be accurately anticipated so that heavily guarded 'magazines' (i.e. distribution centres) would await the arrival of the armies. It is easy nowadays to forget the demands of the horse, essential to an unmechanised army. A horse consumes 60 lbs of fodder a day. Louvois solved that one as well. Until the Nine Years War broke out (1688), the French conspicuously outclassed their enemies in equipment – but also in morale and discipline because an unfed, unpaid soldier will misbehave or desert or mutiny, and an unfed horse will catch cold and die.

What was Louis' role? While he invariably contributed his considerable military expertise, his chief value was to give Louvois his support against his many critics. The generals loathed Louvois – for his rudeness, his arrogance, and his interference. 'The lowliest bourgeois would not accept a missive like that!' Turenne complained after receiving a rebuke from the minister. 'This is no doubt a good plan if you happen to be in an office at Versailles,' Luxembourg remarked after Louvois saw fit to tell him his business, 'but it does not look so impressive in the Rhineland.' Louvois retorted: 'You have put yourself in a position where His Majesty can justly reproach you, that during the entire campaign you have made the finest French army which was ever in Germany entirely useless.' Mme de Sévigné described Louvois' approach to a prominent aristocrat:

> Monsieur de Louvois said the other day to Monsieur de Nogaret, 'Sir, your company is in a very poor state'. 'I did not know that, Sir', replied Nogaret. 'Then, Sir,

you should have known it', retorted Louvois, 'Have you seen your company?'
'No, Sir'. 'Then you should have done so, Sir. You must choose, Sir, either to be
a mere courtier, or to perform your duties if you are going to be an officer'.[16]

In addition to his self-imposed defects, Louvois was *not* an aristocrat.
'You've only to look at M. de Louvois to see that he is a complete pleb',
remarked the duchess of Orléans. But that was one of the reasons why
Louis supported him, just as he was glad to pay the dowries for Colbert's
daughters to marry dukes. In contrast to his somewhat edgy relationship
with Colbert, however, Louis seems to have liked Louvois. For one thing
he was slightly younger than the king, so Louis could regard him as his
protégé. To be fair to Louis, above all he rated Louvois' ability and appreciated his unique achievements. Furthermore, he shared Louvois' dislike
for the duc de Luxembourg who came from a *frondeur* background and
whose father was executed as a duellist while the future marshal was still
in the womb. So the king and the minister cooperated in the disgrace of
Luxembourg during the *affaire* of the poisons, though Luxembourg was
almost certainly innocent – a shabby business.

Geoffrey Treasure compares Louvois' relationship with the generals
to Lloyd George's run-ins with Haig. It is a thought-provoking comparison in which the contrasts perhaps outweigh the similarities. For
instance, George V backed Haig and not Lloyd George. Perhaps there is
also a valid comparison between Louvois and Lesley Hore-Belisha, the
British secretary of state for war (1937–40) who did so much for the
common soldier. He too alienated the generals, but, unlike Louvois, was
not supported by the monarchy, especially when he interfered with strategy. Come to think of it, perhaps Vauban was more like Hore-Belisha.
In 1670 he quarrelled with Louvois over the provision of wheelbarrows, as opposed to hods, to be used by soldiers constructing field works
at Dunkirk. Wheelbarrows, in Louvois' judgement, were 'appallingly
expensive', whereas hods cost only 6 sous each – and the broken backs of
soldiers driven to exhaustion nothing at all.[17]

Louvois' logistics were firmly rooted in the seventeenth century.
Recent research by Lynn, by Rowlands and by Satterfield[18] has shown how
Louvois' work was based on exploitation, especially of the communities
unlucky enough to be overrun by the French army. Satterfield in par-
ticular has investigated the role of the partisans during the Dutch War.
These were in effect licensed, organised, official plunderers. Whereas in

Richelieu's army the soldiers could only survive through 'do-it-yourself' exploitation of civilians, in which their officers connived at best or alternatively preferred not to notice, Louvois typically *organised* the plunder of civilians. Partisans (the word is derived from 'parti', a gang) were equipped with certificates from their officers so that they could compete successfully for the cooperation of their civilian victims with Spanish marauders and French highwaymen. Their loot would then be distributed by their officers among the regiments and garrisons. The role of the partisan was specialised, demanding knowledge of the locality and its inhabitants. Dragoons were ideal and were most frequently employed in this role. Their mobility and loose organisation were especially appropriate. What a picture of military cruelty and civilian helplessness! And it could get worse. The houses of peasants or townsfolk who favoured the Spaniards, or tried to play off the partisans against their rivals, would be torched. Sometimes whole villages would be destroyed. Sometimes the king would support the minister in authorising the laying waste of whole areas in Holland and the Rhineland – a grim precedent anticipating the horrors of the Nine Years War.

So was the Dutch War worth it? Or was it 'probably the greatest mistake that Louis XIV made in international affairs'?[19] Louis did not think so. With reference to the peace settlement (1678–9), he wrote: 'I fully rejoice at my clever conduct whereby I was able to extend the boundaries of my kingdom at the expense of my enemies.' Indeed France made solid gains at Nijmegen: Franche-Comté was retained, Ypres, Cambrai and Valenciennes were the most notable of several conquests which Louis was allowed to keep, though he had to restore Ghent, Coutrai and Charleroi to Spain. But the emperor handed over Breisach and Freiburg to France. Louis bribed the elector of Brandenburg with 900,000 livres, to restore his Pomeranian conquests to Sweden – though T.C.W. Blanning quotes Frederick William's withdrawal as a significant illustration of Louis' moral authority, a reflection of his Europe-wide prestige, given that French troops were hundreds of miles away from the disputed territory. Whatever the explanation, Louis clearly called the shots.

For all Louis' boasting, however, the results of so much blood and cash were disappointing. Without abusing the historian's privilege of hindsight, one can argue that militarily Louis got it wrong. He failed to deliver the expected *blitzkrieg*, while the spoils acquired at Nijmegen were adequate rather than spectacular. On the whole, throughout his reign Louis

accepted responsibility when things were not quite right. But on this occasion he unfairly castigated Pomponne: 'I have suffered for many years from
his weakness, his obstinacy, his laziness and his incompetence. He has cost
me dearly and I have not profited from all the advantages that I could have
had. I must finally order him to withdraw.'[20] These alleged defects did not
prevent Louis from subsequently reappointing Pomponne. In the meantime Pomponne and his friends, such as Mme de Sévigné, were devastated.
As Bluche felicitously puts it: 'Louis thanked Pomponne for his services
and replaced him with Croissy.'[21]

Nevertheless, despite a vague feeling of dissatisfaction, Louis had
thoroughly enjoyed the war. By his criteria, it significantly enhanced his
gloire. He had extended the boundaries of his territory, giving Vauban
the opportunity to improve France's security. Louis had proved himself
a great captain. What if a few thousand soldiers and civilians had per-
ished! The city of Paris hailed him as Louis le Grand. Yes, the Dutch
War, despite its disappointing results, had definitely been worth it.

The historian can be more critical. Leaving aside moral considerations (for the time being), there certainly were positive achievements.
As we have said, France was now strategically more secure. Louis' own
political power was significantly enhanced by his enlargement and domination of the army. He led, his nobility followed. The road was clear for
even more military growth and even more absolutist authority during
the next decade. Louis had exuded self-confidence, conquering fortresses
abroad and nubile women at home. Versailles and its accompanying
palaces were approaching completion. On the debit side, however, the
economy was ruined. The reforms of the 1660s were forgotten as the
harassed Colbert had been obliged to return to *affaires extraordinaires*. In
fact Colbert was deeply hurt by Louis' complaints about the shortage of
money and the lack of progress at Versailles. 'Have another look at those
figures. If you can't find the money, I'll find someone else who can', Louis
brusquely told Colbert. Meanwhile, his hated rival Louvois basked in
the Sun's rays. But there were problems. Louis complacently referred in
his *Mémoires* to the jealousy that his successes had provoked among his
rivals abroad. But king and minister had no idea how alarmed and dis-
gusted Europe had become with French aggression and atrocities. Louis
lacked one of the politician's most essential qualities – the ability to see
the other person's point of view. He was particularly blind to the reactions of whole nations such as the English, the Germans and the Dutch.

As a result France was now surrounded by enemies who were not prepared to believe the king's assurances of future peaceful intentions.

EXPLOITATION OF A POWER VACUUM: NIJMEGEN TO RATISBON (1679–84)

Regensburg

In the immediate aftermath of the Dutch War there was not much that France's neighbours could do when Louis returned to the offensive. For while Colbert's work on behalf of the French economy was in tatters, France's enemies were even more exhausted. In particular the German princes had temporarily had enough, the Dutch had reverted to their preference for peace despite William's pleadings, the English were involved in a major political crisis over the possible succession of the Catholic James, duke of York. As for the emperor, he was distracted by problems in Hungary and on his own doorstep, due to one of Louis' most effective ploys, bribery. English and Swedish politicians were especially favoured by French pensions and jewellery. Now the Sun King embarked on a secret (it had to be) policy of massively subsidising the infidel Turk – while the pope was appealing for a European crusade. Financed by Louis XIV, the Turks threatened Vienna. On his own the king of Spain could only watch helplessly while Louis exploited the power vacuum that now prevailed.

The Sun King, however, had learnt from experience. While he was perpetually surrounded by the clouds of incense dispensed by poets, dramatists, courtiers and lovers at his royal temple of Versailles, Louis never entirely abandoned the common sense he believed was the God-given characteristic of monarchs. So now he temporarily reined in his warlords, despite the fact that unlike everybody else he kept his standing army on full alert. His weapon now was the law, wielded by the cynical, hard-nosed Colbert de Croissy, who replaced the urbane and peaceable Pomponne. Like his unlovable brother the great Colbert, Croissy was a bruiser. His job was to exploit the confusion that still prevailed as a result of recent peace treaties, going back to Westphalia (1648). Many contentious issues had been deliberately fudged, especially by Mazarin, so that his successors could profit from them. Feudal law still applied in western Europe. The assumption still prevailed that a town or a fortress had obscure dependencies that a clever lawyer could maximise. Croissy was a very clever lawyer. Moreover he knew the treaties backwards and was familiar with the ground, having been the intendant in Alsace.

So there now occurred the 'reunions'. Courts known as *chambres de réunion* were established at Breisach, Metz, Tournai and Besançon to investigate claims by the French king with regard to his newly acquired properties. Staffed by French lawyers, inspired by Colbert de Croissy, they consistently 'found' for Louis the Great. Territory between the Moselle and the Rhine, including much of Alsace and Luxembourg, became French. The land acquired was considerable, economically valuable and strategically significant. If Colbert de Croissy provided the cutting edge, Vauban was the consolidator, and Louvois and his king the masterminds in the background. The years after the Dutch War constituted a period of ceaseless activity for the great engineer during which he created a defensible frontier in Flanders and along the Rhine. The concept of the *pré carré* was thus realised. The losers were the princes of the Empire and the kings of Spain and Sweden. What was new was the way that these former allies of France were now so heedlessly alienated.

The climax of this 'robust foreign policy' as Bluche called it, was the seizure of Strasbourg in 1681. All Vauban's plans hinged on this great city, the 'gate' opening into Germany for French aggressors or into France for the Germans. This time Louis threatened force. In September Louvois moved up a sizeable army, which browbeat the city fathers into surrender. Within days Vauban floated stone and mortar down the Rhine in 600 barges for the construction of massive outworks. Strasbourg cathedral reverted to the Roman faith. In October the Sun King himself, attended by his queen, courtiers and Lully's brass band, arrived to receive the applause of his new subjects. A medal was struck: Clausa Germanis Gallia (France protected from the Germans). Strasbourg's Protestants, on the other hand, sang the 137th psalm: 'By the waters of Babylon we sat down and wept.' Louvois told Dietrich, the senior Protestant minister in Strasbourg, to study 1 Maccabees 2:18: 'Do the commandments of the king as all the nations have done.' Unfortunately the minister knew his scripture and continued the quotation: 'If all the nations hearken unto him, I and my sons and my brethren will walk in the covenant of our fathers.' Louvois, humiliated in front of the courtiers, exiled the minister for two years. On the very same day that Strasbourg fell, Louis' troops also captured Casale, the capital of Montferrat, which dominated northern Italy. More work for Vauban!

Louis XIV now confidently stepped up his campaign of aggression. His reasoning was that the emperor was distracted from developments in western Europe by his fight for survival against the age-old enemies of Christendom, the Turks. The Hungarian Magyars, the Transylvanian irregulars and the grand vizier Kara Mustafa, backed by a horde of infidels, surrounded Vienna. Pope Innocent XI appealed for crusaders. The Most Christian King virtuously halted his siege of Luxembourg for a few weeks – but then resumed his attack. 'Crusades are no longer in fashion', he observed complacently. At last he was confronted with armed defiance. As he advanced on Luxembourg, Louis XIV found himself at war with Spain. His opponent was the 21-year-old Habsburg Carlos II, whom we last met as a sickly toddler. The poor man had now grown into 'a rachitic and feeble-minded weakling, the last stunted sprig of a degenerate line', 'afflicted with convulsive fits',[22] illiterate, incapable of lasting the duration of a council meeting without fidgeting for his release like a bored schoolboy. Yet he was still capable of displaying the most forthright emotion of his sad life: hatred of France. The war that he had unwisely entered was an uneven contest. A feeble Spanish mission to relieve Luxembourg was beaten off. The starving garrison was mortared into submission. Carlos II's troops could not prevent the fall of Luxembourg in June 1682. Meanwhile, Genoa had the effrontery to offer Spanish ships hospitality. After ten days' bombardment by the French navy, which had perfected the seaborne mortar, the smouldering ruins of Genoa surrendered. The Doge was obliged to travel across France in order to grovel at Versailles. Louis received his delegation graciously. The Genoese were sent home with bejewelled complimentary portraits of the Sun King.

But alas, Louis' master plan had already begun to unravel. On 12 September 1683 a Christian army led by King John Sobieski of Poland and Duke Charles of Lorraine swept down upon the Turks besieging Vienna and drove them back to Budapest, which fell two years later. Leopold was thus able to regroup and address the situation in western Europe. His unfortunate ally Carlos of Spain had no alternative but to accept the truce of Ratisbon (August 1684), mediated by the Emperor, by which Louis was allowed to keep Strasbourg, Luxembourg and the territory acquired through the reunions for twenty years. But it was only a truce. For the rest of his reign Louis' ambition was to persuade the powers to accept the Ratisbon settlement as permanent. When he anticipated another later land-grabber by claiming that Ratisbon represented his last territorial claim in Europe, he was almost certainly sincere. But was it too late? Had he already squandered too much moral capital for his affronted victims to believe him?

There is a purple passage in Bluche's partial biography of Louis XIV where he defends the Sun King's foreign policy, especially during the aftermath of the Dutch War.[23] Calling up Ragnhild Hatton as an ally, he maintains that Louis' goals were fundamentally defensive, conceived in order to preserve the security of France. Other contemporaries were more aggressive and warlike such as Emperor Leopold or William of Orange. France's foreign policy was no more imperialist than that of any other seventeenth-century power. Bluche demolishes allegations that his hero aimed at world conquest, or the imperial throne, or the conversion of the civilised world to Catholicism – though these are objectives that Louis' critics nowadays no longer attribute to him. Even so, Bluche's and Hatton's interpretations of Louis' actions between 1679 and 1684 clearly have much to be said for them. If his enemies had accepted the Ratisbon settlement, no doubt Louis would have settled down to digest his gains, like a contented boa constrictor that has swallowed a pig and wants to be left alone.

So what was the problem? Are Bluche and Hatton right to agree with Louis that his rivals were too mean and jealous to accept his amazing achievements? Or perhaps Fénelon *was* correct: Louis had fatally alienated his contemporaries by declaring war on Holland in 1672. For his motives then were clearly selfish and irresponsible. Indeed Hatton concedes the case against Louis still more by criticising his greed displayed during the War of Devolution. The fact is that when we consider the aggression and arrogance of European powers in the latter half of the seventeenth century, *Louis started it*. Similarly, the wasteful and counter-productive arms race, which involved all the European powers between 1688 and 1713 in horrendous warfare, was initiated by Louis. On his own admission, there was no threat to France in 1661. By unnecessarily going over to the offensive and by developing what John Lynn strikingly calls 'the giant of the seventeenth century' – the French army of, eventually, 400,000 men and women – Louis provoked the formation of rival 'giants'. The road to Armageddon beckoned.

Having embarked on a career of aggressive land-grabbing backed by overwhelming military and naval might, he further provoked his contemporaries with his gung-ho propaganda. So the elector of Hanover's wife Sophia predicted that 'the grand doge, if we allow him, will soon leave to the German princes no throne but a tomb'. Exaggerated and one-sided perhaps, but that was how she felt, as did many others throughout Europe. They were fed up with the 'clink-clank' of the Sun King's armies and his tendentious self-justification. Meanwhile, Louis was multiplying his strategic problems by adopting disastrously counter-productive religious policies, to which we now turn. The impressions created by these, and their knock-on effects, were to have dire consequences for his foreign policy during the latter half of his reign.

8

LOUIS XIV AND RELIGION

THE MOST CHRISTIAN KING

Louis XIV intervened decisively, frequently and disastrously in religious affairs. He crossed swords with the Papacy, the Gallicans, the Huguenots, the Jansenists and the Pietists – among others. These essentially theological confrontations had profound repercussions for the Sun King's social and political policies both at home and abroad. For this reason the two chapters devoted to Louis' foreign policy sandwich this chapter, which covers his religious objectives and achievements, both positive and negative.

First, the motivation for Louis XIV's frequent religious initiatives and confrontations must be sought in his upbringing, his opinions and his loyalties. Louis cared deeply about his religious responsibilities. He was a serious Catholic. He imbibed the more conservative tenets of the Counter-Reformation with his mother's milk, so to speak. From her he acquired the devotional practices which he faithfully followed throughout his life: he said his prayers when he got up and when he went to bed, he attended mass every day and the appropriate services at major festivals, he confessed his sins frequently, he washed the feet of the poor during Holy Week. Bluche[1] reckons that Louis heard over a thousand Advent and Lenten sermons during his personal rule (1661–1715), when he would sit with his hands on the top of his cane, gazing intently at the preacher. Some historians have suggested that Louis became more devout after he married Mme de Maintenon in 1683. She certainly made him more prudish. But, thanks to his mother's influence, he had always been both devout and a prude, even when cavorting with his mistresses.

On the other hand, Louis never acquired a deep understanding of Christian theology. While analysing the king's conscientious approach to religious matters, Joseph Bergin defends him against 'ignorance of religious questions per se – one of the most absurd charges levelled against him by generations of historians'.[2] But on the whole the historians seem to have been right. 'It is not for me to play the theologian', Louis himself wrote in his *Mémoires*. His sister-in-law Liselotte agreed: 'It is amazing how simple the great man is when it comes to religion. The reason is that he has never read anything about religion, nor the Bible either, and just goes on believing whatever he is told about religion.' Mme de Maintenon made the same complaint. Louis was never bookish and, to his great regret, had little Latin, the language of the church's liturgy and of much devotional literature. So his faith tended to be a matter of performing duties in a mechanical way, with a view to avoiding hell-fire. Though he said his rosary at mass, Anthony Levi is probably right to suggest that this was compensation for his own failure to understand what the sacrament was all about, and for his inability to participate in the service that re-enacted Christ's redemptive atonement for the sins of the world. In other words, there is no evidence that he understood the saving theology of the mass – or indeed any of the other major doctrines of the Catholic church.

Did Louis' ignorance matter? His mother never worried her head about theology. 'Fi! Fi! Fi! De la Grace' ('That's enough talk about grace!'),[3] was her comment on predestination. If Louis had been equally laid back, no harm would have come. The problem was that he did care. He profoundly detested opinions that he instinctively felt were in conflict with his own conservative orthodoxy and exaltation of kingship, for he was completely incapable of understanding or sympathising with other people's theological standpoints. Thus he assumed that the Huguenots were just being tiresome by persisting in their faith. Similarly, Jansenists were merely political troublemakers. Louis' confessor La Chaise once remarked: 'I have often heard His Majesty say that cabals of people in revolt against the decisions and opinions of the church were no less damaging to the state than to religion.' This is a revealing comment.

The one doctrine that Louis could appreciate was the divine right of kings. He believed that God had chosen him and had given him all the necessary skills and qualities. Louis derived this self-belief from his upbringing, culminating in his coronation at Reims. While the glamorous youngster had impressed one and all with his natural poise and dignity on that glorious June day in 1654, this popular enthusiasm was as nothing compared to the excitement experienced by the young king himself. Louis was entranced by the mystic drama of the occasion. The Sunday Child, the Gift of God to the French nation, had spiritually come of age. Anointed with the oil of Clovis, he would be indefatigable in his crusade on behalf of France and the church. Traditionally the king of France was known as 'the Most Christian King' and 'the Eldest Son of the Church'. Descended from Charlemagne and Saint Louis, he inherited their virtues. Louis touched thousands of sufferers from scrofula in the belief that he had inherited miraculous healing powers. He nodded with approval when Bossuet, the high priest of royal bombast, thundered: 'The royal throne is the very throne of God', or 'Majesty is the image of the greatness of God in a prince.'

Louis' belief in his semi-divine status doesn't just explain his self-confidence in presiding over ecclesiastical affairs and pronouncing on dogmatic issues, despite his outstanding ignorance. It also explains his remarkable self-satisfaction and readiness to judge others even while stepping out of line himself. We have seen that, despite committing adultery with his mistresses, he frequently rebuked his brother for his homosexuality. Louis believed that kings had a special relationship with the Almighty, which allowed them a certain latitude in moral conduct. He faithfully followed the example of his royal ancestors, such as the promiscuous Henri the Great. Like his great-grandson, Louis XV, he believed that an immediate 'peccavi' ('I have sinned'), plus a satisfactory deathbed repentance, would suffice for day-to-day sexual misdemeanours. He probably agreed with his cousin Charles II who felt sure that 'God would not mind him having a little pleasure along the way', or Henry VIII who had boasted that 'God and my conscience are on excellent terms.'

So when court preachers such as Bossuet compared Louis to David, who made Bathsheba his mistress after arranging her husband's death in the front line,[4] Louis could retort that he had never stooped as low as that. But Bossuet's criticism of the king was embarrassingly perceptive when he quoted the second letter of Peter about the dog returning to its vomit. In Louis' case it was adultery, confession, communion and adultery again. Eventually Louis lost patience with Bossuet, dispatching him to the remote bishopric of Condom. Once he felt a censorious nobleman's head and asked him if he felt in sound health. Only Mme de Maintenon could halt the royal lecher.

But divine right went much further. Louis took his coronation oaths seriously. He had promised God that he would promote the interests of Heaven (whatever that meant), look after his people's spiritual welfare and extirpate heresy. Every Friday Louis presided over the Council of Conscience, attended by the archbishop of Paris and by the king's confessor. This council helped the king to keep his coronation promises. It also helped him to make senior appointments in the French church, especially bishops. Louis tried hard to make appropriate appointments, once instructing La Chaise to get rid of ambitious careerists at court: 'Tell all those young abbés that they would do far better to go and reside in their benefices, conduct missions and instruct the poor rather than to stay here at court, and that I shall remember them all the better for not seeing them. I have a very good memory.'[5]

Louis' combination of arrogance and ignorance made him vulnerable to manipulation. Although naturally autocratic, he could be influenced without realising it. His confessors were invariably Jesuits – Annat (1654–70), Ferrier (1670–4), La Chaise (1674–1709) and Le Tellier (1709–15). Jesuit influence was widely feared and resented. The Society's monopoly of the post of confessor to the king did Louis' reputation no good. Others influenced him too. In his *Mémoires* Louis had told his son that there was no harm in having mistresses provided that women were not allowed to influence policies and appointments. There was real irony here. Mme de Maintenon certainly influenced the king during his later years, especially in his religious policies, even though, to her fury, he rejected her pacifist condemnation of war.

THE ELDEST SON OF THE CHURCH

How much does it say for Louis' intelligence or for his religious principles that for prolonged periods during the first half of his personal rule he was at odds with the pope? So much for being the Eldest Son of the Church. At least this seems a reasonable criticism today. To be fair, the contemporary French *mentalité* saw the pope as a foreigner and believed that his influence should be curtailed. Even more open to criticism, however, is the

Plate 1 King Carlos II of Spain defied his doctors by living to the age of thirty-nine. He presided with relish over the burning of heretics. His portrait effectively captures the Habsburg jaw, his tortured soul and matted dirty hair. (Carlos II. Museo Nacional del Prado)

Plate 2 Louis' favourite portrait of himself. Aged 63, his eyes and sunken cheeks betray his own and his dentist's inadequacy. His arrogant pose conveys impregnable majesty. (Louis XIV in royal costume, 1701, by Hyacinthe Rigaud [1659–1743]. Bridgeman Art Library)

Plate 3 Louis, painted unflatteringly at age 68, has experienced the humiliations of Blenheim and Ramillies. He defies the world nonetheless, prepared to gamble France's resources on future battlefields. He was shaved every other day. (Louis XIV, 1706, by Antoine Benoist [1632–1717]. Bridgeman Art Library)

Rex. Ludovicus. Ludovicus Rex.

NO. 1.—AN HISTORICAL STUDY.

Plate 4 While Louis' courtiers remained obsequious, this satire by Thackeray pokes fun at the Rigaud portrait (Plate 2). Strip away the wig, robes, high heels and panoply of state and we are left with a pot-bellied, bald, middle-aged little man. (Cartoon by William Thackeray. Mary Evans Picture Library)

Plate 5 Mme de Montespan was witty and malicious, although basically good natured. Surprisingly devout, she explained that 'just because I commit one sin, I don't have to commit them all'. (Madame de Montespan [1640–1707], reclining in front of the gallery of the Chateau de Clagny. Bridgeman Art Library)

Plate 6 The 'violet in the long grass' who was ashamed of her sexual conduct. She loved Louis for himself. According to her rivals, Louise was emaciated and dim, though Louis appreciated her looks and her horsemanship. (Françoise Louise de la Baume le Blanc [1644–1710], duchesse de Vaujour, also known as Mademoiselle de La Vallière. Bridgeman Art Library)

Plate 7 The fascinating governess whose sex appeal (despite her double chin) and well-stocked mind captured Louis' admiration. Here, she poses with her niece whom she frogmarched into Catholicism. (Françoise d'Aubigné [1635–1719], marquise de Maintenon, and her niece Françoise d'Aubigné, the future duchesse d'Noailles. Bridgeman Art Library)

Plate 8 Louis envied and feared François-Henri de Montmorency-Bouteville, the maréchal-duc de Luxembourg, his best general after the deaths of Condé and Turenne. He was wrongly accused of involvement in the poisons affair, but survived to become 'the furnisher of Nôtre-Dame' with captured enemy standards. (François-Henri de Montmorency-Bouteville [1628–95]. Bridgeman Art Library)

Plate 9 According to Cardinal de Retz, Anne was smart enough to conceal her own stupidity. Her niece, however, fooled no one, and was condemned to a life of political and sexual irrelevance by her disloyal husband. (Anne of Austria [1601–66] and her niece and stepdaughter Marie Thérèse of Austria [1638–83], *c.* 1664. Bridgeman Art Library)

Plate 10 The peasants were the real victims of Louis' reign. He squandered their money and their lives in his pursuit of *gloire*. Mitchelin's family of bakers were by no means the poorest of the Sun King's subjects, but note their rags and dejected faces. (*The Baker's Cart*, 1656, by Jean Mitchelin. The Metropolitan Museum of Art, New York.)

fact that this conflict ended in Louis' defeat and humiliation. But it certainly did not start that way. In May 1662 Louis saw fit to make a great deal out of a minor brawl in Rome between the pope's Corsican guards and some French embassy staff. Blood was shed, shots were fired at the French ambassador. The whole episode could easily have been sorted out, given good will and common sense. But, as we saw in Chapter 7, Louis had enjoyed humiliating his father-in-law the king of Spain in the previous year after a similar fracas in London. Why not take the elderly pope down a peg as well? So Louis sent troops into the papal state of Avignon in order to bring his Holy Father to heel. It worked a treat. The pope sent his nephew to Fontainebleau to apologise and erected a monument in Rome recording his climbdown. Clearly it was as easy to bully the vicar of Christ as it was to humiliate the Catholic king.

Louis' next run-in with Rome was not so straightforward. By the decrees of the Council of Lyon (1274), king and pope had divided between them the spoils of the French church. Part of the deal was that the king received the *regale* – the income from a vacant bishopric. This perk, however, had not been extended to parts of France incorporated since 1274, such as Brittany and Languedoc. In February 1673, because the Dutch war was proving more expensive than had been anticipated, Louis arbitrarily extended the *regale* to the whole of France. Two tiresome bishops – Pavillon of Alet and Caulet of Pamiers – refused to acknowledge Louis' claim and in 1677, to the king's outraged disgust, appealed to Rome.

A new, vigorous pope, the inappropriately named Innocent XI, proved fully capable of confronting the Most Christian King. When Louis deprived the defiant bishops of their revenues, Innocent threatened Louis with excommunication. Louis retaliated by summoning a council of hand-picked bishops to put the pope in his place. The result was the issue of the four outrageously provocative Gallican articles (1682). It was war! There is no reason to suppose that Louis wanted war. Nor was it necessary in that Louis certainly had a case. Logically the *regale*'s extension could be defended, while he was correct in his belief that the church was extremely rich, even if it spent its wealth more responsibly than the royal government. It was certainly undertaxed. Compromise should therefore have been possible. But Louis' offensive tactics provoked a row that, as events were to prove, he could not win, even by playing the Gallican card.

Gallicanism was an amorphous movement that could be traced back to medieval times. It was a kind of proto-nationalism, based on a gut feeling that France belonged to the French. It had various manifestations. The Gallican lawyers of the Parlement of Paris excluded foreign jurisdictions such as the pope's. Royal Gallicanism stressed the rights of the king to exclusive control of the church and the realm. *Rex in regno suo imperator* ('the king is the boss in his own kingdom') was the appropriate medieval tag. Ecclesiastical Gallicanism went back at least to the Council of Constance (1419) when French cardinals helped to end the papal schism. Gallican conciliarism (the doctrine that a general council could overrule a pope in faith and doctrine) was entrenched in the Pragmatic Sanction of Bourges (1438), which divided the spoils of the French church between crown and nobility to the exclusion of Rome. The king wielded 'ista pragmatica', as the pope called it ('that frightful pragmatic sanction'), as a stick with which to beat the pope until the signing of the Concordat of Bologna (1516). Louis now proved how easy it was to dust down his Gallican armoury.

French clergy gladly evoked the tradition of conciliarism in the Gallican articles of 1682, which asserted the independence of the crown, the superiority of councils to the pope whose authority in doctrinal matters had to be approved by the whole church, and the indisputable authority of French law. These measures, which reflected the opinions of the accommodating Harlay, archbishop of Paris, and the more forthright Bossuet, now bishop of Meaux, were highly offensive to Rome – and probably went further than Louis himself would have wished. But it was obviously advantageous to brandish the Gallican stick once again. The pope, however, showed his alarm and disgust by refusing to consecrate any more French bishops. By 1688 thirty-five sees were vacant – a chaotic state of affairs. In fact, stalemate.

Louis further embittered relations with Rome when he refused to cooperate over the pope's campaign to improve law and order. Innocent XI wanted to send his police into embassy compounds where criminals were claiming immunity. Louis typically saw this as calculated provocation and dispatched the blustering soldier Lavardin as his ambassador. Innocent excommunicated both the bruiser and his master, though he delayed publication for the time being. Again, deadlock prevailed. Neither pope nor king would back down.

The folly of Louis' tactics reached a climax in 1688 when there was a disputed succession to the archbishopric of Cologne. Was it to be the pro-French candidate, Egon von Furstenburg (known as 'Bishop

Bacchus'), who as assistant to the archbishop was the sitting tenant and had proved a reliable French stooge for years, or the imperial candidate, a seventeen-year-old Bavarian aristocrat? Since the chapter was divided, the case went to Rome. Cologne was absolutely crucial to Louis' military and diplomatic ambitions. He tried bribery, bullying, bluff, propaganda. All was in vain. The pope, who was notoriously incorruptible, awarded the archbishopric to the Bavarian. Louis had only himself to blame for this damaging disaster. This was the climax to the row that he himself had provoked, despite the fact that he was unlikely to win – the ultimate folly.

This wholly avoidable catastrophe did in fact lead to a cooling-off period. Innocent XI died in 1689, his successor was more accommodating and a compromise was reached in 1693. The French bishops were consecrated and Louis promised not to implement the Gallican articles, though the Cologne debacle could not be reversed with its damaging implications for Louis' foreign policy. A new chapter in Franco-Papal relations began with regard to the control of the French church. Pope and king, having reached agreement over the appointment of senior clerics, supported the French bishops in an edict of 1695 against their own junior clergy, who were becoming worryingly independent – many of them tainted with Jansenism. Subsequently, Louis XIV became a suppliant at the court of Rome for pronouncements against Jansenism. As we shall see later in this chapter, Louis finally had to call in the pope against his own ecclesiastical and parliamentary establishments. It was an unhappy outcome to a dismal story from which Louis emerges with little credit. To some extent, he ended his days as a papal hack.

ONE KING, ONE FAITH, ONE LAW

In September 1685, by the Edict of Fontainebleau, Louis XIV revoked the Edict of Nantes of 1598. By this earlier edict his grandfather Henri IV had granted freedom of worship with built-in political and military guarantees to the Huguenots, as France's one million Protestants were called. His grandson's withdrawal of this act of toleration was one of the most controversial watersheds of the reign. It can be viewed from various angles, not least Louis' conflict with Rome. For Louis hoped to re-establish his credit with Innocent XI by persecuting the Protestants.

Louis did not like the Huguenots. He was always mindful of his coronation oath to suppress heresy. It annoyed him that French Protestants still existed. For the only explanation that he could understand was that they had emerged initially as a protest against corruption in the French church. Since abuses had been rectified, Huguenots had therefore lost their *raison d'être*. Why were they still there? As we have seen, Louis simply could not get his head round the possibility that others might disagree with his own Catholic conservatism. Though French Huguenots had behaved impeccably during the Fronde, English Puritans, dangerously resembling the Huguenots – or so it seemed to Louis – had executed their king in public. So when a delegation of Huguenots appeared before the king of France in December 1659 they got a cool reception. Louis promised to implement the Edict of Nantes, but with no concessions, no good will. In his *Mémoires*, ghosted in 1669, though certainly reflecting his views, Louis explained his Huguenot policy to his son:

> I believed, my son, that the best means to reduce gradually the number of Huguenots in my kingdom was, in the first place, not to press them at all by any new rigour against them, to implement what they had obtained from my predecessors but to grant them nothing further. I carefully put a stop everywhere to the schemes of these religionists, as in the Faubourg Saint-Germain, where I learned that they were beginning to conduct secret meetings and schools of their sect. But as to the favours that depended solely on me, I resolved not to grant them any, and this out of kindness rather than out of bitterness, so as to oblige them to consider if they had some good reason for depriving themselves voluntarily of the advantages which they could share with all my other subjects. But I am still a long way, my son, from having exhausted every thing that I have in mind for recalling peacefully those whom birth, education and most often a zeal without knowledge hold in good faith to these pernicious errors.[6]

Not that kindness is the word that immediately comes to mind as a description of Louis' policy towards the Huguenots. For the first twenty years or so of his personal rule, Louis backed a policy of moral, physical and financial blackmail. Huguenots were excluded from the professions, their children were brought up as Catholics, they were not allowed to employ Catholic servants and they were bribed to convert to Catholicism. After the Dutch War, the campaign to convert Huguenots to Catholicism was intensified. Soldiers now providentially unemployed

were billeted on Huguenot families. In early-modern Europe the imposition of soldiers on civilians was invariably unpopular, for instance in
Charles I's England. But the essence of the '*dragonnades*', as the policy
was called (dragoons were often employed in this missionary work),
was that the soldiers were actually encouraged to misbehave – not that
they would have needed much encouragement. Marillac, the intendant in Poitou, was the first to expedite conversions by such brutality.
Huguenots had to provide hospitality for the wrecking of their properties, the sexual harassment of their wives, daughters and maidservants
and physical bullying. For instance, Thomas Bureau, a bookseller
at Niors, describes how the dragoons threw his stocks into the street
and stabled their horses in his office, before shouting obscenities at his
mother. The *dragonnades* were predictably effective and were introduced
in the Midi. Conversions soared.

What was Louis' responsibility for this barbarism? Others have
been blamed, including Louvois who nevertheless restrained Marillac
('Violence is not to the taste of His Majesty'). Proselytising bishops
quoted Saint Matthew's Gospel ('Compel them to come in'), and intendants boasted of their success. But Louis was the master. If he did not
know what was going on, he should have done.

In truth he probably could not have cared less about the sufferings
of ordinary Huguenots. As Elizabeth Labrousse remarks: 'Louis cared as
little about a Poitevin peasant as a nineteenth-century czar would about
a moujik.'[7] Healthy scepticism should have resulted from the intendant of Languedoc's claim that there were 180,000 Huguenots in the
province and the archbishop of Narbonne's boast that 230,000 had been
converted. As Louis was keen to eradicate heresy in France, he was probably a supporter of the *dragonnades*. It was indeed the supposed success of
this brutalality that justified the revocation. At the current rate of conversion the Huguenot churches would be extinct by 1730. But Louis
would be dead by then. He wanted the credit for extirpating heresy,
not just with the pope but throughout Catholic Europe. The emperor's
prestige had soared due to his victory over the Turks. Louis was jealous.
Victory over heresy at home would redress the balance.

Louis allowed himself to be convinced by his clergy and advisers,
such as chancellor Le Tellier and his new wife Mme de Maintenon, that
the hour was at hand. 'I cannot doubt but that it is the Divine Will that
I should be his instrument in bringing back to his ways all those who

are subject to me.' The text of the Edict spelt out a similar message: the revocation had to happen.

> The best and greater part of our subjects of the R.P.R. [réligion prétendue réformée] have embraced the Catholic faith; and as by reason of this the Edict of Nantes is useless, we have judged that we cannot do better, to efface entirely the memory of the troubles, the confusion, and the evils that the progress of the false religion have caused in our realm than to revoke entirely the above edict.

Thus the Edict of Fontainebleau began by justifying the cancellation of the Edict of Nantes since the 'so-called reformed religion' no longer existed. Pastors were given a fortnight in which to renounce their faith or leave France. Thereafter they would be sent to the galleys if they were found ministering to their flocks. Huguenot laypeople were to conform forthwith or suffer further *dragonnades.* They were forbidden to emigrate. Bribes to the newly converted now ceased as supposedly they were no longer needed. Catholic clergy, supplemented by specially trained missionaries, were ordered to preach to the newly converted and welcome them to mass. The children of Huguenots were to be baptised and educated as Catholics. Recalcitrant adults were permitted to worship in private, though without ministers this was a meaningless concession – merely dust in the eyes of Protestant Europe. Incidentally, the edict did not affect recently incorporated Alsace where Protestantism was adjudged to be too entrenched, especially in Strasbourg.

Controversy has always surrounded the alleged results of the revocation. The French economy was certainly damaged by the emigration of some 200,000 people who defied the law and escaped to Brandenburg-Prussia, England, Holland, Switzerland and the New World. Many of these émigrés were highly skilled. To some extent they were replaced by Catholic immigrants from Ireland. The American historian Warren Scoville[8] proved that the damage to the French economy and the advantages to the host countries have been exaggerated, though Huguenots certainly spearheaded a technological revolution in Brandenburg-Prussia and cardinals' hats were now made in England. Vauban was in no doubt that the French army and navy lost effective combatants (500 army officers, 10,000 soldiers and 8,000 seamen).

The Huguenot movement survived in France, despite continued persecution and investigation by police spies. Ministers who defied the order to leave France and laypeople caught trying to escape were sent to the galleys where naval chaplains forced them to attend mass. Others were punished in different ways. For example, Louis Bazin, the intendant in Guenne, filed a report on a clandestine Huguenot assembly at Lévignac (5 January 1692), based on the evidence of Robert la Roche who turned king's evidence. La Roche failed to identify the visiting preacher, but reported his message: 'Think about your salvation, don't go to mass, pray for the king of France and for the king of England, give to the poor, keep your mouths shut.'[9] The building where the assembly took place was razed to the ground, three women were imprisoned (they were still there in 1705) and a fine of 200 livres was exacted. The minister was never found. La Roche had to excuse himself for possessing a simple alphabet – for Huguenots were forbidden to educate their children. On another occasion police arrested Pierre Pages for practising his religion in his chateau at Margueron; he was fined 1,500 livres, imprisoned in the Trompette at Bordeaux and hanged in front of his wife.[10]

Huguenots were nevertheless strong enough to mount a full-scale rebellion in the Cévennes. This, the so-called Camisards revolt, occupied 20,000 troops led by Marshal Villars, who finally had to negotiate with the rebels in 1704. Would the Huguenot faith have survived if lay-people had been allowed to emigrate, as well as their ministers? Especially due to the bravery of Huguenot women and a few defiant ministers, per-petually a move ahead of the police, those who could not legally escape were condemned to 'internal emigration', risking punishment by their witness to their faith. These 'children of the desert', as they styled them-selves in imitation of the Israelites travelling to the Holy Land, were represented by a secret national synod that met a few days before Louis XIV's death. Their descendants achieved official recognition in 1787, and later from the revolutionaries and from Napoleon.

Stories of defiance and repression circulated throughout Europe. The revocation and its after-effects damaged Louis' reputation irreparably. Quite possibly William of Orange would have failed to bring England and Holland into the Nine Years War had there not been the threat of further Catholic persecution. Louis succeeded in adding two new words to European languages: *refugees* were people who would not be *dragooned*.

While it is easy to mount a case against the revocation, it was cer-tainly popular with the majority of French people. Indeed, it was the most 'democratic' measure of the reign. The Huguenots were disliked because of their arrogance and envied because of their wealth. Plenty of people agreed with Louis that there should only be one religion practised in the state: One King, One Faith, One Law. The reliable Bossuet boomed out the official line, which no doubt reflected the majority opinion: 'Let us praise and thank God for our new Constantine, our new Theodosius.' Louis was rapturously welcomed by the citizens of Paris soon after the revocation. Several influential people approved: Chancellor le Tellier, Louvois the war minister, Mme de Maintenon, and the clergy such as Bossuet.

Archbishop Harlay of Paris, however, was sceptical about the likely results of the revocation, while the king's confessor la Chaise, as a merciful man, deplored persecution. It is worth remembering that both Harley and Bossuet had launched campaigns to incorporate Huguenots in the Catholic church without persecution. Bossuet even showed sympathy with the church of England.[11] Up and down France Catholics and Huguenots had happily coexisted. For instance, at Mens-en-Trèves, Dauphiné, on a Sunday evening in spring 1676, the local curé played cards with the wife of a Huguenot elder and the minister's daughter. After all, were they not all French people? This was better than the scenes that occurred after the revocation when 'new converts', as they were called, were escorted to mass by dragoons.

Surely, Louis XIV's handling of the Huguenot problem is objectionable – if it really was a problem. Certainly, one can see where he was coming from. For most seventeenth-century European rulers religious diversity implied political threats. Ever since the Reformation had burst upon the European scene, the principle had been accepted that the ruler decided the people's religion – though with the rider that dissidents were free to emigrate. It was certainly Louis' view that religious nonconformity led to political defiance, though this had not recently been the case in France. It is also to be remembered that persecution of Catholics took place in contemporary England – for instance, during the exclusion crisis (1679–82) – and persistently in Ireland. Protestant Scotland was a haven of intolerance, dominated by the ayatollahs of the Kirk. Some historians depict the revocation as merely an inevitable stage in the Counter-Reformation. Yet it seems hardly worthy of Christian traditions of charity and humility.

Indeed, the harassment of Huguenots, who meekly put up with this unfair treatment because they trusted the king, and their ultimate repression reminds one of the persecution of the Moors in the sixteenth century and the Jews in the twentieth century. Louis' failure to rise above the prejudices of his time is disappointing. One feels that he was better than that. For he was normally an urbane and civilised man. One cannot envisage him emulating Carlos II, who presided over an *auto-da-fé* on 30 June 1680 in Madrid when eighteen heretics were simultaneously burnt at the stake. Or again when he deterred his grandson Philip V from destroying Barcelona as a punishment for rebellion. When due allowance is made for contemporary *mentalité*, Louis should have been above persecuting his own Protestant subjects. Lest I be suspected of whiggish Francophobia, I cannot improve on the French historian Roland Mousnier's summary: 'The methods he used were inhuman, an affront to the dignity of man, and contrary to the spirit of Christianity, while forced communion was a sin against the Holy Ghost. In this respect Louis was indeed a tyrant.'[12]

PURE AS ANGELS AND PROUD AS LUCIFER: THE JANSENISTS

Louis XIV's conduct with regard to the Jansenists was even more counter-productive than his treatment of the Huguenots – though, to be fair, not as vicious. No Jansenist blood was shed, nor were Jansenists expelled from France, nor were they sent to the galleys. But Louis victimised them in one way or another throughout his personal rule. He remained ineradicably opposed to them. When his nephew the duc d'Orléans wanted to include an alleged Jansenist in his entourage, Louis was only mollified when it turned out that the man was an atheist. Why was he so prejudiced?

The Jansenists were a minority of aristocratic and bourgeois intellectuals, both clerical and lay, inspired by the theologian Cornelius Jansen whose major work, the *Augustinus,* was posthumously published in 1640. Their powerhouse was the Cistercian foundation of Port-Royal, which had two houses – one in Paris, the other in remote countryside only five miles away from Versailles at Port-Royal-des-Champs. The leaders of the community were members of the Arnauld family, traditionally hostile to the Jesuits. At Port-Royal-des-Champs a community of nuns lived in austere self-denial, joined by selected laypeople, on either a permanent or a more informal and temporary basis. Pupils were taught at Port-Royal in Paris and literature was disseminated from both houses.

The essence of the Jansenist message was derived from St Paul and St Augustine: mankind was hopelessly corrupt and could only be saved by grace bestowed arbitrarily by God. By their denial that Christians could achieve their salvation through good works, they clashed with the Society of Jesus. Indeed, Jansenists were described as 'good Catholics who did not agree with the Jesuits'. In particular they criticised the Jesuits' laxity in condoning sin provided it was confessed. Whereas the Jesuits believed that frequent participation in the mass compensated for sin, Jansenists argued that only after the most rigorous contrition could a Christian presume to attend the mass. In general Jansenists could be described as Catholic Puritans. They represented an attitude rather than constituting a party. Indeed, modern historians have described Jansenism as 'a moving target', due to their chameleon-like tendency to adjust their stance to whatever opponents they thought they were morally obliged to encounter.

It must be stressed that Jansenists never questioned the pope's authority or the church's teaching on the sacraments. They rejected Luther's priesthood of all believers. In other words, from a Catholic point of view they were at worst heterodox and were certainly not heretics, unlike the Protestant Huguenots. Though they shared Calvin's admiration for Augustine, their doctrine of predestination was less extreme; Adam's sin had been freely committed, while grace was efficacious, leading to good works as opposed to being irresistible as the Calvinists argued. Whereas Calvinists proved their election by succeeding in the world, Jansenists renounced secular achievement.

Were Jansenists a political threat to the crown? Certainly they implicitly defied absolute monarchy by insisting that the will of God came before that of man. In 1635 Jansen had published *Mars Gallicus,* an indictment of Richelieu's policy of allying with Protestant powers against Catholic Austria and Spain. By repeatedly attacking the Jesuits, Jansenists implicitly criticised the crown, which favoured the Society of Jesus as the Jesuits were known. We have seen that Louis XIV's confessor was invariably a Jesuit.

On the other hand it is impossible to resist the conclusion that Louis XIV in particular made a problem out of a non-problem. There were too few Jansenists to constitute a political threat. Louis XIV gave them significance by persecuting them. He was infuriated by Jansenist success in mobilising public opinion in general and political and ecclesiastical authorities in particular, such as the Parlement of Paris. He instinctively distrusted any deviation from his own conservative orthodoxy.

The authoritarian Counter-Reformation church in which he had been brought up had little time for disagreement and debate. Louis was too ignorant of theology to understand the nuances of the rival approaches to salvation advocated by Jesuit and Jansenist, both morally admirable, both based on traditional Christian teaching.

The clannish, self-righteous superiority of the Arnaulds struck Louis as potentially subversive. Louis allowed himself to be convinced by his Jesuit advisers that prominent *frondeurs* had been influenced by Jansenism. He copied Mazarin in referring to Jansenists as '*républicaines*'. There was indeed a link between such troublemakers as de Retz and his supporters among the Parisian clergy and Port-Royal. Louis had little understanding of the real strengths of Jansenism, described by McManners as 'the glory of the Catholic revival' – the artistic genius of Philippe de Champaigne, the satire of Boileau and the brilliance of Pascal's invective.[13] As well as inventing the computer, Pascal was a satirist of genius and a profound Christian thinker.

Pascal's devastating attack on Jesuit casuistry in his *Provincial Letters* might seem to justify Ronald Knox's claim that Jansenists always had to attack somebody. One could also criticise Pascal for ridiculing the Jesuits. Ridicule is hard to take and inflames passions. One remembers the resentment caused by Disraeli's mockery of the British prime minister, Sir Robert Peel (1846), who could take criticism, opposition and abuse but could not handle ridicule. Peel's disciples, such as Gladstone, never forgave Disraeli for humiliating their leader. So Pascal raised the stakes by satirising the Jesuits' apparent willingness to forgive anything. At the beginning of the *Fifth Letter*, Pascal wittily alleges that the Jesuits forgive sins according to circumstances. In other words, they have no absolute standards of right and wrong:

Know then that their object is not to corrupt manners; that is not their intention. But neither is it their only aim to reform them; that were bad policy. Their view is this; they have a good enough opinion of themselves to believe that it is conducive, and in a manner necessary to the welfare of religion, that they should be everywhere in repute, and govern all consciences. And because strict Gospel maxims are fitted to govern some sorts of persons, they use them on the occasions when they are suitable. But as these maxims are not in accordance with the views of most people, they, in those cases, abandon them, that they may be able to satisfy all and sundry. Hence it is that having to do with persons of all classes, and with nations differing widely from each other, they require to have casuists assorted to this great diversity.

Pascal was doubly effective because he was no frivolous clown but a genuine and profound Christian thinker. His teaching on the atonement places him squarely within traditional Christian teaching. In his *The Mystery of Jesus* Pascal urges the Christian to identify with Christ's humiliation and resurrection. 'In Gethsemane Christ tears himself away from his disciples to enter into his agony; we must tear ourselves away from those who are nearest to us in order to imitate him. I must add my tears to his and join with him.' Is the hidden God unknowable? No, he reveals himself in the suffering Christ, available to those who possess the necessary humility to welcome him. There is nothing heretical here, just sound Christian teaching.[14]

One wonders what Louis XIV made of all this. He had enough sense of the ridiculous to enjoy Molière. Pascal's satire, however, was presumably too near the bone for Louis. Similarly, he had too little awareness of the importance of humility to appreciate Pascal's teaching on the cross. Be that as it may, having closed his mind to Jansenism, Louis set about its destruction. David Sturdy sees Louis' handling of Jansenism as an example of 'his tendency to become locked in religious controversies of immense complexity and then to attempt a crude, simplistic "solution" '.[15] His tactics were crude indeed. First, he appointed clerics who were opposed to Jansenism to influential positions. Second, he brought maximum pressure to bear on the pope to condemn Jansenism.

A good example of an anti-Jansenist promotion was the appointment of Louis' tutor, Hardouin de Péréfixe, as archbishop of Paris. In August 1664 he visited Port-Royal de Paris in order to discipline the nuns for running rings round him and refusing to accept his choice of confessor. 'You are as pure as angels and as proud as Lucifer', he shouted at them – and he gave the aristocratic and saintly abbess a thorough dressing-down: 'You are nothing more than a stuck-up slip of a girl.' He dispersed twelve of the nuns to other convents. Not only did Louis invariably promote Jesuits as his confessors but also anti-Jansenists such as Bossuet and Fénelon as his son's and his grandson's tutors.

Rome had already complied with French pressure to condemn Jansenism before Louis XIV's personal rule began. In a bull of 1653 Innocent X had identified five heretical propositions in the *Augustinus*.

In 1661 the French clergy were required to assent to the papal pronouncement. Some bishops infuriated Louis by dragging their feet, but in 1668 inaugurated 'the peace of the church' by subscribing to a watered-down version. This interlude proved that, given good will on both sides, compromise was possible. In 1679, however, Louis sacked his Jansenist foreign minister Pomponne and dispersed the remaining male *solitaires* from Port-Royal. While the campaign against the Huguenots took the pressure off the Jansenists for the next twenty years, they were not forgotten. A prominent Jansenist, Pasquier Quesnel, who had written a popular best-seller *Réflexions Morales*, was arrested in the Spanish Netherlands. His papers, turned over to the French government in 1703, proved that a Jansenist network still operated in France. Louis pestered Rome for further condemnation of the troublesome sect. In July 1703 Clement XI complied with the bull *Vineam Domini*.

To Louis' disgust the French clergy insisted on their Gallican rights to scrutinise the bull before supporting it. Jansenism was clearly alive and well. French religious and intellectual leaders continued to admire its stance against the Jesuits. Pilgrims wended their way to Port-Royal-des-Champs. Louis therefore demolished the buildings and had the corpses of dead Jansenists dug up and dispersed. The last nuns were carted off by the police and exiled to distant houses, prompting Saint-Simon to observe that they might as well have been whores. Surely that was it. But no, in June 1713 Louis successfully badgered the unwilling Pope – who had a sneaking admiration for Jansenism – into rejecting 101 propositions in Quesnel's *Réflexions Morales* in the bull *Unigenitus Dei Filius* (Only-begotten Son of God). Most of the doctrines targeted by the bull had already been condemned several times. New, however, were prohibitions against lay participation in church services or study of the Bible. The laity were neither to read nor think. The infallible, hierarchical nature of the church was re-emphasised. All attempts at ecumenical compromise with Protestants were forbidden. Authority was magnified, implicitly in preference to truth – though for Louis they were the same thing.

From Louis' point of view *Unigenitus* proved to be an appalling own goal. Having called in the Gallicans to support him against the pope in 1682, he now found himself up against them in Parlement – which refused to register *Unigenitus* – and among the clergy. The Sorbonne rejected the bull, while several French bishops led by Noailles the archbishop of Paris refused to promulgate it. Chancellor Pontchartrain resigned. Louis had provoked his own people's hostility to papal influence. In pursuit of his para-noid vendetta against Jansenism, encouraged by his confessor Le Tellier and his wife de Maintenon, he had made himself ridiculous. He stormed and ranted in vain. He was forced to announce the summoning of a council of the French church, which he proposed to chair himself – but he died before this interesting threat could be implemented. Jansenism survived to plague Louis' successors and to inspire the opposition to Catholic conformity and Bourbon absolutism for the rest of the eighteenth century. *Unigenitus* was his greatest single mistake.

To sum up, the persecution of the Jansenists shows Louis at his worst. It illustrates his vulnerability to influence, especially that of the Jesuits and of Mme de Maintenon, and his obstinate refusal to change his stance, once he had been persuaded to adopt it, in defiance of all the evidence that it was unwise. For instance, Louis allowed his surgeon to treat a nun at Port-Royal provided that he report back to the king. When the surgeon testified as to the holiness and devotion of the nuns, Louis was momentarily impressed. But not for long. He preferred to listen to the edited highlights from Jansenist tracts that Mme de Maintenon read to him every evening. Saint Simon puts it well:

> The King who had vigorously adopted the Jesuits' opinion, who was entirely resolved to listen to none but the most heated of them, who had invested his authority and his conscience in it, who busied and sustained himself with nothing else, regarded the Jansenists as enemies of the church and state, as republicans, as enemies of his authority and his person.

At the peace conference at Rastadt in 1714 a French delegate asked Prince Eugene how the emperor dealt with Jansenism. Eugene replied that he had no idea, nor for the life of him could he understand why the king of France wasted his time on such a matter. Fair comment?

'THEIR INTENSITIES MERGED': QUIETISM

Like Jansenism, Quietism was never *quite* heretical. Indeed the contem-plative life and the surrender of self in God's presence have always been part of Christianity. So it was that a prominent Catholic Quietist, the Spaniard Miguel de Molinos, made a great stir with his *Spiritual Guide*

(1675), though it was subsequently condemned by the pope. Quietism nevertheless survived. It was promulgated in France by a wealthy, attractive, eccentric widow, Jeanne Bouvier de la Motte Guyon, who had written books advocating a passive prayer life in which the individual awaited the Holy Spirit. When she was in one of her trances, she allegedly turned purple. Despite being a little mad, Mme Guyon impressed a number of people, including the duke of Burgundy's charismatic and intellectually gifted tutor Fénelon. As Saint-Simon cynically put it, 'their intensities merged'.

Mme de Maintenon thought that this prayer specialist was just the person to inspire the girls at Saint-Cyr, the school for the daughters of impoverished aristocrats that she had founded and supervised personally with typical bossiness. The girls were soon experiencing trances, fastings, faintings and missing unpopular lessons. Worrying reports reached the bishop of Chartres, Mme de Maintenon's confessor, who soon rumbled Mme Guyon. A committee of theologians, including Noailles and Bossuet, pronounced Mme Guyon heretical (1694). She was imprisoned and exiled.

Why did this apparently absurd business involve the king? Louis was not in the least impressed by Mme Guyon, nor did he understand Quietism. But he was furious with his wife for being so gullible and for allowing Saint-Cyr to be disrupted. He refused to speak to her for several weeks. Indeed, she despaired and fell into a decline until Louis took pity on her. 'Are you going to die of this business, Madame?' he asked her – and she smiled gratefully through her tears.

Unfortunately the affair came into the public domain due to Fénelon's support for Mme Guyon. He was punished for rocking the boat by exile to Cambrai where he had just been appointed archbishop. The French intelligentsia was now treated to a gladiatorial slanging match between Bossuet and Fénelon – 'the Eagle of Meaux' versus 'the Swan of Cambrai'. It was indeed a battle of giants. Fénelon was hero-worshipped as a saint by Burgundy's circle. Ronald Knox suggested that Fénelon was the sort of person one approaches on all fours. He compared the rivals to the Victorian churchmen Cardinals Manning and Newman.[16] The controversy was referred to Rome and reached its climax when Fénelon received the pope's condemnation just as he was about to preach in his cathedral. With a typical instinct for self-dramatisation, the archbishop tore up his sermon, read out the pope's verdict and preached on humility. Bossuet had boasted that 'we have on our side God, the truth, a worthy motive, the king and Mme de Maintenon'. Now the pope too, it seemed, condemned the Swan of Cambrai – though not to permanent silence.

In the devastated Pas de Calais Fénelon had an excellent opportunity of appreciating the effects of Louis XIV's wars. For some time he had questioned the king's priorities. Now he openly expressed his reservations. Perhaps one should allow for Fénelon's bias against the man who had disgraced him. But presumably he knew what he was talking about. One example of his criticism of the king was the allegorical *Télémarc*, a veiled attack on the king. Wholly unveiled was a letter that the archbishop wrote to the king and which he sent to Mme de Maintenon. It is not known if Louis ever saw it, though presumably he was aware of the archbishop's views. It is of interest because one is often warned against condemning Louis' wars on the grounds of anachronism, for one must understand the *mentalité* of the time, especially of Louis' aristocracy. Well, Fénelon was both an aristocrat and presumably aware of contemporary opinion. This is what his *mentalité* had to say:

> Your people, whom you should love as your own children, and who have hitherto loved you so passionately, are now dying of hunger. Cultivation of the land is almost abandoned; the towns and the countryside are becoming depopulated; all the trades are languishing and no longer produce workmen. Thus you have drained away half the inner strength of your state in order to make and defend useless conquests outside it. Instead of drawing money from this poor people, you should give them alms and feed them. The whole of France is now no more than a great devastated hospital, with no provisions. You, Sire, have brought all these troubles upon yourself; for, with the whole kingdom in ruins, you keep everything in your own hands. The very people who loved you so much are losing their affection, trust and respect. Your victories and conquests no longer make them rejoice; they are full of bitterness and despair.[17]

This perhaps goes further to explain Louis' anger with regard to the whole Quietist episode, involving Mme Guyon, Archbishop Fénelon, and his wife. Mark Fumaroli[18] has persuasively linked Fénelon's protest with the Fouquet *affaire* thirty or so years before. Fouquet had stood for just the same principles of peaceful compromise at home and abroad that Fénelon now advocated. Fénelon attributed the nation's misfortunes to the Dutch

War (1672-9), which Louis had willed through his lack of charity and humility. Fouquet's eldest son, the comte de Vaux, had married Mme Guyon's daughter. What did the king's wife, whose first husband Paul Scarron had befriended his fellow-poet La Fontaine, a close friend and client of Fouquet, think she was doing getting tied up with such dangerous people? Fénelon's letter confirmed that a very different Christian ethic, based on humility, mercy and friendship, was still at large. Louis' egotism could not abide such a challenge. If that was what Quietism produced, Louis was determined to smash it. Mme de Maintenon took the hint and promptly ditched her friend, a prudent step of which the loyal Fénelon was incapable.

TOWARDS A CATHOLIC NATION?

Apart from involving the church in unnecessary conflicts, what was Louis XIV's contribution towards the development of France's religious complexion? His coronation oaths committed him not only to the eradication of heresy but also to the interests of Heaven and the spiritual sustenance of his people. In Louis XIV's book these objectives were code for the reduction of France to the conservative, conformist Catholicism in which he had been brought up and that he personally never ceased to practise. How successful was he? How near did he come to his goal?

First, what was the religious context in which Louis operated? The 'long' seventeenth century during which the first three Bourbons reigned (1589–1715) witnessed a remarkable religious movement in the French church. Thanks to the disruptions caused by the wars of religion (1559–98), the Counter-Reformation only reached France late in the day. When it did arrive, the French church was invigorated and reformed, while missionary activities were launched in town and country, not just against Protestants but against paganism, ignorance and sloth in general. The church produced its saints, heroes and heroines – Vincent de Paul, François de Sales, Jacqueline Arnauld, and many others. Actually the most exciting and dramatic developments had already occurred when Louis' personal rule began. His reign was a period of consolidation. But the great reform movement continued; it had by no means run out of steam. As a result the church in 1715 was very different from the church in 1661.

Louis' contribution was, first, his role in staffing the French church. He was advised by the archbishop of Paris and his current Jesuit confessor, who joined him every Friday in the Council of Conscience. Louis took pains in appointing and promoting suitable bishops. It was dangerous getting it wrong in that bishops were irremovable and immune to pressure, being neither venal nor hereditary. Problems could be caused by independent-minded clerics such as the anti-papal bishop of Noyan who used to refer to 'Monsieur de Rome'. If Louis made a mistake, as with the appointment of Noailles to the archbishopric of Paris, he was irretrievably lumbered. But he did not often get it wrong. To some extent there was a shift during Louis' reign from the France of the cardinals when bishops were sometimes appointed for overtly political reasons; some, for instance, were soldiers and sailors, some were patronage brokers and 'creatures' of the cardinals, some were scions of great families, frequently under age or openly pursuing a scandalous private life. Recent research, however, has proved that for the most part Richelieu patronised and promoted godly bishops, a trend Louis continued, seeking to appoint bishops who were theologically and pastorally credible. He genuinely cared about promoting men for the right reasons, even more than his red-hatted predecessors had done.

But not even Louis could transform the episcopate overnight – and some of his own appointees were flagrantly immoral, such as Archbishop Le Tellier of Reims, nicknamed 'the hog', who lived incestuously with his niece. Archbishop Harlay's private life was irregular, and he died suddenly of a stroke while in the company of his mistress before he could receive the last rites. No bishop would deliver a funeral eulogy, there being two problems: Archbishop Harlay's life and his death. But in general Louis' bishops were increasingly clean living, well educated and dedicated to the improvement of their dioceses. Joseph Bergin has described a typical 'Louisquattorzian' bishop: a Paris theology graduate, a product of a major seminary such as Saint-Sulpice, formerly a vicar-general of a diocese, experienced in preaching to Protestants or attacking Jansenists, probably aristocratic, possibly with friends at court such as Mme de Maintenon, well educated, morally blameless, totally professional.[19]

What difference did bishops like this make to the everyday life of French people? Everything depended on the parish priest. As ever, some were better than others. On the whole reformist bishops gingered up their clergy. An absolutely crucial development was the diocesan seminary where priests were trained. During Louis' reign parish priests became better educated, more the products of the urban bourgeoisie, more censorious in their attitude to the sexual practices of their parishioners, perhaps less in touch with the realities of peasant life, given that about 85 per cent of the population lived in the countryside. The clergy were expected to keep a card index of their parishioners' sins – actually an absurd idea that seems to have gone out of use pretty fast. Priests, however, were told to forbid peasant families sleeping together in one bed – ignoring the likelihood of there being only one bed in the house anyway, the necessity of keeping warm in wintertime and the possibility that multiple bed-sharing might actually discourage incest. There was a decline in superstitious practices, the persecution of witches, riotous charivaris, and boozy festivals when village boys and girls cavorted together. Louis himself shared Colbert's enlightened scepticism on the subject of witchcraft, and he had pronounced reservations about the plebs enjoying themselves.

The king spearheaded one of the more questionable features of religious activity during his reign – the campaign for sexual purity. Louis experienced a dramatic moral change of life when he married his mistress Mme de Maintenon after his first wife's death. It was not that his beliefs and attitudes changed. It was his lifestyle. Whereas previously he had bedded an unending succession of women, ranging from princesses of the blood to servant girls, he now became strictly monogamous. This was dramatic and unexpected. When Louis married his illegitimate children's aristocratic governess, he became the most uxorious husband of all time. While he did not necessarily follow Maintenon's ideas on the conduct of foreign policy, he was unquestionably influenced by her in religious and moral affairs.

Louis fully supported the church's campaign to reform the nation's morals – described by Robin Briggs as 'one of the greatest repressive enterprises in European history'.[20] As well as cleaning up the court at Versailles, the king kept his beady eye on his courtiers when they fled to Paris. The chiefs of police, de la Reynie and his successor d'Argesson, were ordered by the king to round up sodomites, atheists, prostitutes, beggars and blasphemers. Aristocratic and bourgeois sinners were dispatched to 'my chateau the bastille' where their imprisonment might last an unspecified time, but conditions were reasonable (one husband refused to come out after his wife had petitioned successfully for his release). Lower-class sinners were sent to the Saltpetrière and other prisons that were little better than plague pits. Louis took an especial interest in the prosecution of abortionists. In one case where a surgeon and his wife were running a profitable clinic, Louis sent the wife to the Saltpetrière and the husband to the army where medical officers were badly needed.[21]

This case was typical of the church's prejudice against women, which Louis shared. It was always the woman's fault. Women were exhorted to model themselves on 'the second Eve'; that is to say, the Virgin Mary. Whether beggars, street-walkers in the Paris slums, high-class courtesans or 'grandes horizontales' at court, they were 'soldiers of Satan'. No action was taken against the men who exploited them. On Louis' initiative thirty Parisian women were imprisoned for selling their daughters into prostitution. He prosecuted women guilty of infanticide with fanatical self-righteousness.

But the question still tugs: did Louis get it right? To a great extent the church and the monarch, who directed and defended it, lost touch with the French people. Louis' 'back to basics' campaign was open to ridicule and charges of hypocrisy and inconsistency – not only because of his own dubious past but also for his patent inability to reform his own family and court. Even Bluche admits that Louis' decision that his bastards could inherit the throne 'violated the principle of Catholicity, which implied "that anyone capable of succeeding must be the issue of a canonically valid marriage" '.[22] Similarly his censorship campaign repressed originality of thought, and drove independent thinkers underground or abroad. While Louis used the pulpit as the mouthpiece of government propaganda, and bishops were entrusted with the propagation of the king's appeal to the nation in 1709, his campaign for a unified Catholic French nation based on crown, altar and persecution of Protestants and sexual deviants was unrealistically ambitious.

Louis' priorities were challenged both by atheistic sceptics, such as his own nephew the duc d'Orléans, and by Christian moral rigorists, such as the Burgundy circle led by his grandson and Archbishop Fénelon, and also by the indestructible Jansenists. Inspired (if that is the right word) by his wife and his confessor Le Tellier, Louis constantly saw Jansenist influence everywhere: 'ces Messieurs de Port-Royal, toujours ces Messieurs' ('these Gentlemen of Port-Royal, always these Gentlemen'). As we have seen, his paranoia led to the hopelessly bungled Unigenitus campaign.

This highlighted his failure. That Louis had to bring in the pope against his own people showed how tragically he had mismanaged his attempt to unify France theologically.

In his handling of religious issues in general Louis XIV had consistently failed to bring to bear the cautious realism that normally made him such an effective politician. It is indeed ironic that he should be so disastrously assertive in the field in which he was so ignorant and unqualified. Arguably, the damage wrought by Louis XIV's religious policies stretched far beyond his lifetime. His successors were plagued by Jansenist opposition and by controversies prompted by the Jesuits. Enlightenment thinkers treated the church with contempt so that, in Paul Hazard's much-quoted and somewhat simplistic words, 'Frenchmen began by speaking like Bossuet and ended by speaking like Voltaire'.[23] Certainly the virulent anticlericalism of the revolutionaries could be attributed to the oppressive religiosity of Louis XIV's ecclesiastical establishment.

Warfare between clericals and anticlericals lasted into the twentieth century. Frenchwomen were denied the vote until 1945 because anticlerical republican politicians feared that priestly influence would dominate gullible female minds. Recent satirical references in France to the German Benedict XVI as 'Pope Adolf XVI' perpetuate the tradition of bitter reaction to Louis XIV's authoritarian campaign for an exclusively Catholic France. His attempt to create a Catholic ultra-conservative France based on his own sacred divinity and the suppression of independent thought proved to be profoundly counterproductive.[24] In Dale Van Kley's words, the monarchy was committed 'to a defence of a pre-Reformation Catholicism increasingly unacceptable to many literate Frenchmen, making any challenge to the Catholic Church into one against the state and thereby provoking opposition to the monarchy itself.'[25] Louis got the worst of all possible worlds.

[handwritten note:] Louis made the Church less of everything Christian, provoking the Enlightenment reaction or at least making it more plausible.

9

NEMESIS

FOREIGN POLICY, 1684–1715

A DREADFUL STORY

The Sun King's reign ended in a blood-red sunset – the twenty-five-year war that wrecked Europe in general and France in particular. It was a dreadful tragedy. On the face of it, this was not a predictable or inevitable sequel to the truce of Ratisbon, brokered by the emperor in August 1684. Seemingly something went wrong soon afterwards. So there is a case for dividing the Sun King's foreign policy at 1684 as we have done in this book. David Sturdy argues that 'the year 1684 turned out to be the apogee of Louis XIV's fortunes in international affairs'.[1] Ragnild Hatton agrees that to regard the truce of Ratisbon as the key moment after which things fell apart is 'an interesting idea'. So what were the problems that caused the cataclysm?

Part of the trouble was that from the French point of view the truce of Ratisbon was acceptable only if in due course it became a permanent settlement. Unfortunately for Louis XIV, however, the leaders of the great powers (Holland, England, the Empire, Spain and the German princes) were by no means prepared to grant his wish that the Ratisbon truce should become a long-lasting peace. Were the opportunity to arise – if, for instance, the balance of power were to swing against France – her enemies might well impose revisions. This was why Louis could never settle for any scenario where weaknesses in France's defences could still be seen.

There were always improvements to be made, as was certainly the case in 1684. In other words, the truce was fine provided that France's enemies allowed it to be permanent. If not, not. So the depiction of Ratisbon as a watershed can be overdrawn. The shadows were already lengthening.

Furthermore, there was a basic continuity of priorities and method during the whole period from the Treaty of Nijmegen (1679) to the outbreak of the Nine Years War (1688). Throughout this decade Louis played a strong hand badly. His insensitive acquisitiveness displayed in the reunions did not stop at Ratisbon. He continued to be counselled by men who shared his arrogance and willingness to cut corners by appealing to force. Prominent among such advisers were Colbert de Croissy and Louvois. The latter was now at the height of his power, especially after Jean-Baptiste Colbert's death in 1683. Louvois took over his rival's responsibilities for buildings and manufactures, as well as the whole artistic campaign to promote the king's image, while remaining secretary for war, in charge of postal services and so forth. He was disappointed not to get Colbert's responsibility for the navy as well, but Louis, true to his policy of 'divide and rule', gave the job to Colbert's son, Seignelay. France continued to exploit the power vacuum in Europe in her own interests, which she had shown during the reunions, notably while the emperor was occupied with the Turkish threat. Louis' harsh treatment of his Huguenot subjects and mishandling of his relations with Rome were all of a piece with his punitive foreign policy. Indeed, historians have wondered if there was something wrong with the man. Were his egregious mistakes, his disastrous overacting, his appeals to force, due to some mid-life crisis? Did he feel the need to throw his weight around to compensate for the termination of his sexual adventures? Who knows? What is clear is that he displayed all the exhibitionist, hubristic symptoms of a Greek tragic hero, which in due course led predictably to the nemesis of the twenty-five-year war (1688–1713), a war that even Louis could see France did not need.

'IF YOU WANT WAR, PREPARE FOR WAR' (1684–8)

The usual version of the adage is, 'if you want peace, prepare for war'. But if Louis XIV truly wanted peace – and he may well have done – his preparations for war were so offensive and provocative that nobody believed his pacific protestations. For example, strategic strong points acquired through the reunions were fortified in a distinctly permanent manner. Whereas expenditure on fortifications between 1662 and 1668 had been 2.3 million livres per annum, it averaged 8 million between 1682 and 1688. Vauban was extremely busy. France's magnificent armed forces were kept busy as well. The navy, fresh from its triumphs in reducing Genoa to ashes, now applied the same methods to Algiers and Tripoli in the pursuit of Muslim pirates. As for the army, it was deployed on an unusual battlefield for professional soldiers, the terrorising of French people whose Christianity did not accord with the Sun King's.

Strictly speaking, after the revocation of the Edict of Nantes the 'so-called reformed faith' no longer existed. Even so it was considered advisable to vandalise the property and rape the women of ex-Protestants who might still hanker after their former commitments. Conversions soared, thanks to the king's dragoons. Louis found still further mission-ary work for his army as Louvois' boast that the frontiers could be closed to Protestant fugitives proved overambitious. Refugees who flocked to England, Brandenburg and Holland got away. But several thousand who were given hospitality by the Protestant Vaudois were not so lucky.

The Vaudois were subjects of France's ally Victor Amadeus, the duke of Savoy. They were still only too accessible to Louis' troops. Louis forced a reluctant Victor Amadeus to accept French reinforcements with a mis-sion to eradicate Protestantism and thus close down this particular escape hatch. Five regiments of infantry and ten squadrons of cavalry commanded by Marshal Catinat arrived in April 1686. Lynn calls this war 'the most rapacious and reprehensible of the reign'. It was soon all over. The Vaudois, incapable of meeting the French on the battlefield, resorted to guerrilla warfare. But the instant hanging of the captured and the laying waste of their villages enabled Catinat to report on 9 May: 'The country is completely desolated; there are no longer any people or livestock at all.' Of 12,000 Vaudois imprisoned, a high proportion died from starvation and disease. Louis had this to say: 'I see that sick-ness delivers the duke of Savoy of some of the embarrassment caused by having to guard the rebels. I do not doubt that he easily consoles himself for the loss of such subjects who make room for better or more faithful ones.'[2] In the meantime Louis' troops were ready for the next challenge.

The persecution of Protestants, which caused an exodus of bitter, dis-affected critics of the Sun King all over Europe, the prowess of France's

mighty armed forces, the propaganda of French arts and crafts, all combined to create a profound sense of unease among Louis' other rulers.
This gave birth to the League of Augsburg, formed in August 1686
between Spain, Bavaria, Sweden and the Elector Palatine. It was initially defensive, designed to block any further French incursions into
Germany. The signatories promised each other assistance if they were
attacked by France. The League was soon joined by the Empire, Holland
and England. This early attempt at the balance of power spelt trouble
for Louis XIV's France. It behoved Louis to work out the wisest tactics
– whether to break up the League by punitive action against its weaker
members or whether to reassure everyone of his harmlessness. Much
depended on what explosive issues would next arise in Europe.

Unfortunately two flashpoints soon flared up in the highly sensitive
area of western Germany. In 1686 the Elector's death created a vacancy
in the Palatinate that was speedily occupied by the emperor's nephew.
Louis protested on behalf of the late elector's sister Liselotte, Monsieur's
wife, but held his hand for the time being. Then another elector died,
the pro-French archbishop of Cologne. As we noted in the previous
chapter, Louis supported the bishop of Strasbourg, the reliable French
stooge Cardinal Furstenburg. The emperor backed Joseph Clement, the
seventeen-year-old son of the elector of Bavaria. The canons of Cologne
could not reach a satisfactory verdict. So the matter went to Rome.
Louis' natural reaction would have been to try bribery. But Innocent
XI was tiresomely upright. There now emerged the imbecilic stupidity of Louis' policy towards the papacy over the previous decade. Indeed
there had just been another fracas, which caused the new French envoy
Lavardin to be excommunicated. Louis therefore resorted to his other
favourite approach – violence. He threatened to invade the papal territory of Avignon. In addition he sent a special envoy, the marquis de
Chamlay, to deliver an eloquent appeal to the Holy Father from His
Most Christian Majesty:

> Any refusal by His Holiness to grant the necessary bulls in favour of
> Furstenburg would only serve to set off a war in the Empire which it would
> be hard to end, and which would cause Christendom to lose all those advan-
> tages which have been secured only because I have not wished to profit from
> favourable circumstances to press the claims of my crown against neighbour-
> ing states while the emperor's forces were occupied in Hungary.[3]

We shall never know what the pope would have made of this appeal, because he refused to receive Chalmay and promptly appointed the seventeen-year-old Bavarian to the archbishopric (August 1688). A month later Louis retaliated by issuing a declaration: his enemies were clearly motivated by malice, displayed by the formation of the League of Augsburg, the rejection of his sister-in-law's rights in the Palatinate and of his favoured candidate at Cologne, whereas he had been the personification of peace, trustworthiness and goodwill. He gave his enemies until the end of the year to accept the permanence of Ratisbon.

In the meantime, just to concentrate their minds and prove his own pacific nature, Louis sent his armies into the papal state of Avignon and into the Palatinate. The ancient and beautiful cities of Worms, Heidelburg, Speyer and Mannheim were burnt, the crops destroyed, the inhabitants expelled. Louis' actions were defensive, his goal to make the Palatinate useless as a base for his enemies' troops. No doubt this goal was achieved. But this further 'triumph' was to alienate German public opinion, so that when the historian Leopold von Ranke was asked whom the Germans were fighting in the Franco-Prussian War (1870–1), he replied, 'Louis XIV'.[4] The heartbroken Liselotte complained to the king, but he snapped at her that she had better work out whose side she was on. Soon Cologne was under siege. So was the crucial fortress of Philippsburg. Here Louis entrusted the siege to his son the Grand Dauphin. He seems to have done well, listening carefully to his professional advisers, keeping his father in the picture, and earning the loyalty and affection of his troops. The League of Augsburg retaliated by declaring war on France. The war that no one wanted had begun.

Was there ever such an unpleasant, costly and *unnecessary* war? While to some extent all wars result from misunderstandings and miscalculations, both sides entered the Nine Years War with only the vaguest notions of what was at stake or what was on the cards. When Louis started the war with his assault on Philippsburg and his devastation of the Palatinate, the last thing he wanted or expected was a crippling conflict that would continue for nine years. However self-deceiving he may have been, his thinking was genuinely defensive: to protect France by making the Palatinate militarily useless and by hustling the League into accepting the permanence of the Ratisbon truce. There is something decidedly paradoxical about *starting* a defensive war. But that is what Louis XIV did. As for the League, which Holland and England were to join a few months after the outbreak of war, how could the member states possibly have common aims, given their differences of race, religion, political complexion and geographical location? Louis' defenders (Bluche, Hatton, Black) argue that Leopold and William were as aggressive and acquisitive as Louis. So they may have been, but their objectives were different from each other's and from those of their allies. One preoccupation alone united the League: fear, hatred and distrust of France. So Louis bears a heavy responsibility for the war through his thoughtless, insensitive acts of aggression ever since 1672.

THE NINE YEARS WAR

The Nine Years War (or the War of the League of Augsburg, as it is sometimes called) began unusually with a sideshow. Whereas the main theatre of operations was to be the eternally blood-soaked fields of Flanders, the first campaign involving the French and their Anglo-Dutch opponents led by William III took place in Ireland. It was as though the First World War began with the Gallipoli campaign. This was partly because Louis was understandably keen to retrieve what has sometimes been described as the supreme blunder of his career – the assault on Philippsburg in October 1688 that gave William of Orange the green light to invade England. Louis, however, can hardly be blamed for not anticipating the normally cautious William's decision to invade from the sea a hostile country defended by a standing army and navy in *November*, and his equally astonishing success. While James II had a deserved reputation for stupidity and incompetence, not even he could have been expected to abandon his sizeable, loyal armed forces and run away. Louis, always generous to friends down on their luck, welcomed the English royal family and awarded them the palace of Saint-Germaine plus a sizeable pension. Futhermore, he decided to back James's willingness to reverse the disaster of 1688 by invading Ireland where the mainly Catholic population would support him. 'I hope I shall never see you again', Louis remarked to his departing guest. If this campaign went well, it would distract William from Flanders, which was bound to be the decisive theatre in the long run.

The Irish campaign was made possible by the impressive strength of the French navy. This was due primarily to Colbert's enthusiastic initiatives, capably continued by his son Seignelay. Louis deserves credit as well, although he was a confirmed landlubber and regarded the navy as subordinate to the army. Even so he had approved the expenditure, which gave France a navy twice the size of the Dutch by the peace of Nijmegen and capable of taking on the allied Anglo-Dutch fleet in 1690 (89 French warships as against 135 Anglo-Dutch). The English navy on its own could not prevent the French descent on Ireland, even though the campaign ended disastrously for James II at the Boyne (July 1690). On the same day Tourville inflicted a heavy defeat on the Anglo-Dutch navy off Beachy Head, sinking eight Dutch warships. Despite the Irish debacle, the way was clear for a French descent on England. But Louis' heart was not in it. The French navy waited for its chance to win the war, but eventually sailed to its downfall at La Hogue (1692) when Tourville, ordered by Louis to fight, obeyed against his better judgement and was defeated. Courtiers maliciously expected the admiral to be lambasted when he reported to his monarch at Versailles, but Louis displayed his customarily high standards of decency and fairness towards unlucky commanders:

> I am entirely happy with your conduct and with that of all the navy. We have been defeated, but you have earned glory, both for yourself and for the nation. It has cost us some ships, but that will be put right during the coming year, and assuredly we will defeat the enemy.[5]

The decision was now taken to resort to piracy – and an inspired decision it was, even though it was necessitated by financial realism. Issuing from Dunkirk and the Breton ports, equipped with official approval from the crown, French privateers massacred Anglo-Dutch shipping. It was the golden age of the great pirate-chieftains Jean Bart and René Duguay-Trouin. Raids on enemy harbours where the merchantmen gathered yielded profits of 10 million livres. Tourville masterminded a wolf-pack operation against the Anglo-Dutch Smyrna convoy off Lagos in April 1693. Over 5,000 English merchant ships had been captured or sunk by the end of the war – a highly persuasive inducement for the English government to make peace.

Predictably the crucial campaign was fought in Flanders – a gruesome bloodbath in which neither side established an advantage. Thanks to Vauban and the skilled Dutch engineers, the ground was pitted with fortresses and defensive lines. Pitched battles were few and indecisive. Luxembourg, Louis' best general, was the only commander on either side

who seemed to know how to win – certainly William III had no idea.
Has there been any other war in history in which the opposing com-
manders-in-chief were both hunchbacked gnomes of doubtful sexual
orientation? 'How does William know I have a hump? I've never shown
it to him!', Luxembourg boasted. He triumphed at Fleurus in July 1690
and at Steenkirke in August 1692 when William surprised the French
but lost control of the chaotic scrimmage that ensued. Luxembourg
intuitively committed his cavalry before his officers had time to tie
their cravats, so that at Versailles courtiers took to wearing their cravats *à la Steenkirke*. Victory at Neerwinden in July 1693 delivered so
many enemy standards that Luxembourg became known as '*le tapissier de
Nôtre Dame*' (the furnisher of Notre Dame). Louis presided over several
sieges, including the capture of Mons (1691) and Namur (1692). But he
remained at Versailles after the 1693 campaign and so was not there to
stop William III recapturing Namur in 1695 – perhaps William's finest
military achievement, though it cost the attackers almost twice as many
casualties as the defenders. Meanwhile, French troops fought successfully in northern Italy, led by Catinat, and in Spain where Noailles and
Vendôme took Barcelona.

War-weariness now dominated both sides. Winter 1693–4 was especially severe in France, combining with high taxation and war casualties to
cripple the economy. Controller-General Pontchartrain even introduced
the *capitation*, which taxed the rich. Louis' victories were little consolation. In Voltaire's memorable words, 'the people died of want to the
sound of the *Te Deum*'. Versailles was peopled by soldiers on crutches and
widows in mourning. The English and Dutch had had enough as well,
despite effective methods of financing the war such as the national debt.
Negotiations began in the summer of 1694 at William's villa of Ryswick,
outside Amsterdam. But sticking points such as William's status as king
of England, which Louis was reluctant to recognise, created deadlock.
Colbert de Croissy's attempts to bring pressure to bear on the emperor
by forming a third party in Germany broke down on the princes' distrust
of Louis XIV. Leopold was a nuisance to both sides. William refused to
continue the war to gratify the emperor's ambitions. When Leopold suggested that Louis should give up all his gains since Westphalia, Louis
exploded: 'What? Am I to give up the work of thirty years, I who have
struggled so hard lest my enemies should come into my house?' The
log jam was broken when France and Savoy signed a separate peace in

June 1696. In the end the maritime powers, represented by William's friend Bentinck, and the French, represented by Marshal Boufflers, hammered out a compromise. Louis surrendered his gains since Nijmegen apart from Strasbourg and recognised William as king. His sudden willingness to make concessions was caused both by France's exhaustion and by the news from Madrid that Carlos II's sad life was coming to a close. So Louis' self-congratulation may sound a little hollow:

> The happy successes with which God has favoured my arms in the course of so long a war have never removed me from the sincere desire I have for peace, which was the unique purpose I aimed for in all my enterprises ... I have made it my rule to consecrate the fruits of my conquests to the repose of Europe. I am sufficiently recompensed for everything that this moderation costs me by the end it makes of all the evils of war. The prompt comfort which will accrue to my people and the pleasure I receive in rendering them happy are sufficient compensation for everything I sacrifice on their behalf.[6]

While church- and government-sponsored processions, Te Deums, speeches and so forth may or may not have reflected people's gratitude, Louis XIV certainly deserved admiration for the way he had conducted the war. He was a remarkable warlord, never more so than during the Nine Years War. We have seen how France's armed forces grew in size during the Sun King's personal rule. By the 1690s his army neared 400,000 men on paper, and probably around 320,000 in fact. Add the thousands of horses, the more sophisticated weapons such as mortars, the immensely complex business of recruiting, equipping, feeding, caring for and disciplining such an army. Take for instance the single problem of the *passe-volants*; that is to say, fraudulently paraded soldiers who had already been counted, so that more money could be claimed. Or take the problem of feeding horses. A horse consumed fifty pounds of fresh grass per day, plus oats. And needless to say there were plenty of four-legged *passe-volants*. Recruitment presented an increasingly insoluble problem. Soon the very old, the very young and the criminal swelled the army's ranks. Luxembourg returned thousands of recruits without bothering to train them, describing them as 'children'. Louis was especially instrumental in drilling and disciplining his military juggernaut. To get such a force into the field was an astonishing feat of organisation for which he can personally take much credit. Two historians have independently researched this impressive story – John Lynn and Guy Rowlands. While they do not always agree on such matters as the size of contributions made by regimental commanders out of their own pockets, there is a broad consensus on the growth of royal power, both cause and effect of the creation of such a magnificent army.

This revolution, brought to fruition by Louis, was implemented by the Le Tellier family: first Michel who administered the army in succession to Richelieu's man Sublet de Noyer, then Louvois until his death in 1691, and after him his son Barbézieux. Louis backed these men – and it was not always easy. Le Tellier was a reasonable, rather colourless civil servant who knew his place – an ideal number two, or, as an unkind acquaintance remarked, an ideal number twenty-two. There was nothing colourless about Louvois, however. From the Dutch war onwards Louis refereed fights between his war minister and his generals. In 1690, for instance, the king had to reassure Luxembourg that Louvois would behave himself. Louvois had such a cutting edge that few could stand up to him. And unlike his father he did not remain in his office behind the lines, but toured the front himself, dealing with administrative problems on the spot, to say nothing of recalcitrant generals.

Rumours circulated in 1691 that even Louis had had enough of him and that he was about to be dismissed. Louvois was certainly under pressure. 'You don't look well', Louis remarked to him in a council meeting. Louvois asked to be excused, left the room, had a fit and died. Later in the day Louis was seen pacing up and down, lost in thought. When James II sent condolences, Louis replied: 'It is true that I have lost a good minister, but there are other able men who will serve the state.' Whether Louis found the ablest is a fair question. True to his loyalty to family succession, he appointed Louvois' son, Barbézieux, to succeed him. Barbézieux was only twenty-three, drank and wenched. He was frequently 'absent' from council meetings. Rowlands has rescued Barbézieux from contemporaries and historians. He obviously had ability. When he died in 1701 as a result of ill-advised dissipation, Louis remarked, 'What a pity! He was beginning to overcome his weaknesses.'

Louis was an increasingly 'hands-on' commander-in-chief during the Nine Years War, especially due to Barbézieux's inexperience. He sometimes interfered with the conduct of sieges and battles, especially in Flanders where he knew the ground and where instructions could speedily be conveyed from nearby Versailles. Louis, however, was in awe of

Luxembourg whom he disliked, though he recognised his ability to win battles. Commanders in more remote theatres such as Catinat in Italy and Vendôme in Spain inevitably enjoyed more freedom of manoeuvre. Ironically, despite his ignorance of naval affairs, Louis had no hesitation in telling his admirals their business, as when he ordered Tourville to fight at La Hogue, while he often behaved diffidently to his generals whose trade he had thoroughly mastered.

Perhaps Louis' happiest and most productive professional relationship was with Vauban, who certainly needed royal patronage. Unlike Luxembourg, who was a Montmorency and never let you forget it, Vauban came from a minor provincial family. Worse still, he was an engineer. Previously, no engineer had risen beyond the rank of captain. But now Vauban was promoted to brigadier, lieutenant-general and, shortly before his death, marshal. When other generals objected to taking orders from this low-class engineer, the king put them in their places. Louvois too supported Vauban, appreciating his expertise and reluctance to waste blood and treasure. Vauban was just the sort of expert Louis liked: modest, loyal, hardworking and competent. While he is famed for his fortifications, Vauban in fact demolished more than he built, saving the king money and soldiers who could be better deployed elsewhere. Indeed, Vauban wore himself out, travelling all over France to see for himself what needed doing. Unfortunately defences were static, unlike soldiers who could march to be inspected by their commander. As Vauban humorously remarked, 'There is not a single watchtower in all the king's fortresses which will move so much as an inch at my command.'

Louis derived immense satisfaction from French victories and suffered on his troops' behalf when things went wrong. By and large France's armies effectively exploited their superior equipment, manpower and leadership during the Nine Years War, her geographical ability to operate on interior lines and the dynamic encouragement of her king. France's performance – even though outright victory eluded her – alarmed and impressed Europe. Despite William III's gutsy performance and the improving military standards of the now thoroughly blooded English and Dutch armies, France still dominated Europe. The compromise peace to which Louis XIV agreed in 1697 was roundly condemned by his more belligerent courtiers and soldiers. But, more to the point, Carlos II was impressed by France's overall military efficiency and the leadership of her redoubtable monarch.

CARLOS II'S BOMBSHELL

Louis XIV continued to behave in a statesmanlike way for the next three years. He retained his vast standing army, which displayed itself in insolent pride at a review at Compiègne in the summer of 1699, an event that all Europe noted with consternation. Yet he was simultaneously receiving cautious and responsible advice. The abrasive Colbert de Croissy was replaced by Pomponne, recalled from disgrace, and by Croissy's son Torcy who became secretary for foreign affairs in 1696 and a minister in 1699. If there was a warmonger at large, it was Emperor Leopold. Unlike Louis and William who were aware of conditions in their relatively compact domains, Leopold was ignorant of his people's sufferings in his far-flung empire, and so continued to adopt policies that could lead to the resumption of war. This was an outcome that Louis XIV and William III genuinely wished to avoid. Clearly the flashpoint would be the death of Carlos II. So the two statesmen did their best to negotiate a settlement that would be acceptable to all parties involved.

The results were two partition treaties. The first (1698) awarded the bulk of the Spanish inheritance to the eight-year-old Prince Joseph Ferdinand of Bavaria, the emperor's grandson. France and Austria would be compensated with territory in Italy. Neither Leopold nor the Spaniards were consulted, but it was hoped that there was enough in the treaty to please everyone. We shall never know, since Joseph Ferdinand died in the following year. So it was back to the drawing board. The second partition treaty (1700) awarded Spain and the colonies to Leopold's second son Charles with increased Italian compensation for France. These proposals were rejected in both Vienna and Madrid. The Spaniards would not countenance any attempts to split their empire, while Leopold objected to French domination of Italy. Perhaps the Habsburg powers should have been consulted at the earliest opportunity, though there is no reason to suppose that they would have concurred.

Indeed, quite the reverse. For when Carlos II's sufferings came to an end on 1 November 1700, his published will left his whole empire to Louis XIV's second grandson, Philip of Anjou. This was totally unexpected, certainly in London where there was baffled disgust that the Spaniards had let the side down, but no less at Versailles. The French envoy at Madrid, Harcourt, who had played a sensible and thoroughly diplomatic hand, was as astonished as everyone else. What had happened was that the dying king had become fed up with the nagging of his pro-Austrian second wife and was convinced that only Louis XIV could effectively save the Spanish inheritance from being torn apart. The will stipulated that 'Philip V' was not to become king of France as well and that if the French rejected the will, the whole inheritance was to go the emperor's son instead.

What was Louis to do? This unexpected bonanza, exceeding Louis' wildest dreams over forty years, was arguably too good to be true. Was it a trap it would be a mistake to fall into without looking carefully at the consequences? After all, to accept would be to break a treaty with William III that Louis had only just helped to negotiate – and the Sun King was proud of his reputation for keeping his word. War would undoubtedly follow the acceptance of the will. On the other hand the latest partition treaty would also involve war, and against a Catholic coalition. Louis' family pride was undoubtedly gratified by Carlos II's amazing compliment. Furthermore, while he genuinely had no ambition to unite the two crowns, close collaboration between the great Catholic monarchies of France and Spain appealed to him.

Several discussions took place in Mme de Maintenon's rooms, though in his memoirs Torcy is adamant that the lady was not there when the final decision was taken.[7] Monseigneur, the Grand Dauphin, spoke forcefully, making it clear that he would gladly surrender his own and his eldest son's rights on behalf of Philip, his second son. Behind the scene Mme de Maintenon and Torcy argued for acceptance, especially when they realised that this was Louis' own preference. In the end Louis accepted on his grandson's behalf. The courtiers were summoned, the great doors that separated the king's apartments and had never been opened were now unlocked, and Louis presented his grandson as the king of Spain. Louis, clearly deeply moved, told the young man to become a good Spaniard, but never to forget that he was a Frenchman too. The Spanish ambassador declared that the Pyrenees had ceased to exist.

This was surely a justifiable decision on Louis' part. He was influenced by family pride, imperial ambition in that he had worked for this outcome for forty years, belief in the God-given rights of heredity, and not least a hard-nosed calculation that it was the wisest move all round. After all, what was the point of refusing, when this would simply dispatch the Spanish delegation to Vienna? The seventeen-year-old Philip was given several intense tutorials by his grandfather, and was then escorted down the road to Bordeaux by his weeping relations. Meanwhile, in firm but courteous terms, the acceptance of Carlos II's bequest was conveyed to the courts of Europe. It was portrayed as the will of God and of the Spanish people. Louis' letter to William III, for instance, could hardly be bettered. Written at Versailles on 7 December 1700, it addresses William in flattering terms and, only a little disingenuously, stresses Louis' self-sacrifice in surrendering France's gains envisaged in the second partition treaty:

> Very high, very excellent and very powerful Prince, Our own dear and very loved good brother, cousin and ancient Ally, We are sending to you the Count de Tallard, Lieutenant-General of our armies. He will particularly explain to you the just reasons which have obliged us to prefer the public tranquillity, rather than our personal interests in accepting as we have the testament of the late Catholic King in favour of the King our grandson. We have no doubt that after being informed of our decision you will agree that nothing will be capable in the future of troubling the general tranquillity of Europe.[8]

While most historians agree that there was a perfectly sound case for Louis' decision to accept the will, controversy arises over what he did next. Louis' critics accuse him of committing several unnecessary mistakes that alienated potential allies. More recently, revisionist historians, sympathetic to Louis, have argued that the Sun King had a case for all these alleged 'own goals', and that these mistakes, if such they were, really made very little difference. What are the facts?

The first provocative act occurred in February 1701 when Louis promulgated a decision by the Parlement of Paris that Philip V had not given up his rights to the throne of France. Louis' argument was simply that if the worst happened and all the other legitimate heirs to the French throne died, Philip would still be eligible. Louis did not envisage his grandson ruling both France and Spain. He was in no doubt that in this eventuality Philip would leave Spain in order to return to the land of his birth, while the Spanish would have to find another king. Unfortunately this was not made clear. It was therefore open to speculation that the way remained open for precisely the Franco-Spanish empire Louis' enemies had always dreaded. They did not trust him. Perhaps the Pyrenees really would cease to exist.

2   Second, in the same month Louis XIV expelled the Dutch troops from the barrier fortresses they had been permitted to garrison by the Treaty of Ryswick. This looked bad. In actual fact the French had been invited to take this step by the Spanish government to protect the frontiers of the Spanish Netherlands. Philip V's accession was by no means universally popular in Spain. Louis knew this and wanted to make his grandson as acceptable as possible in the eyes of his own people. Such a step would, Louis hoped, depict the French connection in a favourable light. But obviously it did not reassure the maritime powers.

3   The most defensible of Louis' alleged 'own goals' was his third. He persuaded the new Spanish government to award the monopoly of slave traffic from Africa to the Spanish New World (known as 'the asiento') to the French Guinea company. Well, why on earth shouldn't he? Louis has frequently been criticised for his snobbish lack of interest in French trade. Now here he was at last doing the right thing for his own merchants. Naturally Louis alarmed and offended English and Dutch trading interests. But his action was neither unreasonable nor unethical. Incidentally, the legal provisions for the treatment of slaves Louis promulgated were an improvement on everybody else's.

4   Perhaps Louis' most celebrated 'blunder' was to recognise the dying James II's son as James III (September 1701). Louis went against his ministers' advice in so doing, the prevailing influence being Mme de Maintenon – plus, it has to be said, his own monarchist prejudices. Maintenon always referred to William as 'the Prince of Orange' and Anne as 'the Princess of Denmark'. So she was being consistent in preferring the claims of James II and his son. Louis, however, was breaking his own promise made in the Treaty of Ryswick. Torcy admitted that 'the whole English nation looked upon it as the greatest indignity that France should pretend to arrogate a right to give them a king'.[9] Even Bluche reckons that Louis was in the wrong. It was an unnecessary and sentimental gesture to cheer up his dying friend. Louis' defenders point out that the alliance between his enemies had already been formed. Nevertheless, it rallied the English political nation behind its unpopular Dutch leader, whose capacity to conduct his own foreign policy had just been drastically reduced by the grossly insulting Act of Settlement. Nor was Louis able to exploit a huge slice of luck when a few weeks later William was thrown from his horse, broke his collarbone and died. The coalition's mainspring had gone. But thanks to Louis' provocation it continued to function, activated by anti-French sentiment.

None of Louis' actions was unreasonable. He had a case in each instant. But it is a strange story. Louis had accepted the will – fair enough. His enemies would undoubtedly be alarmed. But would they take their disapproval as far as a declaration of war? In the case of Leopold, almost certainly. As for the rest, quite possibly not. Louis' priority should have been to make his acceptance of the will as inoffensive as possible. Instead he just could not leave well alone. He seems to have gone out of his way to provoke his potential opponents. He seems to have assumed that war was inevitable. And in a sense it was. But what sort of a war, against whom? Emperor Leopold would fight. France and Spain could easily and quickly have seen him off if he was on his own, but not if he was supported by the maritime powers and the Germans. Maybe Louis was a victim of the prevailing system. Because rulers seldom met each other, there was ample opportunity for misunderstandings and miscalculations. Furthermore, the widespread admiration of war as the only fit activity for gentlemen meant that rulers did not regard war as the ultimate tragedy to be avoided at all cost. So Louis and his contemporaries gambled light-heartedly with the prospect of war, without troubling too much about its consequences.

Still, it is clear that in winter 1700–1 Louis genuinely did not want war on a disadvantageous playing field. Yet he eventually got the wrong war against the wrong opponents – a war, as it turned out, he could not win. Mark Thomson attributes to Louis a failure of nerve during these decisive months. It seems to me that the king failed to identify the right priorities, combined with an obtuseness with regard to public opinion among the Dutch, German and English political nations. Louis should have followed up his excellent letter to William III with further demonstrations of his peaceful intentions. He should not have occupied the barrier forts. He should have cut the English in on the slave trade. For what should have been *the* priority? The avoidance of war with the maritime powers! Louis cannot be absolved of insensitivity, arrogance and stupidity. Regrettably, he was clearly willing to fight another war. He might do at least as well as he had done in the last war. After all, God was a Catholic, and could usually be relied on to be a Frenchman as well. Unfortunately, hubris was still Louis the Great's God-given reaction. He had yet to learn.[10] Nemesis was waiting in the wings.

THE WAR OF THE SPANISH SUCCESSION (1701–14)

The French people, the French economy, the French armed forces and their redoubtable leader had had little more than four years in which to recover from the last bruising encounter before they were involved in a yet more horrendous ordeal. Furthermore, while the Nine Years War could be described as a winning draw in which France had achieved notable victories, now she was to experience bitter, catastrophic defeats from which she was to make an incomplete recovery, leading to an unsatisfactory peace. Decades of hubris now inexorably led to nemesis.

As this book is a biography of Louis XIV and not a history of European warfare, a brief summary of the War of the Spanish Succession must suffice, in which France and Spain faced a coalition of more or less the rest of Europe. Then Louis' own contribution, reactions and achievements can be analysed at greater length. First, it must be stressed that this was an important war, affecting the future of Europe for decades to come. Momentous issues were at stake and were decisively settled. Most obviously, was a Bourbon to remain on the throne of Spain? What was to be the future of the Spanish low countries over which so much blood had been shed? Given that in March 1702 William III was succeeded by another childless monarch, his sister-in-law Queen Anne, could Louis' ambitions to restore a Catholic ruler on the English throne finally be satisfied? Indeed the war could justifiably be called the War of the English Succession. Perhaps in the long term the settlement of the wider world was the issue that affected the maritime powers above more parochial questions. Certainly the struggle for control of the Spanish Empire and the war at sea mattered as much as the continuous fighting in the Iberian peninsula where Philip V defended his throne against his imperial rivals and their Anglo-Dutch allies. Were his Italian domains to be seized from him? Were France's enemies to succeed in breaking through her eternally vulnerable frontiers to the east and north-east? Flanders and the Rhine valley were to be drenched in blood once more. So was the Danube.

Louis XIV waged war on less favourable terms than he had enjoyed in the last conflict. While once again he fought on interior lines and exercised unifying control, his armed forces, though still immense, were weaker in quantity and quality. His navy, for instance, could no longer mount a battle fleet in the North Sea and the Atlantic but had

to resort again to commerce raiding. The army was exhausted before
the war began. The attitude of the nobility had become far more sober
and realistic, reflecting the fact that this was not a war France wanted
or one likely to be enjoyed as a glamorous adventure. The king's former
allies were now on the other side, with the sole exceptions of the elector of Bavaria and the duke of Savoy – and the latter joined the allies
in 1703. While there were talented commanders who had made their
reputation in the previous war – Villars, Vendôme, Berwick, Boufflers
– the great strategists of earlier times were dead. No one equalled the
capacity of Condé, Turenne or Luxembourg. Indeed, the great captains
trained by the French had been prodigally discarded: Marlborough, who
owed everything he knew to Turenne, and Eugène, who had applied for
promotion in the French army but had been contemptuously dismissed
by Louis because he looked like a daffodil: 'You don't seriously suggest that I shall regret letting him go? I don't like the insolent way he
looks at me.' Even more serious was the failure to replace Louvois. After
Barbézieux had died of drink in 1701, Chamillart's grip on affairs was
limited, even if he was not as incompetent as his detractors alleged. The
old king in his office at Versailles could not make up for the lack of flair
of his generals or the administrative shortcomings of his war depart-
ment. He tried his best. But it was uphill work, given the depressed
state of the economy and the incidence of popular discontent. For much
of the time he himself was weary and sad.

The imperialists started the war by attacking the Spanish Empire.
First they invaded Spain's Italian territory in July 1701. Eugène drove off
Catinat, defeated Villeroy twice and took him prisoner for six months.
Soon after William III's death in March 1702 the new queen's minis-
ters declared war. 'Things have come to a pretty pass when *women* attack
me!' was Louis' reaction. But women were to prop up the king of Spain.
Madame des Ursins represented the French interest in Madrid, corre-
sponding frequently with her friend Mme de Maintenon at Versailles.
In Spain Louis' grandson Philip V faced defeat and discouragement
during the long campaign to defend his realm. But he kept going.
He was supported by such able commanders as Berwick, Vendôme and
Orléans and managed to attract the loyalty of the Spanish people, who
reflected that he *was* their late king's choice. Furthermore, 'Charles
III' (as the archduke styled himself) led a motley array of heretics –
Lutherans, Calvinists, Anglicans, Presbyterians – who blasphemed,

sacked churches and assaulted priests and nuns. When a shocked Louis XIV recounted the latest outrage, the Spanish ambassador rubbed his hands: 'Splendid! Splendid!' Although the imperialists at one stage drove Philip out of Madrid, he ended the war in undisputed mastery of his country. Vendôme's victory at Villaviciosa (December 1710), in Torcy's words, 'changed beyond doubt the affairs of Spain, and, with that, those of Europe as well'. Similarly, Philip's lieutenants held on to his Italian territories despite the treachery of the duke of Savoy.

It was clearly good tactics to carry the war to the enemy's nerve centre. But Louis' imaginative attempts to combine with his ally the elector of Bavaria in a march on Vienna unfortunately met a fatal reverse at Blenheim (13 August 1704) when Marlborough and Eugène outmanoeuvred Tallard and the elector. Indeed, more than the Sun King's strategy was demolished on that summer day. Thirty thousand French and Bavarian troops were killed or captured, and their commander Marshal Tallard taken prisoner. This was a turning point in European history. The Sun King's brilliant forces had been checked in the past, but it was unheard of that one of his armies should be soundly thrashed. Louis' courtiers hardly dared break it to him that he was no longer invincible. A monument erected on the battlefield carried a Latin inscription: 'Let Louis XIV acknowledge that no one should be considered happy or great before his death.' Voltaire maintained that the battle of Rossbach (1757), when the French army was humiliated by Prussia and her allies, marked the end of French European hegemony. Maybe, but the world was never quite the same after Blenheim.

Marlborough's genius likewise threatened Louis' own nerve centre. A series of victories in the Low Countries brought the allies nearer and nearer to Paris and encouraged them to make outrageous demands, such as the return of all territory acquired by France since the Peace of Westphalia (1648). The fate of northern France depended on the French army's ability to check Marlborough. For six years it was a tale of disaster, abandonment of fortresses and humiliating retreats, notably after Ramillies (1706) and Oudenarde (1708). But Vauban's defence lines held, Villars drew the battle of Malplaquet (1709) and defeated Eugène at Denain (1712) after Marlborough had been sacked by the Tory government that had replaced the Whig warlords in 1711.

Later imperial successes by Britain's Royal Navy have been read back by her patriotic historians into Louis XIV's time. In truth the French navy acquitted itself creditably between 1702 and 1713. Although

Britain's Mediterranean hegemony was established by the acquisition of Gibraltar and Minorca, and although a Jacobite assault on Scotland in 1708 proved abortive, the French commerce raiders based on Dunkirk and Saint-Malo were apparently unstoppable. Between 1702 and 1707 the English lost 1,146 merchant ships. French sailors and privateers ravaged the West Indies. Duguay-Trouin, the toast of Saint-Malo, captured a convoy bound for 'Charles III's' Portuguese allies in autumn 1707. The Franco-Spanish war effort was assisted by the navy's success in escorting the bullion fleets from the New World.

The peace treaties that concluded the war were less hard on France than the terms Louis offered the allies in 1710. This was due not only to French naval resurgence but to continued success by Philip V in firmly grasping his Spanish inheritance. Denain proved that without Anglo-Dutch help the imperialists could not defeat the French. Leopold's death in 1705 had brought his elder son Joseph to the imperial throne. But Joseph's death in 1711 meant that 'Charles III' became emperor. To continue to support him as king of Spain was absurd. What was the point of upsetting the balance of power by reviving the empire of Charles V? So the British and Dutch conceded to Louis the triumph of his grandson's retention of the Spanish throne, even if the bigoted old dynast had to accept the Protestant succession to the throne of Great Britain. Britain and Austria benefited most from Utrecht and Rastadt. But from France's point of view, it could have been much worse.

THE OLD WARLORD, 1701–13

As in his previous wars, Louis XIV was the master. His contribution was immense, his responsibility for both success and failure unquestionable. He continued to supervise recruitment, discipline and training. In 1701 he raised morale by appointing twenty-three lieutenant-generals in one go. Although he continued to interfere far too much, especially with regard to Flanders, he kept away from the actual fighting, exercising control from Versailles (or Fontainebleau, or Marly). He kept in touch by correspondence, receiving detailed reports in writing or interviewing generals or ministers who had reported to headquarters. Louis was at his best in praising the successful or consoling the unfortunate, for example Villeroy after Ramillies.

One of Louis' most influential contributions was in the matter of appointments. Here he made mistakes. In general he rated loyalty too highly, as against ability. Hence his choice of Tallard, the diplomat who 'commanded' ('if that is right word' – Bluche[11]) at Blenheim. Villeroy, who similarly allowed himself to be wrong-footed by Marlborough at Ramillies, was a courtier, one of Louis' oldest friends since boyhood and the son of his tutor. It was said of him that he impressed the ladies more than the enemy. Perhaps Louis' worst choice was his grandson Burgundy, supposedly under the tutelage of Vendôme. Burgundy was a humourless young prig, Vendôme a cynical old reprobate. His nose ravaged by syphilis, he instructed his staff while sitting on his commode, which he would then use for shaving. This combination of virtue leaning on vice was bound to fail. Together they wrecked the Oudenarde campaign – and continued to quarrel with each other during the bitter aftermath. Louis retained Chamillart, his billiards opponent, far too long. According to Saint-Simon, he was a charming man who worked hard. But it was absurd to expect such a second-rater to hold down the war ministry and the control of the economy, responsibilities that had fully taxed both Louvois and Colbert.

Louis was slow to revise his opinions when he had clearly been wrong. Thus he allowed Mme de Maintenon to prejudice him against the uncouth Vendôme and the abrasive Berwick, whom Maintenon called 'her unsmiling Englishman'. Both Louis and his wife detested Orléans, who finally doomed himself with a drunken toast at an officers' party in Spain to 'our con-capitaine and our con-lieutenant'.[12] This disrespectful reference to Mmes de Maintenon and her friend des Ursins did not go down well at Versailles, and Orléans was never employed in the field again. Despite the debt France owed him, Louis never forgave Vauban for writing the *Dîme Royale*.

On the other hand, Louis did eventually change his mind about the courageous and impulsive Villars, who 'treated Louis XIV, Chamillart, Voisin and Mme de Maintenon in much the same way as he did his subordinate officers'.[13] Disgraced in 1703 for insubordination to Maximilian of Bavaria, he was recalled to resolve the Camisards revolt where his judicious mixture of firmness and generosity anticipated Templar's 'hearts and minds' campaign in Malaya (1950–3). Louis, in desperation after everyone else had failed, put Villars in command of the Flanders front. Soon after taking over, he rode all night to Versailles where he turfed Chamillart out of bed: 'You're supposed to be the secretary for war, so how is it that we don't even have boots and bread, and that our weapons are unserviceable?' Two day later, in the *conseil d'en haut*, when Villars shouted and banged the table, a shaken Louis replied: 'All I have left is my confidence in God and in you, my outspoken friend.'[14] Villars was to repay the king's confidence by holding Marlborough and Eugène to a draw at Malplaquet when the allies lost nearly twice as many men as the French. Villar's knee was shattered, his return to a grateful monarch being on a stretcher. Louis had no hesitation in retaining Villars for the crucial campaign of 1712 when he outfoxed Eugène at Denain.

All the while Louis exercised his responsibilities as head of state. In the context of war this meant raising money. He worked closely with his controller-generals – Pontchartrain, Chamillart and, after that supreme billiard-player's disgrace in 1709, Desmarets. All pretence at orthodox state finance had long been abandoned in favour of *affaires extraordinaires*; that is to say, sale of offices and borrowing. Sale of offices brought in less and less money as purchasers lost interest.[15] So not only was the *capitation* reimposed, but a new tax, the *dixième*, was dreamed up by Desmarets in 1710; in theory it taxed everyone in proportion to their income. The government's greatest challenge was the appalling winter of 1709–10. Louis did his best to encourage the wealthy to be charitable by offering his own gold dinner service. He ordered well-provisioned provinces to dispatch corn to those hardest hit. He escorted convoys of grain from abroad. Nevertheless, thousands died from cold and starvation. Partridges froze in the fields, as did the wine on the king's table.

Always concerned with image, Louis tackled the problem of his government's unpopularity. What with starvation, the collapse of trade, disease and war casualties, people reflected that not much *soulagement* was in evidence. And the war was going badly. During his previous wars Louis requested his bishops to organise the singing of the *Te Deum* to flag up his victories. Now a wit suggested that the *Miserere Nobis* ('Have pity on us') would be more appropriate. Scurrilous rhymes circulated attacking the king's government. Louis reacted to criticism in two ways. First, he hammered his critics, imposing rigid censorship, disgracing Fénelon and Vauban, and renewing the persecution of the Jansenists. Second, he appealed to public opinion for sympathetic understanding of his difficulties in obtaining peace. Torcy showed flair in implementing the king's wishes. For instance, he had Jonathan Swift's famous pamphlet, *The Conduct of the Allies*, which criticised Britain's subsidising of Dutch selfishness, translated into French and marketed in Paris. Minister and king were anxious that the greed and intransigence of France's enemies should be known. When the allies demanded most of Louis' territorial gains, plus his active cooperation in driving his grandson out of Spain, Louis wrote a remarkable letter of June 1709 to the archbishop of Paris and provincial governors and bishops, which parish priests were to read from their pulpits:

> The hope of peace soon is so widespread in my kingdom that I owe it to the fidelity which my people have demonstrated during the course of my reign to inform them of the reasons why they are not yet enjoying the repose which I intended to procure for them. I would have had to accept in order to achieve this, conditions highly dangerous for the safety of my frontier provinces, but the more I demonstrated a willingness and desire to dissipate the suspicions which my enemies still claimed to have of my powers and intentions, the more they multiplied their demands. I pass over in silence the proposal that I should join my forces with those of the league and force the king my grandson to quit his throne. It is against all humanity that they should even conceive of asking me to promise such an alliance with them ... I am certain that my subjects would be opposed to accepting peace upon conditions contrary to both the justice and the honour of France.[16]

Evidence is lacking as to the reception of the king's letter, just as it is not clear how the English people received Churchill's speeches during the Second World War. Certainly the French went on fighting – and on occasions fought well. Arguably this was a significant development in the story of French nationalism – the response of a whole people to their leader's call. It was certainly an unprecedented decision on Louis' part to humble himself by appealing to his people. It was probably Torcy's idea, quite possibly Torcy's prose. Nevertheless, Louis agreed to its publication over his name.

Louis continued to dictate France's foreign policy. He was fortunate in his secretary for foreign affairs, Colbert de Torcy, who was one of his better appointments. Realistic, well-informed, flexible, Torcy was just the man to make the most of an increasingly weak hand. His objective was peace on the best possible terms. But after Oudenarde and Turin and the winter of 1708–9, the position deteriorated almost daily. The triumphant allies pursued their own agendas: the emperor wanted his son to rule the complete Spanish Empire, the Dutch wanted an enlarged barrier to protect them from the man who had called them 'maggots', the English wanted their share of the slave trade and of the Spanish Empire, plus the expulsion of 'James III' from France. All these objectives were there for the taking, given the collapse of French hegemony. Louis' plenipotentiary at The Hague, the Rouen magistrate Rouillé, could do little to achieve peace, though Torcy admitted that 'there was not the least fault to be found with President Rouillé'. But the desperate situation in spring 1709 demanded desperate measures. Torcy submitted a master plan to the king, who always regarded foreign policy as his specialism.

Torcy proposed to go to The Hague himself. This unprecedented and unconventional suggestion – that the Most Christian King's foreign minister should go uninvited, cap in hand, to an enemy capital – carried risks. Would not such a measure be an admission of weakness? One thinks of Chamberlain's flights to Germany in September 1938. Torcy's reasoning was this. France's plight was so dire that speed was of the essence. A junior negotiator such as Rouillé would have to refer any new proposals back to Versailles, thus wasting time. Torcy, on the other hand, knew his master's mind so well that he would not have to refer anything back, but could take instant decisions and achieve immediate peace. That is to say, if the king agreed to place such trust in his minister. Torcy's proposal was discussed by the *conseil d'en haut*. The other members feared that 'it ill became one of the king's ministers to apply in a suppliant form for peace to his enemies'.[17] But Torcy goes on to recount how 'His Majesty relished the proposal of his secretary, who stayed behind after the other ministers had gone out of the cabinet-room.' So Louis agreed that Torcy should go. Louis knew perhaps better than the ministers how desperately France needed peace. He gave Torcy a list of bribes for Marlborough in return for concessions to France's strategic needs, a kind of tariff that illustrated Louis' profound cynicism about human motivation. Marlborough was certainly greedy, but it was probably a misreading of his character to think that he would stoop so low. Louis was now prepared to give up most of his gains except Strasbourg and to abandon Philip V. Compare Lenin sending Trotsky to Brest-Litovsk to negotiate with the Germans in March 1918: 'Sign anything!' Well, not quite, in Louis' case.

Indeed, that was why Torcy's mission was probably a mistake, since, unlike Trotsky, he could not sign anything. Torcy enjoyed meeting Heinsius. He was impressed by the modesty of the great man's household: a secretary, a coachman, a footman and a maid-servant. But Heinsius had not forgotten the treatment he had received from Louvois in 1679 who had threatened to send him to the Bastille. In the event the Dutch prevaricated: they had to wait for Marlborough, who was delayed by contrary winds. Torcy was fascinated by Marlborough when he eventually arrived. What a *smoothy*! All his victories were attributable to God alone. All his skill, if any, he had learnt from Turenne. He apologised for Townsend's presence whom the Whig lords had sent as a kind of political commissar to keep an eye on him. Would Torcy please pay his respects to the king and to the 'Prince of Wales'.[18]

This was all very civilised. But the 'Preliminaries of The Hague' communicated to Torcy were far from civilised: Louis was to recognise 'Carlos III' as ruler of the whole Spanish Empire; the 'duc d'Anjou' was to be given Sicily and Naples, and was to be allowed two months in which to leave Spain, or be forced out by the allies *and* the king of France; French trade was forbidden to the Spanish New World; Louis was to surrender Strasbourg, Breisach and Landeau; the defences of Dunkirk were to be raised; the Protestant succession was to be recognised and the Pretender expelled. Torcy could not possibly agree to this package and left The Hague in disgust. The only profit that accrued was that on his way home he was able to communicate the terms to Villars, who raised morale in the army by informing his troops. Hence Malplaquet a few days later. Hence Louis XIV's appeal to the nation.[19]

When negotiations were renewed at Geertruidenburg a year later, the allies insisted on even harsher terms. They offered just Sicily to Philip and insisted that Louis should actually make war on his grandson if he failed to leave Spain. Villars joined a majority of ministers in recommending acceptance so that France could at last have peace. Torcy advised further negotiations in pursuit of a modified acceptance. Louis listened carefully before rejecting the terms and sending Vendôme to Spain, whom Philip had requested as commander-in-chief. Louis deserves respect for keeping his nerve. He had gone as far as he possibly could by way of concessions. Events were to justify his determination to concede no more. On the other hand, while coalitions always have enormous problems ending wars, the allies deserve contempt for their arrogance, greed and stupidity. While coalitions always have problems reconciling conflicting priorities, did their understandable distrust of Louis XIV really justify such intransigence? They could have had a settlement markedly more favourable than Utrecht/Radstadt (1713–14). Their hubris exactly mirrored Louis XIV's refusal to be generous to the Dutch in 1672–3. But Louis had to endure many further months of anxiety and discouragement. On 12 April 1712 Villars reported to Louis on his way to the front. He was moved by the old king's grief after his recent family bereavements. Louis then changed the subject. What was Villars' advice if misfortune persisted on the battlefield? Villars was momentarily stunned. So Louis continued:

> While giving you a little time to collect your thoughts, I will tell you mine. I have heard all the arguments of my counsellors – that I must retire to Blois and not remain in Paris if you are beaten. I know also that your army will not be routed and that it will be able to reform behind the Somme. I know that river. It is very difficult to cross. I intend to come to Peronne or Saint-Quentin, to gather there all my remaining troops and to make a last effort by which you and I will save the state or perish together. I do not intend to live to see the enemy in my capital.[20]

Villars, intensely moved, agreed that 'the bravest counsel is often the wisest'. In July he outmanoeuvred and defeated Eugène at Denain. France's two old soldiers – the king and the marshal – had saved the state.

PEACE AT LAST

The Sun King's courage, common sense and belated humility were now rewarded by good luck. Not only did the god of battles smile again, the god of politics did as well. In London the Whig warlords were replaced by the Tory peace lovers. Marlborough was sacked after Swift had assassinated his character. Britain's allies were sidetracked. Bolingbroke hammered out with Torcy the details of the peace of Utrecht. Abandoned by the British and the Dutch, the emperor reluctantly empowered Eugène to negotiate the Treaty of Rastadt with Villars, who was thus able to realise his diplomatic ambitions. Partly because Villars could not understand any other language, the treaty was negotiated in French. This was also a compliment to the Sun King's cultural if not to his military domination of Europe.

Not for nothing did contemporaries refer to the *paix Anglaise*. Just as Louis in his pomp used to reward himself for 'granting peace to Europe', so the English benefited from 'granting peace' by awarding themselves the top prizes. Louis was obliged to acknowledge the Protestant succession to the English throne and promised that the French and Spanish crowns would never unite. He agreed to the raising of Dunkirk's fortifications. The *asiento*, the lucrative right to ship slaves to the Caribbean and thereby to perpetrate the greatest crime against humanity of the eighteenth century, was transferred from France to Britain. Britain acquired Gibraltar and Minorca from Spain, and Nova Scotia, Acadia, Newfoundland and St Kitts from France. Austria did well too. She acquired the Spanish Netherlands, Milan, Naples, Sardinia and Louis' conquests on the right bank of the Rhine. The Dutch fared badly, having to console themselves that France was no longer their neighbour since they kept their barrier fortresses. Louis XIV might well have reflected that France could have done much worse, especially bearing in mind the concessions he had offered the allies in 1710. His grandson remained on the Spanish throne. France retained Strasbourg, Franche-Comté, Lille and Bethune. Overseas, Louisiana (named after the Sun King), bases in Madagascar and Senegal, and the Newfoundland fishing rights formed the nucleus of a future empire.

Historians suggest that the peace settlement marked the replacement of the Old World dynastic kingly state by the New World territorial state. In other words, concepts such as the balance of power counted for more than dynastic preoccupations. For instance, the British representative Viscount Bolingbroke insisted that Philip V had to renounce either the throne of France or the throne of Spain. Louis XIV assumed that his grandson would prefer France: 'Should gratitude and affection for your Spanish subjects be strong inducements with you to adhere to them, I can tell you that you owe those same sentiments to me, to your family, and to France.' But Philip shocked his grandfather by ignoring his dynastic commitments and opting for his new territorial acquisition. But then Louis himself had to betray dynasticism by recognising the Protestant succession to the English throne at the expense of 'James III'.[21]

CONCLUSION

Had it all been worth it? Villars tactlessly claimed that Louis XIV's wars had been unnecessary, in that France's acquisitions could have been obtained by negotiation. This is not fair. Strasbourg and many of Louis' other conquests could only have been won by force. During his personal rule, Louis built on Mazarin's achievements. Vauban's *pré carré* was now well established, having proved its worth against Marlborough and Eugène. France no longer feared invasion, especially with a Bourbon on the throne of Spain. But Louis had made enemies where once there had been friends and had created an atmosphere of hatred and suspicion. The defeats and humiliations of the War of the Spanish Succession meant that France, despite her partial recovery, no longer dominated western Europe as she had done between 1661 and 1702. Not until Napoleon bestrode Europe was this to be the case again.

What about 'the unavoidable question' with which this survey of Louis' foreign policy began?[22] There is no way of accurately knowing the damage caused by the wars in which Louis XIV was involved. Lynn reckons that over a million died in the War of the Spanish Succession alone, Bluche goes for half a million[23] – though it is not clear whether he is referring to French deaths only. Who can remotely guess at the lives ruined by bereavement, wounds or disease? How to assess the material damage of cities bombarded, villages torched, fields laid waste? And there again, how many starving peasants was a town in Flanders worth? Arguably one dead soldier, one raped countrywoman, one hanged Rhinelander is one too many.

It is clear that Louis alone did not cause all this suffering. He was not the only warmonger in Europe. Leopold's imperialism in the Balkans was just as aggressive, successive rulers of Brandenburg-Prussia just as acquisitive, Peter the Great an even more terrifying dynast. As for William III, to invade his father-in-law's country, chase him out and usurp his throne goes far beyond any of Louis XIV's contraventions of contemporary morality. Louis lacked all these rulers' willingness to overturn the status quo. His foreign policy was fundamentally conservative and defensive. Furthermore, in assessing Louis' policies and achievements, hindsight must not be abused. The fate of the Spanish Empire when Carlos II finally died was not only a window of opportunity but also a threat should it pass into the wrong hands. We know what eventually happened. Louis did not. What he did know was that under the cardinals the united Habsburg power bloc very nearly strangled France. So it is unfair to blame Louis for pursuing objectives that Richelieu and Mazarin are praised for identifying as French priorities. Whether they were the right priorities is a question to put to all seventeenth-century France's rulers.

If the causation of 'Louis' wars must in fact be shared, there remains the question of relative responsibility when each conflict is assessed. What is striking here is not Louis' wickedness but his incompetence. Louis certainly has a case to answer with regard to the causes and course of the Dutch War. Nor can Louis escape the charge of incompetence when he precipitated the Nine Years War – despite not actually wanting it. Above all the War of the Spanish Succession should never have involved France. Many have speculated what Louis XIV's standing in history would have been if he had died, say, in 1684: Louis the Great, indeed. What if he had died in the winter of 1700–1, immediately after the publication and acceptance of Carlos II's will? Louis the even Greater, surely. He had just led France to unprecedented triumphs against the rest of Europe. Carlos had reacted by awarding France the prize of prizes. But Louis lived to make a diplomatic hash of his relations with other powers over the next few months, so that once again he found himself fighting the rest of Europe. He lived to lead France into a chasm of military and economic bankruptcy. And he ended his reign distrusted by his fellow rulers and disliked and despised by his long-suffering subjects.

Louis the incompetent!

10

THE SUN KING AND HIS PEOPLE, 1684–1715

What about the coronation oaths sworn by the Sun King all those years ago to his bride, La France,[1] now that the shades had begun to lengthen? One promise he did his best to keep, and that was to extirpate heresy. Similarly he could claim to have honoured his undertaking to protect France's frontiers, especially during the course of the horrendous twenty-five-year war (1688–1713). This chapter explores the Sun King's impact on the daily lives of his people, taking up the themes developed in the course of Chapter 3. To what extent did he keep faith with his many and varied subjects? For that matter, did they keep faith with him?

NOT MUCH *SOULAGEMENT*

The sufferings of most of the French people during the last three decades of Louis XIV's reign cannot be denied. Whether he cared very much or whether there was much that he could do about it are questions we shall consider shortly. First, the facts. France suffered from the European recession that prevailed during most of the later seventeenth century. Shortage of coin, falling wages and prices, declining trade, uneven population growth – such depressing problems affected not just France, but the 80 per cent of the French population who lived in the countryside or in the poorer quarters of the towns had an especially grim time. Intendants' reports of suffering due to poverty, starvation and disease are confirmed by travellers and diarists.

[handwritten margin notes:] In the last 30 years, France suffered

1) Recession

2) Suffering Due to Poverty

The appalling physical condition of the French peasant was caused by malnutrition, physical toil, disease and deprivation. These factors were exacerbated by high taxation and bad harvests. Here is the result:

> One meets with certain wild animals, male and female, scattered over the country, dark, livid and tanned by the sun, bound to the soil which they till with invincible obstinacy; they have something like an articulate voice, and, when they rise to their feet they reveal a human face. They are in fact men. At night they retire to their hovels where they live on black bread, water and roots.[2]

There are many references to the miserable diet to which peasants were reduced – at best, rye bread and water. Corpses were found with grass or nettles in their mouths. The carcases of horses, dogs and cats were devoured. The English philosopher John Locke, who travelled in France during the 1680s, was nauseated by a peasants' 'Sunday joint' – in fact, fried congealed blood. No wonder that during the period of bad harvests of 1688–94 a tenth of the population died. Diseases such as dysentery found ready victims, especially among the old and the young. The bell tolled repeatedly for funerals, but not very often for marriages.

If a French Rip van Winkle had gone to sleep in 1661 and woken up in 1715 what would he have made of conditions in his own village? He would have been shocked by the deterioration of French agriculture, which, far from improving during Louis' personal rule, if anything regressed due to shortage of labour as men were recruited for the armed forces and as the amount of land in cultivation declined. Indeed, if our friend had gone to sleep in the reign of 'Saint' Louis (Louis IX, 1226–70) he would have been at home in the reign of Louis the Great. Wooden ploughs pushed or drawn by men and women, seed sown by hand, harvests gathered manually with back-breaking toil condemned the peasants to life lived on the very edge of subsistence – as one commentator remarked, like men with water up to their chins, helpless if the ground fell away at all. A typical harvest yielded only six times the seed sown. When it failed, the alternatives were to run into debt, eat the seed corn, join the army – or starve.

Or they took to the road, maybe heading for the nearest town or hoping for survival through begging from passers-by. Vagrancy posed severe problems of law and order to the authorities, giving rise to what historians have called 'the great confinement' of the seventeenth century when the desperate poor would be locked up with the old, the criminal, the syphilitic and the mad. More often a vagrant presented merely a problem of disposal. On 22 December 1684 Gabriel Georges died of starvation in the poorhouse of a village in the Cévennes. Ironically it was freezing, as he had walked from his home in Poitou in search of food, work and the warmth of the Mediterranean. He was typical of thousands who had degenerated from ownership of land to tenancy, to day labouring, to debt, to the open road. Boisguilbert, the lieutenant-general for Rouen, writing in 1697, testified on behalf of another disadvantaged segment of society, the thousands of children who died before reaching adulthood. Initially deprived of their mothers' milk through shortage of food and overwork, 'at a greater age, having only bread and water, without beds, clothes or any remedies for their illnesses, they perish before completing half their lives'.[3] Typical of this tragic state of affairs was a dead woman found with a baby sucking at her breast.

The problems highlighted here were infinitely exacerbated by high taxation. Boisguilbert again:

> In effect the arbitrary *taille* compels a merchant to hide his money, and a farmer to let his land lie fallow, for if one wished to do business and the other to plough they would alike be crushed with the *taille* by powerful men, who themselves are in the position of paying little or nothing. The *aides*, customs and taxes on goods coming in and out of the kingdom bring it about that a man sees his cellar full of wines rotting, whilst they are very dear in his neighbourhood, so that five hundred millions are lost to the revenues of the kingdom.[4]

Not only were taxes levied to fund Louis' wars cripplingly high, but they were unjustly levied. This anomaly was pilloried by the austere, outraged and angry soldier of fortune, Sebastian Vauban, in his 1698 best-seller *Dîme Royale:*

> I write without any other passion but to preserve the interests of the king, of those who serve him and the welfare and repose of his people. The wandering life I have led for above forty years has given me opportunities of seeing and observing the state and condition of the people, whose poverty having often moved me to compassion has put me on an enquiry into the causes of it. Our problems are caused by the armies of financiers, sub-financiers and their assistant leeches of whom their numbers would fill the galleys ... Near a tenth part

of the people are actually reduced to beggary; but of the other nine parts, not five of them are in a condition to give alms to the tenth, by reason of the miserable conditions they are reduced to, and the small pittance that is left them. In effect the establishment of a royal tithe, laid upon all the fruits of the earth, on one hand, and on all that produces yearly incomes on the other, seems to me to be the most equal and proportional of all other methods of taxation. As a result, fewer great fortunes would be made, while greater happiness and justice would be achieved.[5]

If knowledgeable and compassionate people such as Vauban and Boisguilbert not only reported their findings but also advocated solutions, what was the Sun King's role? Louis quite often showed awareness of his people's plight and his wish to help them – for example in his letter to governors and bishops (June 1709): 'My affections towards my people are no less great than those I feel for my own children, while I share in all the evils which war has inflicted upon them.'[6] How seriously should he be taken? Under the influence of Mme de Maintenon he became less addicted to pleasure and self-indulgence. Nevertheless, Versailles, that gigantic monument to royal self-glorification, continued to be staffed and maintained to the end of the reign, concerts, parades and hunts continued throughout the grimmest famines, and the king still consumed colossal meals consisting of pheasants and partridges, joints of beef, trifles and fruit while his people starved. Still, he led the way by donating silver and gold from palace decorations and dinner services in order to encourage other rich people to make sacrifices. And, to be fair, although Louis resented Vauban's criticisms and behaved coldly towards him when he presented his book at court, the capitation tax on all classes of society was followed by the *dixième*, which implemented Vauban's scheme.

But it was too little too late. First, the sheer size of taxation to fund war must be established: 42 per cent of total state expenditure was devoted to war between 1662 and 1669, 66 per cent between 1670 and 1679, 78 per cent from 1690 onwards. Estimates of total expenditure go like this: 77 million livres in 1670, 96 in 1680, 198 in 1685, 182 in 1700, 264 in 1711. The state debt is generally agreed to have been over 2 billion livres at the end of the reign. Second, society was riddled with injustice and economic inequality, taking its lead from the king. Despite the capitation and the *dixième,* the poor paid most while the rich escaped more or less unscathed. In March 1688 Nicholas Guenichot, a prominent member of the Normandy parlement, reported on the dissolute behaviour of the gilded youth of Dijon who shocked decent folk by their gargantuan feasts washed down with unlimited wine. What was more, their gluttony occurred during Lent. It was all right for some, from Louis downwards. This inequality was accentuated by the system of taxation, which Louis tolerated for most of his reign. *Soulagement* was out of the question due to the sheer scale of the taxation necessitated by Louis' wars. J.-C. Petitfils argues that the French were less heavily taxed than the English.[7] But the French were too overburdened with other handicaps to afford royal taxes on a par with their more robust contemporaries across the Channel. These various taxes, unjustly and cruelly levied, set against the poverty of those most heavily taxed, were to a considerable extent Louis' fault. Alas, here was a coronation oath he failed to honour.

POSITIVE ACHIEVEMENT

We have seen that Louis XIV was a conscientious and professional ruler. So was all his hard work in vain? Did he wholly fail to benefit his people? By no means. Indeed many of Louis' domestic policies were remarkably successful, certainly according to his own priorities; but the French benefited as well.

His most striking achievement was to create a disciplined society in which royal authority was respected. Perhaps there is no better proof of Louis' success here than the lack of protest against the raising of taxation during the latter part of the reign. There was a major revolt in Brittany in 1675. The Tard-Avisés rebelled in Quercy in 1707. But apart from the Camisards in the Cévennes, who were religiously motivated, there were no other major protests against the government – in sharp contrast to the revolts against Richelieu's and Mazarin's fiscal terrorism. Historians have debated the reasons for this docility, especially remarkable given the doubling of taxation in real terms during the twenty-five-year war (1688–1713). Certainly the ruthless suppression of revolts earlier in the reign, in the Boulonnais for instance, and in 1675, discouraged further protest. But perhaps the chief reason was the underlying respect for royal government, based on the mutually beneficial cooperation between crown and local oligarchies. Maybe Louis was not the only one to conclude from the Fronde that royal authority was best.

The crown's success was based on Louis' charismatic leadership of his nobility and at the same time the efficiency of royal administrators such as the intendants. But this success must not be exaggerated. Historians used to refer to a revolution in government achieved by 'le roi bureaucrat'. Nowadays assessments are more cautious. The very partial and imperfect nature of Louis' reforms is stressed. For example, he could not even abolish the anomaly of the pays d'États and the pays d'élections. Petitfils criticises Louis for not being more of a reformer. He emphasises the conservatism of Louis' outlook, comparing royal administration at the end of the reign to an old, worn-out car, kept going by a mechanic skilled at tinkering but refusing to buy a new engine.[8] Similarly, Sturdy reckons that 'by present-day standards, the France of Louis XIV was under-governed and under-administered ... Louis and his ministers were seeking seventeenth-century solutions to seventeenth-century problems'.[9] It is indeed the case that Louis was handicapped by the inevitable constraints of time and distance. France is a big place. There were a lot of French people, by no means all of them well disposed to the distant Bourbon. All one can say is that given the circumstances Louis and his collaborators made a fair job of ruling France, achieving definite though limited improvements in efficiency and public expectations.

The contrast between aspiration and achievement is well illustrated by Louis' legal reforms. Most of these were masterminded by Colbert, such as the Code Louis (1667), the Ordonnance Criminelle (1670) and the Ordonnance de Commerce (1673). The Ordonnance des Colonnies, otherwise known as the Code Noir, was published in 1685, two years after Colbert's death. Petitfils calls it 'terrible', because it legalised slavery and the slave-trade. In actual fact it was humane for its time, allowing slaves to marry, stipulating the appropriate food and medical care, making emancipation easier and establishing punishments for cruel owners. Would it be too cynical, though, to suggest that this ordonnance par excellence illustrates the problems of enforcement? Although Louis' laws were a creditable anticipation of the Code Napoléon (1804), there were so many vested interests, so many local laws already in existence, so much obstruction from provincial parlements that people benefited spasmodically. One of Molière's characters complains: 'My cause is just, but I have lost my case.'

A similar verdict has to be pronounced on the economic reforms attempted by Louis' ministers. Colbert's greatest achievement was to improve the efficiency of the tax system, reducing waste and corruption and ensuring that the king got something like his due. Real progress was made in the improvement of postal services and communications. The Canal du Midi linking the Atlantic and the Mediterranean was the most ambitious of many such projects. France had the best roads in Europe. But vested interests triumphed over such measures as Colbert's well-meaning dirigisme, involving detailed regulation of manufactures and trade. Louis showed that he had learnt from experience by reconvening the council of commerce in 1700, which he staffed with merchants. Mercantilism was replaced by free trade. War, which caused such damage to the agricultural economy, boosted the various industries that clothed and armed the king's warriors. But the expulsion of the Huguenots was on balance an economic own goal. Tariff war against England and Holland damaged French interests rather than the enemy. Above all the survival of tolls and internal trade barriers disrupted and delayed internal reform. At the end of Louis' reign England and Scotland constituted the largest common market in Europe. All in all a mixed picture. And nothing was done for agriculture.[10]

OPPOSITION

If Louis' subjects had plenty of grounds for complaint, can one identify a recognisable opposition? The answer is, yes and no. When does acute dissatisfaction with the government justify the term 'opposition'? Obviously armed rebellion is at one extreme of the picture, passive dissatisfaction at the other. The problem of identifying political dissent in the France of the *ancien régime* is that there was no such thing as a 'loyal opposition', in contrast to developments in early eighteenth-century Britain. Any opposition in France was *ipso facto* disloyal and indeed half way to treason. Furthermore, Louis XIV was a formidable and self-regarding monarch who was well aware that it was part of his job to maintain his untarnished prestige. It was therefore also his job to smash criticism in whatever form it emerged. Thus when the chevalier de Rohan conspired with the Dutch in 1674 to mount a rebellion in Normandy, he and three of his collaborators went to the scaffold. Mind you, Rohan's self-publicising placards were eccentric, to say the least, promising not only cooperation with the peasants but even with

Huguenots.[11] So he really had to go. Nevertheless, part of the problem of improving royal government was this concurrence of any form of criticism with treason. Apart from courageous court preachers such as Bossuet, opponents did not dare to criticise Louis to his face. When Monseigneur the Grand Dauphin timidly dared to mention the poor, he was slapped down with a vengeance. With his deeply conservative loyalty to his few ministerial clans, the Sun King too rarely saw new faces or listened to new ideas. So he rarely had to take on board suggestions as to where he had gone wrong and where he could put matters right.

One way round the problem was to publish criticism abroad and smuggle it into France. Especially after the expulsion of the Huguenots, this form of opposition became widespread. Some of this criticism was of a high literary quality and of real political content, such as the bitter invectives of the Protestant Pierre Jurieu who predicted in 1686 that 'the Beast' would fall from power within three years. Some of it, on the other hand, was scurrilous knock-about stuff, passed from hand to hand in smoky taverns and coffee shops, defying the attention of de la Reynie, d'Argesson and the Paris police. For instance, one such pamphlet described in loving detail Père La Chaise in bed with Mme de Maintenon – who thought that the Jesuit was in fact the king: 'She embraced him with such amorous embrace that the poor Father thought that he would expire in this charming exercise.'[12] London competed with Amsterdam, for example exporting *The Most Christian Turk, Or a View of the Life and Bloody Reign of Louis XIV containing an account of his monstrous Birth, afterwards his own unjust enterprises in War and Peace, the blasphemous titles given him, his treachery to England.*[13] Or Parisians enjoyed reading: 'The grandfather is a braggart, the son an imbecile, the grandson a clown, what a lovely family. How I pity you, you poor French people, having to submit to this regime. Do as the English have done, that's good enough advice for you.'

Whatever the origin – and some of this invective was home grown – no one could miss the frequent references to 'the holy whore' and to the king's unpopular ministers: 'If the situation were not so tragic, we would die of laughter.' Especially damaging was a parody of the Lord's Prayer: 'Our Father at Versailles, / Your name is no longer hallowed, / Your kingdom is a shambles, / Your will is no longer done. / Give us the bread which we lack, / May our enemies forgive our blunders, / Save us from Chamillart and La Maintenon'. It is impossible to assess the impact of such satirical invective. Possibly it had real impact on the

Satire

desacralisation of the monarchy (see Chapter 11). It is worth bearing in mind that a drunken mob hooted and jeered at Louis' corpse on its way to burial at Saint Denis.

Towards the end of the Nine Years War a serious opposition movement emerged in Louis' own household – just about the only place where explicit criticism could survive. Peace treaties traditionally created opportunities for reform as the pressures of war subsided. While long-drawn-out negotiations finally produced the Treaty of Ryswick, a group of idealistic aristocrats and clergy gathered round the duc de Bourgogne, Louis' grandson, who, it was assumed, would eventually succeed to the throne.

The leading light was the duc's tutor, François de Salignac de la Mothe-Fénelon. His letter to the king describing France as a great charnel house has been quoted as evidence for the state of France at the end of the seventeenth century. Louis may or may not have read this letter. Similar criticism, however, appeared in Fénelon's widely read novel, Les Aventures de Télémaque, which was published in 1699. It tells how Telemachus, Odysseus' son and heir (Burgundy), was advised by the elderly statesman Mentor (Fénelon). The whole book is a thinly disguised criticism of Louis XIV's policies and methods: 'The king owes the people all of his time, labour and affection … he is worthy of kingship only if he forgets himself and sacrifices himself for the public good.' Where have we heard this before? They appeared in Louis' memoirs, composed for his son thirty-five years before. Fénelon's point is that Louis has not adhered to his own principles. Fénelon was especially dangerous, as his pupil the duke was devoted to him – and with good reason, for Fénelon was a most attractive and impressive man.

Another luminary was Saint-Simon, the brilliant diarist who wrote in sorrow rather than in anger, in that he admired and liked the king. But alas! He had gone wrong. Saint-Simon's basic philosophy was that the aristocracy should be restored at the centre of government. He believed that Louis XIV had erred disastrously by excluding the ancient nobility in favour of low-born bureaucrats. Louis was 'run' by his ministers and his mistresses. Saint-Simon had a particular loathing for 'the old trollop', Mme de Maintenon, and for the king's bastards whom Louis had scandalously legitimised and promoted. It was the bastards' golden age. It was no coincidence that Saint-Simon admired the king's nephew Orléans, who emerged at the end of the reign as the rightful, legitimate regent, contrary to the wishes of Louis and Mme de Maintenon who promoted the cause of the odious 'limping bastard', the duc de Maine.

Had these embittered noblemen and clerics anything worth saying or any serious proposals to offer? What were their policies? Certainly Fénelon favoured a peaceful foreign policy – but then so did the king by this late stage of his reign. Fénelon was joined by Abbé Claude Fleury and by Boisguilbert in their advocacy of 'Christian agrarianism'. Agricultural reforms would improve the economic plight of the peasantry *and their morality*. It says a lot for the unworldliness of these admirable philanthropists that they were as concerned for the peasants' souls as for their bodies. Indeed they fought shy of the real improvement needed in the countryside, an increase in the amount of coin in circulation, which they believed would encourage pride and avarice. When Orléans did eventually become regent, Burgundy and Fénelon were dead, having narrowly predeceased Louis XIV. Nevertheless, Orléans and his aristocratic friends made a fair job of helping France to recover from defeat and bankruptcy.

In the short term, however, Burgundy was absorbed into the bosom of the royal family when in 1699 he married Marie-Adelaide of Savoy, who rapidly became the child-bride favourite of Louis and Maintenon. Burgundy was then groomed for high command in the army, with disastrous results. Orléans was disgraced after his father's death in 1701. Fénelon fell out of favour because of his loyalty to Madame Guyon. But he also infuriated the controller-general Louis de Pontchartrain by opposing the government's economic policies. As a result he was packed off to his archdiocese of Cambrai where he had a unique opportunity of observing at first hand the deplorable results of the Sun King's foreign policy. Burgundy kept sneaking the odd surreptitious visit to his guru in his exile at Cambrai. Although Vauban courageously published his *Dîme Royale*, which pleaded for a just system of taxation, to all intents and purposes the opposition was condemned to watching and waiting for the Sun King's demise.[14]

Not, however, before there mushroomed a massive crisis for the monarchy in which the 'opposition' mounted a final challenge to the ultimate display of Ludoquattorzian idiocy. In 1713, under intense pressure from Louis, who in his turn was under intense pressure from his wife and from his confessor, Pope Innocent XII reluctantly issued the bull *Unigenitus*. This papal pronouncement not only condemned Jansenism but forbade the laity to read such subversive books as the Bible. It was clearly a triumph for Jesuit ultramontanism against French Gallicanism. It brought down on Louis' thoroughly deserving head a storm of protest. Fénelon, who disliked the Jesuits, kept out of it, but the bull was rejected by the Parlement of Paris, by the Sorbonne and by the archbishop of Paris and a significant proportion of bishops who appealed to a General Council of the Church. Pontchartrain, the chancellor and long-serving royalist minister, resigned. Now this *was* opposition! The national cause was no longer represented by the crown. It had been hijacked by the Jansenists and their admirers.

Louis reacted furiously, bullying the Parlement and the Sorbonne into compliance, and threatening to call his own French General Council, though he died before this interesting proposal could be implemented. Archbishop Noailles remained defiant, and the Jansenist protest survived into the next reign and indeed until the Revolution of 1789. Louis' resort to *Unigenitus* was his greatest own goal and ensured that his reign ended in bitterness and frustration. The one-time exponent of nationalist Gallicanism had been compelled to call in the papacy against his own people. Louis had turned his back on the tradition of defending France against papal interference. The monarchy was thereby desacrilised and denationalised. What a result! Who says there was no opposition!

THE BETTER HALF, OR SOLDIERS OF SATAN?

The latter part of Louis XIV's personal rule was not exactly the golden age of feminism. How could it be when all the old structures that made women legal minors and excluded them from public office and the universities remained in place? Women who bucked the trend could be counted on the fingers of one hand. The Margaret Thatcher of Louis XIV's last years was the amazing, unique Françoise de Maintenon, the uncrowned queen of France and unacknowledged National Mother Superior – to whom we shall return. Adelaide of Savoy was the favourite to whom nothing could be denied. Louise-Renée de Kéroualle, duchess of Portsmouth, was Louis XIV's unofficial ambassador to the Court of St James, promoting French interests as a reward for slaking Charles II's lust. Mme de Scudéry advocated the education of women, but she was a lone voice. Mme Guyon, the prayer specialist, had her brief moment of glory before the Bastille swallowed her up and then spewed her into ignominious exile.

French women's most high-profiled political activity was the bread riot, housewives being naturally aware of the ever-increasing cost of living. Their most notable acts of ideological defiance were performed by Huguenot women who courageously kept the flame of Protestantism alive when their more high-profiled husbands sought safety in obscurity. Similarly, the redoubtable Jansenist nuns at Port-Royal continued to defy official bigotry before they were carted off to remote nunneries.

Women continued to get a shabby deal from the medical profession, though the normal bias to the rich was reversed in childbirth. The poor had a better chance of survival. Let Princess Marie-Anne-Christine-Victoire of Bavaria, the dauphin's ugly wife who was nonetheless a capable linguist, a graceful dancer and a clean eater, represent her high-born sisters. When she was brought to bed on 5 August 1682 with the future duc de Bourgogne, Louis XIV thoughtfully imposed Clément the surgeon on the proceedings instead of the usual midwife. Masses were said throughout Versailles. The king personally supervised the birth, together with assorted ambassadors, foreign princes and courtiers. The dauphine suffered excruciatingly. The weaker she got, the more Clément bled her. She dreaded the arrival of a girl, though Louis gallantly assured her that he would not hold it against her. At last the baby emerged. The news that it was a boy prompted the courtiers to hug the king and make a bonfire of the available furniture and parquet floors. Meanwhile Clément wrapped the dauphine in the skin of a newly flayed sheep and prevented her from sleeping for several days. As an additional precaution, she was kept in suffocating darkness for a fortnight.

Not surprisingly women were the chief victims of the Sun King's crusade to stamp out vice, inspired by his moralistic second wife, Mme de Maintenon. Seventeenth-century Catholic reformers consistently saw Eve rearing her ugly head as the betrayer and seducer of men. Women were described as 'soldiers of Satan'. Friendship with a wicked man was alleged to be less dangerous than with a virtuous woman. Prostitution was always caused by 'fallen women', never 'fallen men'. Women were exhorted to follow the example of 'the Second Eve' – that is to say, Mary the Virgin – and dedicate themselves to the service of God or, as a second best, their husbands and children. But this ideal was infrequently attained, so that wives, daughters and female servants were regularly beaten. 'Hé! Quelq'un!' was the imperious demand for service, usually female. Under the strictest supervision, reliably orthodox women were allowed to instruct newly converted ex-Protestants. But female progress in the medical profession, for instance through training as midwives, was dealt a fatal blow by the revelations of the poisons affair. The close links between prostitution, fortune telling and murder suggested that the old Eve was still alive and well.

Not that there was a shortage of vice to clear up, if the women of the Court were taken as an example. Even after the king had reformed himself, he found it hard to reform his court. Vice went underground, as it were. Various forms of dissipation continued, though more and more behind the scenes, or in Paris. Louis' illegitimate daughters, for instance, surreptitiously borrowed tobacco and pipes from the king's Swiss guards, as smoking in public by women was frowned upon until the turn of the century. Court ladies continued to gamble, eat voraciously and get drunk. Sexual activities flourished. In 1702 Comtesse de Murat was exiled for lesbianism. The Englishman Philip Skippon was shocked by French women's coarse language. At court he would have heard the Duchesse Mazarin boasting of her own sexual equipment or the princess of Monaco belittling the king's. Ladies' dresses became increasingly revealing, as cleavages plunged and hemlines were raised – even for attendance at church. Several court ladies such as Mmes de Saulx and de la Trimouilles became lax with regard to personal hygiene, relieving themselves where they stood or tipping their excrement over the balcony at the opera. Dissipation flourished in Paris and in the provinces, beyond the baleful gaze of the monarch and his wife. The poison affair briefly lifted the curtain, which concealed spectacular vice not only at court but in the capital. Louis overreacted to the affair, partly because he was so appalled by it.[15]

Louis, however, was determined that female conduct should revert to the high standards of his mother's time. He now launched a great moral offensive against female vice. Prostitutes were whipped and locked up. Abortionists were hanged as murderers. Adulteresses were sent to the Saltpetrière jail if their husbands refused to take them back. The police were perpetually kept busy pursuing vice – and all the while they were exhorted to supply the king with more details. Louis took a particular interest in the discouragement of prostitution in the army. Prostitutes caught servicing the troops were whipped and disfigured by losing their ears and noses. One general was commended for throwing 800 prostitutes off a high bridge into a river. All the more bizarre was the survival of a handful of women who served as soldiers and whose sex was often only discovered when they were killed or wounded. But then, recruitment had become such an acute problem that Louis could not be choosy. Jeanne Bensa, who served first as a valet and then signed up as a soldier with the Regiment de Bourbon, served in Italy and was discharged with a royal gratuity of 40 écus. She had proved her worth in a man's world.

Were men totally immune to the royal crusader's campaign? Almost, so it seemed. Since the Counter-Reformation church reiterated that 'Satan's soldiers' were usually the culprits, men were only disciplined when women were not involved. Sodomy logically demanded the punishment of men only. Louis watched with approval when his adolescent bastard the count de Vermandois was stripped and thrashed for homosexual relations with an older courtier. Louis approved the lash for laziness as well, witness Bossuet's 'tutorials'. Once Montausier, the dauphin's governor, was asked why he had just beaten his charge – 'Can't remember', he replied. The magistrates, policemen and other officials were all men, however, who relished the king's determination that women should pay the most frequent penalties. Rousseau inherited seventeenth-century prejudices when he described women as 'the sex which must obey'. Eighteenth-century Londoners, it should be remembered, regarded a trip to Bridewell to see the female inmates stripped to the waist and beaten as an appropriate Sunday afternoon pastime.

MME DE MAINTENON: A CASE-STUDY

The assumptions, prejudices and priorities of the later part of Louis' reign are illustrated by the extraordinary career of Mme de Maintenon. She makes an appropriate case-study, both with regard to the status of women in the latter part of Louis XIV's reign, and his own contribution and attitudes. What are we to make of her? 'Hating Mme de Maintenon is a durable French pastime', according to John Conley.[16] Certainly she was loathed by many of her contemporaries – Montespan, Liselotte, Saint-Simon, Orléans. Indeed, there was much to loathe. 'The Old Turd' was smug, sanctimonious and vindictive, especially towards those she disliked, often for no apparent reason. But she was also intelligent, affectionate and idealistic – contrasting qualities that make her so fascinating. Certainly her influence was widely resented, though just how widespread that influence was is a question about which modern historians are sceptical. Robin Briggs, for example, writes: 'Madame de Maintenon is one of those irritating insoluble problems, I fear – I just don't see how one can ever hope to know what her influence really amounted to. The king talked to a lot of people – that was one of his techniques – and was very careful to keep everyone guessing about what advice he took seriously.'[17] Louis certainly consulted her. 'What does Your Solidity think?' he would say during the council meetings held in her room while she meekly bowed her head over her embroidery. But Briggs is right: Louis – to Maintenon's disgust – quite often ignored her. She disapproved of his foreign policy, for instance. She was perhaps more influential over the matter of appointments than policies. In particular she boosted the prospects of her favourite, the duc de Maine, at the expense of Philip d'Orléans who outraged her by reading Rabelais during Mass, or Chamillart, or Villeroy. There is also her correspondence with her friend Mme des Ursins – letters from the uncrowned queen of France to the uncrowned queen of Spain. Maybe.

Mme de Maintenon's actual career was indisputably spectacular: from impoverished orphan, to wife and then widow of the Z-shaped Scarron, to governess of the Sun King's illegitimate children, to the Sun King's bed – first in all probability as mistress, than as wife. No wonder she was envied and feared. Hypocrisy is the main charge levelled against her by contemporaries and historians. Françoise's brother frequently dined out on his hilarious stories about his sister's sexual adventures in her younger days, which included lesbian relationships and various affairs with male aristocratic lovers. Once Racine disgraced himself by referring to Scarron's obscene verses; Maintenon went scarlet and Louis remembered that he had some paperwork to finish. But here is the lady herself, attempting to give her pupils a different picture. Consider her account of the famous chair-tipping episode with the king, mentioned in Chapter 3, which she coyly recalls in the third person:

> You must avoid men and never give them the least liberty with you. One day I was in the company of the king. In the room were many other women seated on chairs, because His Majesty gives many privileges to those who have the honour of seeing him often. The king was still young and, as he chatted away, he pulled out the chairs of these ladies, letting them fall on the floor. They

ended up in some very comical postures. However, he came to one lady – who wasn't from a more noble house than the others – and said, 'Ah! I wouldn't dare with this one.' In these few words he pronounced an entire eulogy about this lady. It's not by some affectation that you establish your reputation. It's by proper reserve in the presence of men.

No one would guess that 'this lady' would subsequently share the king's bed. Quite the reverse – the only way to preserve one's reputation is to allow men no liberties whatsoever. 'You must realise how swiftly men notice the particular weaknesses of our sex and just how we may be conquered.' Madame then went on to analyse and condemn a woman who had joined injudiciously in male laughter – and she had been so unwise as to walk out alone, apart from a male servant who followed behind her. She should have had an older, female, companion.

She moaned frequently about her life at court. Yesterday and today are full of people in high office who protest that 'I never wanted the job in the first place', none more so than Mme de Maintenon. 'What I find so consoling in the state where I am is that God has placed me here. I never wanted for a single moment to be in it. When I arrived at court, I thought that when I had accumulated a little wealth – because I had none on arrival – I would retire to a private house somewhere.' Her girls would have been unaware of the governess's excitement when the king began to court her, or the ruthlessness with which she outmanoeuvred and replaced her friend and former employer Madame de Montespan. She complains with surprisingly indiscreet disloyalty about the king's demands on her: 'The prince thinks that my only pleasure lies in seeing him and being loved by him … There is nothing so cruel as to sacrifice your life, your work, and your time for someone whom you don't really love.'

Perhaps the most remarkable passages concern the education of women. Mme de Maintenon told her staff at Saint-Cyr to discourage the girls from reading books, for instance about Alexander, king of Macedon. That was by definition a profane book. Only works of devotion were permissible. And they must be the right works of devotion: 'The Jansenists have written defamatory letters, full of bitterness and animosity and falsehoods, against the Jesuits, because this order has always been the firmest in denouncing innovations.' Mme de Maintenon, who was the personification of unctuous religiosity, claimed that 'heretics have always appeared under a mask of feigned piety'. As an ex-Huguenot, she presumably knew all about that. Nor were the girls to be encouraged to think for themselves, even on theological issues. 'I am grateful for being a woman, because we women are incapable of understanding theology. Women always settle for half-knowledge. The little they know usually makes them vain, disdainful, garrulous, and contemptuous of solid things.' Who would have guessed that it was Françoise's well-stocked mind as much as her shapely body that had first attracted Louis?[18]

But this was the woman the king delighted to honour, just as Louis was her man. Like any loving married couple they grew old together, reinforcing each other's prejudices. Together they moulded France socially. One must not generalise too much. Wendy Gibson portrays a colourful, varied picture of feminine activity, which contradicts sweeping allegations of gloomy repression of women by men. Nevertheless Louis and Françoise ensured that it remained a man's world. One would expect nothing else from Louis. What is extraordinary is that Françoise clearly reinforced his chauvinism. She had risen to the highest position available to her sex. A witty courtier suggested to her that when she got to Heaven she would marry God the Father. But, despite her marriage to Louis XIV, she allowed her position to be in many ways lower than the lowest position available to men. Her views on the woman's place in society, on the education of women, on women's role in the church are as reactionary as her husband's. Given that she had a good mind and plenty of common sense, to say nothing of Christian idealism, she should surely have known better. Was she merely the helpless prisoner of the current *mentalité?* Maybe. Yet it is fascinating to reflect that she was the contemporary of Queen Anne – who may not have been very bright but was assuredly no push-over in a man's world – and of Sarah, duchess of Marlborough, who had no compunction in pushing men all over the place.

WHAT SORT OF FRANCE?

Louis XIV and Mme de Maintenon knew exactly what sort of France they were trying to create. They wanted the French to be respectful, devout and clean-living. Society was to be dominated by the Counter-Reformation church. Not only heresy, but any form of deviation from the strictest orthodoxy was to be discouraged. One King, One Law, One Faith! France was meant to be a man's world, an orthodox, devout

The values of the Rulers.

Catholic man's world, from the king's palace to the peasant's hovel. Deference was the supreme virtue – the deference of women towards men, Christians towards the Catholic hierarchy, plebeians towards noblemen, everyone towards the king. Abroad, the European states were to be similarly deferential, acknowledging the God-ordained hegemony of the king of France. On the whole the Sun King and his secret wife came astonishingly close to success in achieving their aims, or at least some of them.

For there were flaws in this conformist, conservative structure. The *Unigenitus* affair illustrated the limitations of the king's authority at home. Abroad, half a century of warfare had compelled the Sun King to make concessions to his European rivals, which he bitterly deplored and resented. These flaws will be analysed in the concluding chapter. So far as Louis' relationship with his people is concerned – the subject of Chapter 3 and of this chapter – the following points should be borne in mind. First, not even Louis XIV could stop French people thinking for themselves. The age of the Enlightenment would make the Sun King's backward-looking conservatism increasingly inadequate, indeed absurd. Second, the problems of poverty and injustice had been swept under the carpet, not solved. However successful Louis XIV had been in suppressing revolts (for instance, against his taxes to finance warfare), there was a great seething tide of resentment building up that would eventually burst its banks, sweeping away the *ancien régime*. In other words, the sort of France Louis had created was by no means what he intended. La France contained the seeds of bitter divisions – religious, economic and political. She would eventually become 'Marianne'. Contrary to the Sun King's intentions, she would soon establish the right to speak with conflicting voices, many of them iconoclastic and subversive.

11

CONCLUSION

VIGNETTE: A LAST GLIMPSE OF THE SUN KING (SUNDAY, 11 AUGUST 1715)

As all the windows were open, a gale blew through Mme de Maintenon's sitting-room at Versailles. The Sun King's bleak expression lowered the temperature even more. He was no longer the exuberant, cheerful, upbeat extrovert of happier times, no longer gorgeously apparelled, but now soberly dressed in a forbidding, brown surcoat. He glared at Daguesseau, the Procureur-général, as he apprehensively approached the king. He was right to be apprehensive. After he and two colleagues had led the protests against the papal bull *Unigenitus*, they had been threatened with the Bastille by their enraged monarch. Parlement had responded by refusing to register the bull without reservations. Daguesseau had had the effrontery to hail Noailles, the archbishop of Paris, as the 'man of the nation' for condemning the bull. Daguesseau had even described the bull as 'the idol of Roman grandeur'. He had suggested that *Unigenitus* should be publicly displayed 'as a durable proof and an eternal monument to the pope's fallibility'. Now he had been summoned to the presence, on his own this time, to be rebuked and browbeaten into submission. But he was prepared to resist this last assault by the dying old bully. Daguesseau's wife had ordered him to accept imprisonment rather than give in.

It was not a happy interview. Louis XIV shouted and blustered. He stamped his foot with rage. He broke his cane on the marble desktop. He grabbed Daguesseau by the throat. Louis furiously shouted: 'If the parlementaires persisted in refusing to register the bull, he would resort to a *lit de justice* and would make them crawl on their bellies. Alternatively, he would preside over a national synod of the whole French church to get the result he wanted.' It was a distressing and undignified scene.

Often the king's interviews were witnessed by Mme de Maintenon from her sentry box, covered in red damask, in the furthest corner from the window. We do not know whether she was there on that unhappy Sunday morning. But Louis would certainly have asked for her opinion after the still-defiant Daguesseau had departed. Equally certainly she would have replied: 'God will forgive you for your many, grievous sins because for the last thirty years you have tried to be a good Catholic.'

This vignette forms a fitting farewell to the Sun King as he approached death. It illustrates his frustration as he experienced the result of his miscalculations. He had mishandled the Jansenist problem – and he knew it. Cardinal Noailles was indeed the real 'man of the nation'. Louis had alienated the nation by his own provocative, insensitive ineptitude. If he had enough self-control to stop short of insulting Parlement's representative by imprisoning him, it was he who had boxed himself into a corner. His arrogant bigotry had reaped its deserved reward. The limitations of absolutism were laid bare. As Lavisse put it, Louis' rule constituted 'despotism tempered by disobedience'. Or as Goubert suggests, 'perhaps it was the other way round'. But it was certainly what Louis deserved. On this occasion he had got it hopelessly wrong.

SUNDOWN (1 SEPTEMBER 1715)

The combination of willpower and a magnificent constitution enabled the Sun King to live almost until his seventy-seventh birthday, a vast age for those days. In so doing he had defied crippling misfortunes, both public and private, massive overeating and the ministrations of his doctors. Mme de Maintenon's worst appointment had been the arrogant and incompetent Guy-Crescent Fagon. Louis' fatal tendency to trust the experts had cruelly rebounded on him over the years as his dentists shattered his jaw and his doctors purged, bled and tortured him. Fagon was the worst of the lot, combining ignorance with malice. He happily spread the libel that Philip of Orléans was poisoning the royal family, whereas the truth was that he himself, albeit unintentionally, was their murderer. But not even Fagon could kill the king, even when his heart was broken by military disasters and family bereavements. Indeed it is astonishing how well Louis remained until his last summer. Despite shouldering the conduct of war, peace negotiations and an ever-increasing governmental machine, despite the premature deaths of virtually the whole royal family, despite the medical 'cures' he meekly accepted from Fagon and his fellow quacks, the mid-septuagenarian found the physical and mental resilience to soldier on. Occasionally the old lion could still roar, as when the English ambassador complained that the fortifications at Dunkirk had not been demolished: 'Not so long ago I controlled the houses of other princes – don't remind me by interfering in mine.' But alas, government was no longer a 'delightful pastime'; rather, it was a grim obligation. Nevertheless, Louis never flinched: 'We owe ourselves to the public', as he had observed when Adelaide was reluctant to dance.

The king's nearest and dearest tried to distract him with concerts, hunts and promenades. But Louis was tired and depressed by seemingly intractable problems. Parlement and clergy remained defiant in their rejection of *Unigenitus*. The treasury was 6,500 million livres in debt. Above all, Louis worried about the succession. He shared Mme de Maintenon's detestation of Philip of Orléans who would automatically become regent on behalf of Louis' great-grandson, unless somehow he could be replaced by the old couple's favourite, the 'limping bastard' otherwise known as the duc de Maine. Unfortunately no one rated this superficial lightweight whose skills as a mimic were indisputable, but who had displayed few other abilities. Although Alfred Cobban called him 'pious and honourable',[1] contemporaries did not rate him. When he accompanied the infant dauphin at a parade of the royal guards commanded by Orléans, the troops laughed at the favourite and clustered round their popular commander. Louis did his best, not only by legitimising Maine and his brother Toulouse but by persuading Parlement to recognise their rights to succeed to the throne. But he acknowledged reality when he said to Maine, 'However much I exalt you now, I can do nothing for you when I am gone, for then you will be on your own.'

Shortly before dying, Louis committed a strange letter to Marshal Villeroy, to be handed to Louis XV at the age of fifteen:

> Follow the advice of the duc de Maine. Protect him from the greed of his enemies. If he suffers from their malice, you must restore the situation at my death, as much with regard to religion as for that which applies to the duc de Maine. Have confidence in him, follow his advice, if he dies protect his children.[2]

This revealing letter demonstrates Louis' love for his favourite child (there is no reference to the comte de Toulouse, still less to Louis' illegitimate daughters) and his wish to do precisely what he had warned Maine he could not do – that is, protect him from beyond the grave. However, when Mme de Maintenon and Maine floated the idea of setting up a regency council there and then in order to tie Orléans' hands in Maine's favour, Louis erupted angrily at the implication that he was past it.[3]

During the early summer of 1715 the old king was clearly not himself. Courtiers were saddened by his drawn face and weary demeanour. He had lost weight and had to be propelled round the palace in an armchair with castors. He had even lost his appetite – so something must certainly be wrong. When he hunted, he rode alone in the barouche that he had once shared with his beloved Adelaide, whom nowadays no one could replace. Mme de Maintenon and Fagon dismissed suggestions that Louis was unwell. When his leg began to hurt him, Fagon diagnosed sciatica, wrapped it in bandages soaked in Burgundy and ordered his patient to sleep in feather quilts to make him sweat. As a result Louis could not sleep at all. Torcy 'accidentally' let slip a story in a London newspaper, which he was reading to the king, that bets were being laid as to whether he would last until the end of the month. Louis joked about it at dinner, but he was clearly depressed. A well-meant attempt was made to cheer him up when a Persian entrepreneur was dressed up as the ambassador so that Louis could receive him in his full pomp, recalling the glories of happier days. But the attempt failed.

By August the king was in agony. His leg – that shapely leg that had delighted the spectators of royal ballets long ago and he had still displayed magnificently for Rigaud's portrait only a few years before – had now become blotched and swollen, so that even Fagon recognised the symptoms of gangrene. A committee of doctors and surgeons recommended amputation. But at last Louis rejected the experts' advice.

'I am not afraid to die', he countered – for he realised that he was mortally ill. His death was frightful, acted out in the full glare of publicity demanded by contemporary usage. He was in constant pain. He had no appetite. He soiled his linen without being aware of it. 'How long?' he asked Maréchal, his surgeon, on Sunday, 25 August, the feast of Saint Louis, when he had fainted after listening to a military tattoo. 'We think your Majesty will live until Wednesday', was the educated guess. No such luck. Louis' agony was prolonged until the following Sunday.

Louis, who had always known how to live like a king, knew how to die like one. He bore his suffering with dignity and courage, patiently putting up with tortures imposed by his doctors who hacked at and punctured his suppurating leg and poured quack-medicines down his throat. The dying man was badgered by his wife and confessor to make a new will. There was to be a Council of Regency to keep Orléans in check, while Maine would be responsible for the little king's safety and 'the magnificent cretin' Villeroy for his upbringing. Louis knew perfectly well that the will was not worth the paper on which it was written. But he signed it nevertheless. 'Now perhaps they will leave me in peace', he whispered. Again, what a hope! Maintenon instructed Père Le Tellier to make sure that the king confessed not only his sins but the *right* ones. When the doctors suggested that Louis would be cheered by a visit from Noailles, the temporarily disgraced archbishop of Paris, with whom Louis wished to be reconciled, this was vetoed by his wife unless Noailles condemned Jansenism. Cardinal Rohan was substituted, a bizarre choice for the consolation of the dying sinner as he was probably Louis' son. But Rohan was not a Jansenist.

Louis said goodbye to his tearful courtiers to whom he apologised for not being a better master. He blessed his children. He thanked Mme de Maintenon for her loyalty, despite his failure to make her happy. And then he had a last conversation with his five-year-old great-grandson. After kissing the frightened little boy, the dying king spoke justly famous words:

> Little one, you are about to become a great king. Never forget your obligations to God. Try to relieve your people as much as you can, something that it has been my misfortune to be unable to do, because of the necessities of the state. Do not follow the bad example which I have set you. I have often gone to war too lightly. Do not imitate me in that, but be a prince of peace.

Always think of accounting to God for your actions. I give you Father Tellier as a confessor: follow his advice, and always remember your obligations to your governess, Madame de Ventadour.[4]

According to the incomparable Bluche: 'This confession had been inspired by his confessor. The proof lies in the fact that the king was confessing to faults of which he was innocent. This book has attempted to prove that the wars of the reign, with the exception of the Dutch War, were wholly justified, especially the last.'[5] *This* book has attempted to prove nothing of the kind. That apart, Bluche is surely wrong in imparting to the king's confessor the inspiration for his dying words, which are in fact pure Maintenon. During the whole of their married life she had advocated sheer, uninterrupted pacifism – many would say, to her credit. Her husband had refused to listen – until now when he was dying. The cynics would say that she had at last got him where she wanted him and that he now responded by expressing the politically correct line, out of fear of his wife and of hellfire. A kinder verdict would be that Louis meant what he said. For he was confessing real sins and mistakes he really had committed and that at the last apparently recognised for what they were. According to Saint-Simon, he also regretted that he had been too fond of building. But this admission almost certainly reflects the little duc's view of what the dying king *should* have said.

On his deathbed Louis exclaimed: 'I am going, but the state remains.' He was irritated by the self-indulgent hullabaloo of his female relations: 'Do they think that I am immortal?' he grumbled. To Mme de Maintenon he whispered that he had always thought that dying was a problem – 'but I find it easy'. He gave clear-headed and typically practical instructions for conveying the new king to the healthy environment of Vincennes. He expressed faith in God's mercy. He heartily joined with his priests in the prayers for the dying. According to several witnesses, the Sun King's last words were 'O my God, come to my aid, hasten to help me.' He took extreme unction and fell asleep during the night of 31 August. He died early on 1 September without regaining consciousness, four days short of his seventy-seventh birthday. By this time Mme de Maintenon was tucked up in bed at Saint-Cyr.

After the doctors had enjoyed their final opportunity of poking around in their master's body in order to dispatch Louis' heart to Val des Grâces, his corpse was taken to Saint-Denis. On the way it was insulted by a drunken, delirious mob, which issued forth from strategically sited wine booths. Popular libels celebrating the king's death included: 'Here lies Louis the Little, / He whom the people raved about, / Don't pray to God for his soul, / Such a monster never had one.' Meanwhile Versailles was deserted. The courtiers had gone home now that the old puppet master no longer pulled their strings.

THE MAN IN THE GOLDEN MASK

So what was he like? A recent biographer, Geoffrey Treasure, claims that 'going towards his Christian death, defying pain, considerate to the needs of the state and the feelings of those around him, Louis XIV seems impressively to be the same man essentially as the intense and committed young king who took the Coronation oath and Christian sacrament in the Cathedral of Reims sixty-two years before'.[6] Well, yes and no. Certainly Louis maintained the highest standards of dignity and self-control throughout his long reign, for ever on parade, determinedly keeping his cards close to his chest. At the end of his life he was still the same buttoned-up authoritarian and inflexible Catholic that he had always been. Nevertheless, over such a long period of time there were bound to be changes. For instance, the king's marriage to Françoise de Maintenon (1683) profoundly altered his personality and outlook on the world. Then there were the catastrophes of his last decade, which taught Louis le Grand to be humble. 'God seems to have forgotten all I have done for him' (after Ramillies) became 'God has punished me for my sins' (after Oudenarde). Louis resembled his uncle Charles I whose misfortunes at the end of his disastrous career inculcated a certain measure of self-criticism and undoubtedly made him a kinder and more likeable man. Similarly, one can warm to Louis' brave acceptance of defeat and his heartbroken tears of bereavement.

Whether he was always a likeable man is hard to say, simply because he was so unknowable. He certainly had a sense of humour, though it was sometimes tinged with malice. Take for instance Louis' laughter at Mme de Maintenon's expense when she grieved at the queen's death. He enjoyed the company of children, or at any rate liked to have them around. He was certainly fond of his dogs, and fed them personally. But the mask was always there. From first to last Louis was courteous, urbane and even-tempered, a concise and judicious conversationalist, a well-informed and self-controlled manipulator of women and men. But his emotions hardly ever showed through this impassive exterior. Bluche reckons that Louis only lost his temper on three occasions – with Colbert, Louvois and Lauzun. All these episodes have been covered in this book. He also lost control of himself when Maine was proved to be a coward, and there was the furious shouting match with Monsieur that brought about the latter's fatal stroke. There may have been other lapses, though one suspects very few. Louis wept when Adelaide died. But his self-control following other bereavements, and after the defeats in the War of the Spanish Succession, was phenomenal. Courtiers worried if the king was slightly downcast – for that might indicate bad news from Flanders. But equally he might have been suffering from gout or tooth-ache. He remained a hard man to know.

What are we to make of Louis' insensitivity? Did it result from iron dedication to the task in hand or was he quite simply rather a cold man? He could be so very unfeeling and inconsiderate, especially towards women. The famous coach trip to Flanders during the War of Devolution when Marie Thérèse had to put up with La Vallière and Montespan is an exam-ple. Courtiers were embarrassed when Louis was delighted by the news that Adelaide had miscarried: 'Thank God, I shall no longer be thwarted in my travels, but can now come and go as I please' – and anyway, appar-ently the dead baby was only a girl. Louis consistently ignored Mme de Maintenon's fear of draughts by opening all available windows so that she complained of 'American hurricanes'. Then when she caught cold, he called her '*L'Enrhumée*' ('Sniveller'). On occasions Louis could be down-right cruel, for instance when Vermondois was thrashed in his presence for a homosexual affair or when he had a peasant woman beaten for com-plaining that her son had died during the construction of the waterworks at Versailles. When an old *frondeur* broke cover to feed and shelter a lost hunting party, Louis had him executed. He treated Fouquet ruthlessly, and showed gross brutality towards the Rhinelanders and the Huguenots. In other words, he could behave like a monster.

On the other hand, Louis could be kindness itself – for example, towards the unlucky (James II, or Villeroy), towards his servants (he would greet Le Nôtre with a bear-hug), towards a gatekeeper who was berated by courtiers for not being aware of his duties. He made a point of showing Mary of Modena round the gardens at Versailles when her husband was fighting unsuccessfully in Ireland. His observation that his long-serving valet Bontemps 'never said an unkind word about anyone and said something charitable every day'[7] is as much to Louis' credit as to Bontemps'. Then there was the time he sent Burgundy off to Mass when Chamillart was about to be sacked – which he knew would distress the young man.

So if there was indeed this contrast between unfeeling cruelty and real thoughtfulness, why the inconsistency? Part of the explanation is that Louis was naturally a kind man, but that he was spoiled. Years of adulation and cosseting made him insensitive and selfish. His arrogance and self-love, his vanity and pride, often prevented him from appreciating the feelings of others. For instance, when Marie Thérèse died, his comment that this was the only time that she had caused him any bother was conceivably an example of wry self-reproach, but more probably the reaction of a total egotist. But what could be expected, given the adulation of the god-king? Lavisse's remark that Louis XIV frequently seemed to do God a favour is fair comment. Yet while he ruled his court with a rod of iron, his courtiers not only respected but liked him. A friendly glance or a thoughtful word could make someone's day. 'Madame, you and I are too fat to fit into a barouche', he remarked to the duchesse de Berry who loved him for it, just as Liselotte forgave him for nudging her when she fell asleep during sermons. Louis addressed only three remarks to Saint-Simon in fifteen years, but that ferocious arch-critic treasured every one of them. In other words, every now and again, Louis' better nature and innate humanity triumphed.

Did the Sun King ever let down his guard? Clearly he was more interested in seeing through others than in revealing himself. Astonishingly his courtiers did not resent his habit of opening their mail. Perhaps they realised that his social success was based on genuine interest and affection as well as on the curiosity and omniscience he exploited unhesitatingly. But he kept his own letters sealed, his own cards close to his chest. He was at his most informal at Marly – hence the popularity of an invitation to join him there. Courtiers were allowed to sit in his presence when playing cards with him. Presumably Louis talked with his mistresses in private. His intimate servants, especially his valets, would gossip with Louis when more aristocratic courtiers had withdrawn for the night. Matthieu Da Vinha describes how Louis enjoyed informal chats with Du Bois, who had served as valet to Louis XIII. For instance,

Louis, well aware how talented a musician his father had been, enjoyed the valet's recollection of the pieces he liked to hear. 'Then the two men discussed music like old friends, the king interrogating his valet on the work of Lully.'[8] Just occasionally the king would forget himself so much as to talk informally with Lord Portland, the English ambassador. The two men would laugh and chatter together, for instance at the expense of the duke of Savoy who never ended a war on the side on which he had begun. But then a valet would announce the arrival of some delegation or other, and the king would automatically adopt his usual rather stiff and formidable demeanour. It was his job to keep up the appearances and style of an absolute king.

What do Louis' relationships with women tell us about the man? Antonia Fraser believes that he was happily married twice – to Marie Thérèse, who brought him massive territorial advantages, and Françoise de Maintenon whom he married for love. Whether the queen would have agreed that her marriage was happy is doubtful, while Maintenon was always moaning. Fraser maintains that he was both generous and considerate to his mistresses, who spontaneously curtseyed to the king's bed even when it was empty. Again, this is surely too charitable. Mancini, La Vallière and Montespan were all heart-broken by the way they were treated in the end. As for Louis' more transient lady friends, there are many obscurities. I have not been able to find out how he actually 'dated' his women. Did Bontemps anticipate Napoleon III's valet, who ushered in the girls whom he had procured with the instruction: 'You may kiss the emperor anywhere except on his face'?

Louis was certainly fond of women. Some historians have speculated on his alleged insecurity, which could be countered by female conquests. Others have suggested that he wanted to distance himself from his homosexual brother. Perhaps the obvious explanation is correct – that he was highly sexed, derived little pleasure from his unappealing and dreary first wife and had endless opportunities for gratifying his appetite elsewhere. In other words, just lust. There is a fascinating contrast between his exquisite courtesy towards women – he would raise his hat to a chambermaid – and his exploits as a predator. We have discussed elsewhere the way Louis squared his sex life with his conscience. Certainly Mme de Maintenon made him pay for his promiscuity when she reformed him after their marriage in 1683. Louis' more edifying private life enabled him to form a close friendship with his granddaughter-in-law, Adelaide of Savoy, with whom he was totally natural and uninhibited, even when she sat on his knee as a married woman. Louis learned to love women without bedding them.

Did Louis' women influence his conduct? Perhaps more than he would have liked to admit. His double adultery with Athénaïs de Montespan caused immense problems with his spiritual advisers, who actually rebuked him in public. Antonia Fraser believes, however, that Louis preferred the company of good women such as his mother, and that in Françoise de Maintenon he saw the possibility of a return to a life of Christian virtue. Possibly. But there was more to it than that, in that Louis found Françoise sexually and intellectually stimulating. Still, she certainly dominated the king in his last years, influencing his religious policies and his appointments. Seeing herself as a kind of universal mother-superior, she turned Louis into a prude. These two moral absolutists, now paragons of marital fidelity, joined in a crusade to force the French to behave themselves.

Perhaps Louis XIV could claim the right to do this because deep down he had always been a prude – or at least a man of principle. A devout and conscientious Christian, he attended mass every day, regularly confessed his sins and took communion at major festivals. To what extent he actually understood what Christianity is all about is a fascinating question. But he would have been hurt by the suggestion that he was a disloyal follower of the Christian gospel. However, he let himself down when he resorted to cruelty and brutality. Lavisse may have been right when he criticised Louis for his lack of *social* charity – for instance, his failure to protect his people from starvation and the tax collectors. But essentially Louis was an urbane and civilised man who hated to inflict suffering, at any rate on his own people. One cannot see him emulating Carlos II who presided over the burning of eighteen heretics at an *auto-da-fé* in Madrid on 30 June 1680. If Louis was corrupted by flattery and self-indulgence, it is amazing that his common sense and common decency survived as well as they did.

What else can one say? Maybe not a great deal. Louis had charisma, which enabled him to dominate a room full of people. He had charm, which explains his popularity with his courtiers and his mistresses. On the other hand he could be terrifying. Petitioners were sometimes dumbstruck, while his children were afraid of him. Whether you warm to Louis XIV perhaps depends on the extent to which you are prepared to take him at his own valuation. Did his obligations to the state justify his acceptance of flattery and pursuit of *gloire*? If one chooses, one can accept him as a great and dignified king, an august professional in the highest sense, a devout Catholic deserving the praise of courtiers and churchmen. Or one can see him as a pompous, spoiled bully, a sanctimonious bigot, self-regarding and self-indulgent, the hypocritical fraud of Thackeray's cartoon. The truth is elusive. In not being able to penetrate the golden mask any further, this biographer has to admit defeat. My consolation is that, to the best of my knowledge, better scholars have been equally defeated.

THE SUN KING: A CRITICAL ASSESSMENT

Bluche enthusiastically quotes Leibniz – a Protestant and a German – to the effect that Louis XIV was 'one of the greatest kings who ever lived'. Other sympathetic biographers, from Voltaire to contemporary admirers of the Sun King such as Bluche, Treasure, Fraser and Dunlop, reiterate that Louis was a 'great king'. More critical historians from Lavisse to Briggs are impressed by Louis' mediocrity. He was ordinary, they reckon. Where does the truth lie?

If being a great king entails being good at the job, in some important respects Louis XIV was a very great king indeed. As for mediocrity, like the rest of us Louis no doubt had his weaknesses. But his strengths were far from mediocre. As a self-publicist he was superb. His ability to manage and dominate his court was indisputable – he brilliantly exploited ritual, precedence, favours, promotions and public display. The skill with which he emasculated the nobility meant that rebellious noblemen became a thing of the past. His manipulation of patronage enabled him to dominate the most remote parts of his enormous patrimony. His grasp of political psychology helped him to control his ever-increasing army, which in former times had defied the crown. As an enabler of creative excellence, he masterminded France's cultural domination of Europe for decades to come. He backed able ministers such as Colbert and Pontchartrain, who reformed France's legal and financial administration; Torcy, the brilliant foreign minister; and Louvois, who reformed the army. All in all, an impressive record.

The adjective, however, that I would use to describe Louis XIV is 'dangerous'. He was arguably too proficient at his job. I am reminded of

Clemenceau's adage that 'there's only one thing worse than a bad priest, it's a good priest'. Louis was a first-rate absolutist. He was so successful in establishing his own authority that far too few opportunities arose for questioning his decisions. Louis prided himself on listening to his specialists, and certainly there were occasions when he deferred to them too much. But when it came to decision-making, only too often his ministers knew what the king wanted, and in order to preserve their own positions went along with him. This scenario applied to religious issues such as the persecution of Protestants and Jansenists. But it is most apparent in the conduct of foreign policy – which too often meant war. As a result, the suffering caused on the battlefield and by the king's marauding troops was equalled by the impoverishment of the French population, which had to finance Louis' wars. My argument is supported by a parish priest's obituary of Louis, penned in remote Blois:

> Louis XIV, King of France and Navarre, died on September 1st of this year, scarcely regretted by his whole kingdom, on account of the exorbitant sums and heavy taxes he levied on all his subjects ... It is not permissible to repeat all the verses, all the songs, or all the unfavourable comments which have been written or said against his memory.[9]

Let me clarify what I am and am not saying. I am not judging Louis in the way that J.R. Green dispatched King John to hell[10] – or, as Evelyn Waugh remarked of Lord Beaverbrook, 'he's got a future all right'. I am merely establishing the sheer misery that Louis XIV caused due to his disastrous, dangerously unchecked, irresponsible decisions. Time and again, especially in his conduct of foreign policy, it is not his wickedness that provokes moral judgement, if one is that way inclined, it is his incompetence that needs nailing. Alas, because he was so formidable and so impressive, nobody could stop him. Compare Louis with his pathetic contemporary Carlos II, 'the bewitched'. This mentally retarded, permanently feeble, eternally moribund rachitic paralytic did far less harm to far fewer people than the robust, brilliant Sun King. These are facts, not opinions. I am trying to be objective. If I am indeed playing the moralist, 'bias to the poor'[11] is all I am prepared to admit.

This is not to argue that Louis' warmaking was devoid of positive results. He left France less vulnerable to invasion. Parts of the French economy were stimulated – iron foundries made guns, clothiers made uniforms, timberyards made warships. War may have stimulated patriotism, or at least a growing awareness of national identity. Louis' appeal to the nation (12 June 1709) when France was on her knees was an interesting experiment. Mme de Maintenon claimed that it was widely read and appreciated, though whether her knowledge of the real France stretched beyond Versailles and Saint-Cyr is to be doubted. Certainly there was no massive rally to join the armed forces. The educated classes perhaps responded to Louis' appeal when defeat stared France in the face. Still, those ringing words are thought-provoking: 'I am persuaded that they [his subjects] would themselves oppose the acceptance of conditions equally contrary to justice and to the honour of the name French.' Louis was more than a mere dynast, as he proved on his deathbed: 'I am going, but the state remains.' He understood that there was a difference. So did his subjects who fought for France and joined in the Te Deums celebrating victory.

The Protestant Pierre Jurieu alleged that this triumphalism included the whole population: 'Whenever the king wins a battle, takes a city or subdues a province, we light bonfires and every petty person feels elevated and associates the king's grandeur with himself; this compensates him for all his losses and consoles him in all his misery.' But Jurieu was writing in 1690. Whether starving peasants in 1709 were equally thrilled is another matter. Nevertheless, France's armed forces, including the local militias, learned to speak French and to be proud of their nation. Even if they had been recruited from the most remote province, they would march the length and breadth of France, discovering the hard way that France existed all right, dwarfing their *pays*. And they became aware of France's identity in a hostile, wider world.

It would be wrong, however, to exaggerate the picture of Louis XIV, the proto-nationalist. If anything the awareness of French people's national identity declined from the days when Henri IV declared, 'we are all Frenchmen'. Louis expected loyalty to the state personified by himself. Indeed, he was extremely successful in making himself the focus of loyalty for all classes, thus breaking down many geographical, social and economic barriers. But Louis was a dynast rather than a nationalist. Take for instance his reaction to Leopold's suggestion that he should surrender territory in the cause of peace: 'What? Am I to give up the work of thirty years, I who have struggled so hard lest my enemies should *come into my house?*' (my italics). Or again, Louis clearly saw the establishment of Philip V on the throne of Spain as a Bourbon rather than a French triumph.

Furthermore, by his insistence on 'One King, One Faith, One Law', Louis dangerously divided his people, so that being a conservative and orthodox Catholic mattered more than being French. Not only the Huguenots but the Jansenists discovered that being French did them no good at all in the Sun King's eyes. Bluche believes that the media campaign to boost the Sun King's image encouraged patriotism. Statues, paintings, medals meant that he was never far away. Rather quaintly, Bluche thinks that a Frenchman locking away a coin in his strongbox would be pleased to have a picture of the king. One can, however, turn Bluche on his head by suggesting that a starving peasant, far from treasuring his portrait of the king, would wish that he had more of them. Indeed by impoverishing his subjects Louis dangerously weakened the French crown as a focus for his people's love and loyalty.

Louis alienated popular support in other ways. The *Unigenitus* fiasco was especially damaging. Petitfils only slightly exaggerates when he claims that the anti-Jansenist campaign caused the desacralisation of the French monarchy.[12] Petitfils asks how the French people could revere and respect their king when he openly allied with the pope and the unpopular Jesuits against the best of the French clergy led by the archbishop of Paris, the Sorbonne and the Parlement of Paris. By his pig-headed paranoia Louis had turned Jansenism into a popular movement of national defiance, which ultimately helped to bring down the monarchy. The Jansenists represented the nation, not the king. The sacred monarchy of St Louis and Joan of Arc was replaced by the arrogant and bullying caesaropapism of Philip the Fair.

At the same time Louis devalued the monarchy, if not desacralised it, in several ways. For instance, his policy of legitimising his bastards not only conflicted with the church's traditional emphasis on marriage and sexual continence but also offended the idea of legitimacy as an integral part of royal tradition. No wonder Louis 'touched' far fewer sufferers from scrofula as the reign progressed, though this was partly because he shut himself up at Versailles. The old Valois/Capetian tradition of meeting the people had been kept alive by Henri IV and by the inhibited Louis XIII, who travelled round France making himself accessible. The magnificent Sun King, on the other hand, seldom emerged from his temple.

Would it also be fanciful to suggest that by pandering to his mistresses Louis encouraged the wrong sort of publicity? Louis' palaces for his girlfriends were less damaging than Louis XV's brothel in the park for his 'nymphettes' (readers will recall Nabokov's *Lolita*). But they were nevertheless much more expensive and unquestionably degrading, especially when the king had to clamber over the battlements at the Louvre to bed his latest dolly bird. Maybe this is relatively trivial, compared to the widespread disgust expressed by the priest from Blois at Louis' failure to achieve the *soulagement* of his people. But to an increasing extent the monarch had dangerously failed to live up to the crown's traditional ideals.

What about the claim that Louis XIV's mistakes contributed to the French Revolution? Was he *that* dangerous? Clearly history should not be read backwards. Nor should someone be blamed who had been dead for seventy-four years for something that happened in 1789. Furthermore, in some respects the administrative monarchy of the enlightened *intendants* actually advanced under Louis XV. Yet Louis XIV undoubtedly made problems for his successors by repressing opposition, without enabling criticism and suggestions for improvements and reforms to be expressed. He created a huge army, but failed to match its growth with financial measures that would make it affordable, so a massive debt encumbered his successors. Furthermore the religious, social and economic problems Louis exacerbated continued to create friction. Although he disarmed the aristocrats who had exploited the Fronde, the greater nobles, far from being crushed by the Versailles system, were brought into the heart of political life and developed a sophisticated technique for influencing the monarchy, often with unfortunate results. The explosion of frustration and rage that eventually swept away the *ancien régime* was therefore partly the Sun King's fault.

So while I can respect Louis' undoubted achievements and successes, and even quite like him as a man, I cannot call him 'great'. Indeed, not even the French pay him that compliment. Although the city of Paris, of all places, bestowed the accolade 'Le Grand' on Louis in 1680, it did not stick, despite the fact that, in David Ogg's words, 'France, the most logical nation in the world, has been completely hypnotized by Louis XIV.'[13] 'Greatness' in a king is obviously a vague, indefinable concept, largely a matter of opinion. But if the ability to rise above the prejudices and horizons of contemporaries is a qualification (Peter the Great comes to mind), Louis was more interested in capturing a town in Flanders than in saving

Vienna from the Turks, keener in chasing the Jansenist nuns out of Port-Royal than establishing Christianity in the Far East or America.

If Louis XIV was more dangerous than Carlos II, he does not compare that well with Leopold the Victorious or William the Deliverer. Leopold every now and then had to be wound up like a clock, according to a French diplomat, so enfeebled was he by generations of Habsburg inbreeding. Yet – with a little help from his allies – he inflicted on the Turks their first defeat for 300 years and thereby saved Vienna. As for Dutch William, Pierre Goubert writes that 'with masterly ineptitude the King of France, having made William master of the United Provinces, went on to help make him king of England' and that 'the last quarter of the seventeenth century belongs to William as much as to Louis'[14] – a judgement that would have infuriated Louis, especially coming from a Frenchman. Personally I rate William higher than Louis, both as a man and as a king. I am impressed by the little Dutchman's obstinate courage when his beloved fatherland was attacked by the French bully. I warm to his religious toleration and his own low-key beliefs, which only occasionally emerged – for instance, when he asked Bishop Burnet what he now thought of predestination when they landed at Torbay. I am impressed by his refusal to be held back by ill-health.

Nevertheless, one must be fair to Louis the Sun King. It would be wrong to begrudge him his triumphs: a Bourbon on the throne of Spain, a frontier more secure than in 1661, a continent on which French was now the language of culture and diplomacy. Perhaps his greatest strengths were his political know-how, his devotion to his dynasty and his flair for publicity. His glamour fascinated contemporaries and has continued to bamboozle historians. But there remained the darker side of the Sun. Louis XIV's irresponsible aggression inflicted suffering on millions. He forced Christians to the communion table. He bullied those who disagreed with him. He got the worst of all possible worlds in his struggle with the Jansenists. By his own lights maybe he was great. Indeed, although Michelet argued that 'respect is the death of history',[15] I can respect much of what the Sun King achieved and even warm to what he was. But deference, adulation and hero worship are other matters. We should not be dazzled by the abominable showman. We do not have to compete with the crowd of jabbering, jostling courtiers, buzzing around their hero as he saunters out into his park.

Glossary

ançien régime   form of government and society before the Revolution.

capitation   a graduated poll tax, the amount depending on the rank of the taxpayer.

chambre de justice   special court set up to try financiers.

conseil d'en haut   small, inner governing council, presided over by the king.

dérogeance   loss of status by nobles for being involved in trade.

dévot   a devout Catholic who applied religious criteria to politics.

dixième   income tax, based on a return by the taxpayer.

don gratuit   a supposedly spontaneous tax granted to the king by the clergy or by provincial estates. The assumption was that it was more than the payers would have preferred to pay, but less than they could in fact afford.

dragonnades   billeting of dragoons on Huguenots to force them to become Catholic.

gabelle   monopoly tax on salt.

généralité   area for extraction of taxation.

intendant   government official involved in raising taxation, controlling troops, supplying information to central government. The workhorses of the *ancien régime.*

lettre de cachet   an order from the king that a person should be imprisoned without trial.

lit de justice   a special session of Parlement at which the king could impose measures.

mentalité   contemporary, seventeenth-century attitudes contrasting with today's assumptions.

noblesse d'épée   noblemen from old-established families who served the king as soldiers.

noblesse de robe   senior civil servants who were ennobled for cash or for administrative service to the king.

parlement   there were several of these courts of lawyers and administrators of which the Parlement of Paris was the senior. They were not representative and not elected.

paulette   tax paid by an office-holder enabling him to pass on his office to a relative.

pays d'élection   provinces without estates where the *taille* was more harshly imposed than in *pays d'états* where the *taille* was negotiated.

procureur-général   the king's representative in the Parlement of Paris.

regale   the king's right to collect the revenue from a vacant bishopric.

Religion Prétendue Reformée (R.P.R.)   official title of the Huguenot church.

robin   member of the legal profession and of the robe nobility.

soulagement   process of taking care of people's welfare and living conditions.

sub-delegé   subordinate official working for an *intendant*.

taille   direct tax from which nobles and clergy were exempt.

FURTHER READING

There are several invaluable primary sources. Pride of place goes to Louis XIV's *Mémoires,* translated and introduced by Paul Sonnino (Free Press, 1970), affording unique insight into Louis' attitudes and priorities. Louis wrote thousands of letters; a useful selection was edited by Pierre Gaxotte (Talendier, 1930). See also the collection of Louis' writings, *Louis XIV par lui-même,* edited by Michel Déon (Gallimard, 1991). The court is vividly brought to life by the duc de Saint-Simon, whose memoirs are introduced and translated by Lucy Norton (Hamish Hamilton, 1967). Also quite useful are Primi Visconti, *Sur le Cour de Louis XIV* (Perrin, 1988), and the marquis de Dangeau, *Journal* (Soulié and Dussieux, 1854–60). Torcy's memoirs (London, 1757) are enlightening, as are Pomponne's, edited and translated by Herbert H. Rowen (Kemink en Zoon, 1955). It was the age of letter-writing, Mme de Sévigné being supreme; a selection is translated by Violet Hammersley (Secker and Warburg, 1955). See also: *Correspondance de Mme de Maintenon et de la princesse des Ursins* (Mercure de France, 2002). In a class of its own is Fénelon's *Lettre à Louis XIV* (Sequences, 1994). It is not really a letter at all, rather a moral and political diatribe. The case against Louis' wars is less intemperately put by Vauban's *Dîme Royale,* edited by Jean-Marc Daniel (L'Harmattan, 2004). There is a fascinating edition by John J. Conley of Mme de Maintenon's *Dialogues and Addresses* (Chicago, 2004). These are miscellaneous reminiscences and dialogues prepared for the staff and pupils at Saint-Cyr — unbelievable for their prejudices and complacency. Helpful and sympathetic light is thrown on that superficially unattractive figure Bishop Bossuet by Patrick Riley's translation and edition of *Politics Drawn from the Very Words of Scripture* (Cambridge University Press, 1990). Saint-Evremond throws light on several contemporaries in his *Condé, Turenne et autre figures illustres,* edited by Suzanne Guellouz (Desjonquères, 2003).

There are several useful selections of documents on various aspects of the reign. Roger Mettam's *Government and Society in Louis XIV's France* (Macmillan, 1977) is a marvellous record of the way France was governed;

no student can ignore it. There are briefer selections in David L. Smith, *Louis XIV* (Cambridge University Press, 1992); Victor Mallia-Milanes, *Louis XIV and France* (Macmillan, 1986); Peter Robert Campbell, *Louis XIV* (Longman, 1993); and Alan James, *The Origins of French Absolutism 1598–1661* (Longman, 2006).

A number of general history books helpfully cover Louis XIV's reign. G.R.R. Treasure's admirable *Seventeenth Century France* (John Murray) was updated in 1981. John Lough's *Introduction to Seventeenth Century France* (Longman, 1957) and W.E. Brown's *The First Bourbon Century* (London, 1971) have worn surprisingly well. The best of all is Robin Briggs, *Early Modern France, 1560–1715* (Oxford University Press, 1998) – succinct, readable, always perceptive and thought-provoking. Colin Jones, *The Great Nation* (Penguin, 2002) is mainly concerned with France in the eighteenth century, but the first chapters are brilliant on Louis XIV's reign. Similarly, Jeremy Black, *The Rise of the European Powers 1679–1793* (Edward Arnold, 1990) has much of value on Louis XIV's foreign policy. J.H. Shennan's Lancaster pamphlet on Louis XIV (Routledge, 1986), and the Historical Association pamphlets by Roland Mousnier on Louis XIV (1973) and by J.H. Knecht on the Fronde (1985), are excellent. William F. Church, *The Greatness of Louis XIV* (D.C. Heath, 1972) is still useful.

Those who find biography a painless entrée into a topic are well served. There are numerous biographies of the Sun King, all different, all with their own peculiar merits, from David Ogg's whiggish master-piece (Oxford University Press, 1931) to Anthony Levi's perverse but readable *Louis XIV* (Constable, 2004), which attributes Louis' 'insecurity' to the knowledge that he was not Louis XIII's son but Mazarin's. Nancy Mitford's *The Sun King* (Hamish Hamilton, 1966) never fades. Ian Dunlop, *Louis XIV* (Chatto and Windus, 1999) is readable and schol-arly. If you prefer a more critical approach, Prince Michael of Greece, *Louis XIV: The Other Side of the Sun* (Orbis 1983), sets a cracking pace, as does Philippe Erlanger, *Louis XIV* (Phoenix, 1988). Pierre Goubert, *Louis XIV and Twenty Million Frenchmen* (Allen Lane, 1970), is a critical com-mentator on Louis in his environment. Joanna Richardson (Weidenfeld and Nicolson, 1973) and Vincent Cronin (Collins, 1964) are not to be underestimated. Five biographers seem to me to be in their different ways outstanding. Geoffrey Treasure (Longman, 2001) is thoughtful and com-prehensive, David Sturdy (Macmillan, 1998) has written a masterpiece of concise analysis, though his book has too little about Louis as a man to be considered a true biography. François Bluche, whom I have repeatedly attacked for his nationalistic bias, incorporates detail, sympathy and perception to an amazing degree. His is a splendid book – and splendidly translated by Mark Greengrass (Blackwell, 1990). Fourth, Antonia Fraser, *Love and Louis XIV* (Weidenfeld and Nicolson, 2006) is entertaining and thought-provoking. And fifth, if I had to award a palm, it would be to Jean-Christian Petitfils (Perrin, 2002) – perceptive, judicious, entertaining. If Buche has been translated into English, why not Petitfils?

Biographies abound of major characters in Louis XIV's reign. I have found the following helpful and have enjoyed reading them: John P. Spielman, *Leopold I of Austria* (Thames and Hudson, 1977); Charlotte Haldene, *Mme de Maintenon* (Macmillan, 1967); N.N. Barker, *Brother to the Sun King* (Johns Hopkins University Press, 1989); A. Lloyd Moote, *Louis XIII, the Just* (University of California Press, 1989); J.H.M. Salmon, *Cardinal de Retz* (Weidenfeld and Nicolson, 1969); Ruth Kleinman, *Anne of Austria* (Ohio State University Press, 1985); E.W. Marvick, *The Making of a King* (Yale University Press, 1986); André Corvisier, *Louvois* (Fayard, 1983); G.R.R Treasure, *Mazarin* (Routledge, 1997); M. Forster, *A Woman's Life at the Court of the Sun King (Liselotte von der Pfalz)* (Johns Hopkins University Press, 1984); Daniel Dessert, *Colbert ou le Serpent Venimeux* (Complex, 2000); Lucy Norton, *Adelaide – First Lady of Versailles* (Hamish Hamilton, 1978); Michael Vergé-Franceshi, *Colbert* (Biographie Payot, 2003); V. Sackville-West, *Daughter of France (La Grande Mademoiselle)* (Michael Joseph, 1959); Charles Petrie, *The Marshal Duke of Berwick* (Eyre and Spottiswoode, 1953); Inès Murat, *Colbert* (University Press of Virginia, 1984); J.C. Petitfils, *Louise de La Vallière* (Perrin, 1990); Claude C. Sturgill, *Marshal Villars* (University of Kentucky Press, 1965); J.H. Shennan, *Philippe Duke of Orléans* (Thames and Hudson, 1979); John Callow, *King in Exile* (Sutton, 2004); Daniel Dessert, *Fouquet* (Fayard, 1987); Lisa Hilton, *Athénaïs, The Real Queen of France* (Little, Brown, 2002). These biographies are in no sort of chronological or alphabetical order, still less in any order of merit. In fact I enjoyed the last mentioned – Lisa Hilton's biography of Madame de Montespan – as much as any of them.

Several books that deal with specific issues raised in the course of this biography can be recommended. For instance the question of absolutism – myth or reality – was given prominence by Roger Mettam's *Power and Faction in Louis XIV's France* (Blackwell, 1988), a most impressive discussion of exactly how France was governed. The exercise of social and political control is explored by Sharon Kettering in 'Patronage in Early Modern France' in *French Historical Studies* (Autumn 1992), and at greater length by W. Beik, *Absolutism and Society in Seventeenth Century France* (Cambridge University Press, 1985). The revisionist demolition of absolutism is continued by James B. Collins, *The State in Early Modern France* (Cambridge University Press, 1995); Mark Potter, *Corps and Clienteles* (Ashgate, 2003); and Donna Bohanan, *Crown and Nobility in Early Modern France* (Palgrave, 2001). David Parker, *The Making of French Absolutism* (Arnold, 1983), emphasises the cooperation between crown and nobility at the expense of the poor. The whole revisionist case is effectively summed up by Nicholas Henshall, *The Myth of Absolutism* (Longman, 1992). A counter-revisionist challenge has been mounted by John Hurt in *Louis XIV and the Parlements: The Assertion of Royal Authority* (Manchester University Press, 2002), in which he argues that Louis XIV's dragooning of the Parlement of Paris in particular was nothing if not absolutist. Three brilliant books on the French army similarly demonstrate Louis' acquisition and exploitation of power: John A. Lynn, *The Wars of Louis XIV* (Longman, 1999) and *Giant of the Grand Siècle* (Cambridge University Press, 1997), and Guy Rowlands, *The Dynastic State and the Army under Louis XIV* (Cambridge University Press, 2002). Rowlands demonstrates Louis' success in dominating and financially exploiting the nobility at war. The less pleasant aspects of Louis' militarism come across in Paul W. Bamford, *Fighting Ships and Prisons: The Mediterranean Galleys in the Reign of Louis XIV* (University of Minnesota Press, 1973) and George W. Satterfield, *Princes, Posts and Partisans* (about the exploitation of Dutch and German civilians) (Brill, 2003). See also Daniel Dessert's excellent book on the navy, *La Royale* (Fayard, 1996). Anette Smedley-Weill, *Les Intendants de Louis XIV* (Fayard, 1995) argues that the intendants became more powerful as agents of absolutism towards the end of the reign. The present state of the arguments about absolutism is helpfully summed up by William Beik in 'The Absolutism of Louis XIV as Social Collaboration', *Past and Present* (August 2005), pp. 195–224.

A related issue to the nature and limits of monarchical power is the role of Versailles and Louis XIV's court. The sociologist Norbert Elias, in *The Court Society* (Blackwell, 1983), showed how Louis dominated his nobility through exploitation of court ritual. Elias's findings were questioned by Jeroen Duindam in *Vienna and Versailles* (Cambridge University Press, 2003) and *Myths of Power* (Amsterdam, 2005). The contribution of gardens to the propagation and establishment of royal militarism is argued by Chandra Mukerji, *Territorial Ambitions and the Garden of Versailles* (Cambridge University Press, 1997). The contribution of music to the maintenance of Louis' *gloire* is analysed by Robert M. Isherwood, *Music in the Service of the King* (Cornell University Press, 1973), and by James Gaines, *Evening in the Palace of Reason* (Fourth Estate, 2005). The importance of the palace comes across well in Guy Walton, *Louis XIV's Versailles* (Viking, 1986), and in Ian Dunlop, *Royal Palaces of France* (Hamish Hamilton, 1985). E. Le Roy Ladurie brilliantly analyses the jungle warfare at Versailles in his *Saint-Simon and the Court of Louis XIV* (University of Chicago Press, 2001). The whole campaign to propagate Louis' image is addressed by P. Burke, *The Fabrication of Louis XIV* (Yale University Press, 1992). See also T.C.W. Blanning, *The Culture of Power and the Power of Culture* (Oxford University Press, 2002), for some brilliant comments.

Various books help to make the difficult topic of Louis XIV's religious policies more intelligible. Joseph Bergin, *Crown, Church and Episcopate under Louis XIV* (Yale University Press, 2004) explains the sort of men who became bishops. Robin Briggs, *Communities of Belief* (Oxford University Press, 1989) offers several thought-provoking essays on the nature of religious commitment in seventeenth-century France. Elizabeth Labrousse, *La revocation de l'Édit de Nantes* (Payot, 1990), and Janine Garrison, *L'Edit de Nantes et sa revocation* (Du Seuil, 1985), cover the religious aspects of the Sun King's persecution of his Protestant subjects, while the social and economic consequences are discussed by Warren C. Scoville, *The Persecution of the Huguenots and French Economic Development* (University of California Press, 1960). William Doyle, *Jansenism* (Macmillan, 2000) is a helpful treatment, as is Alexander Sedgwick, *Jansenism in Seventeenth Century France* (University Press of Virginia, 1977). The religious aspects of monarchy are covered by Dale K. Van Kley, *The Religious Origins of the French Revolution* (Yale University Press, 1996), and Paul Kleber Monod, *The Power of Kings* (Yale University Press, 1999).

On Louis XIV's foreign policy, there are several books and essays written or edited by R. Hatton that are essential reading: *Louis XIV and his World* (Thames and Hudson, 1972), *Louis XIV and Europe* (Macmillan,

1976), *William III and Louis XIV* – including Mark Thomson's 'Louis XIV and the Origins of the War of the Spanish Succession (Liverpool University Press, 1968), *Louis XIV and Absolutism* (Macmillan, 1976). Mrs Hatton corrects those of us who have whiggish inclinations. P. Sonnino, *Louis XIV and the Origins of the Dutch War* (Cambridge University Press, 1988) is severely critical of the Sun King, as is Carl J. Ekberg, *The Failure of Louis XIV's Dutch War* (University of North Carolina Press, 1979). Jeremy Black, The *Rise of the European Powers 1679–1793* (Arnold, 1990) has a useful chapter on Louis XIV.

There are some entertaining studies of freedom of thought and opposition to Louis XIV. Paul Hazard's *The European Mind* (Hollis and Carter, 1953) is still immensely worth reading. Lionel Rothkrug, *The Opposition to Louis XIV* (Princeton University Press, 1965) is useful, as are Robert Darnton, *The Forbidden Best-sellers of Pre-revolutionary France* (Norton, 1995) and J. Klaits, *Printed Propaganda Under Louis XIV* (Princeton University Press, 1976). Roger MacDonald, *The Man in the Iron Mask* (Constable, 2005) is scholarly and non-sensationalist. Marc Fumaroli, *The Poet and the King* (University of Nôtre Dame Press, 2002) defends the anti-establishment poet La Fontaine, and in his essay in J.H. Elliott and L.W.B. Brockliss, *The World of the Favourite* (Yale University Press, 1999) he defends the would-be establishment figure Fourquet. M. Da Vinha, *Les Valets de Chambre de Louis XIV* (Perrin, 2004) discusses the backgrounds of Bontemps *et al.*, but they are disappointingly discreet.

These are books that I have found helpful and enjoyable. If you need an excuse to visit Paris, you can trawl through the admirable libraries there (Bibliothèque Nationale etc.), but really the British Library at St Pancras will get you pretty well anything, in any language. Paris, however, is invaluable as a base for visiting Versailles, Fontainebleau, Vaux le Vicomte, Les Invalides, the Louvre and countless buildings in less-frequented streets dating from the Sun King's time – all first-rate, indeed absolutely essential, primary sources.

NOTES

1 INTRODUCTION

1   Louis XIV, *Mémoires*, edited and translated by Paul Sonnino (Free Press, 1970).
2   P. Goubert, *Louis XIV and Twenty Million Frenchmen* (Allen Lane, 1970), p. 289.
3   Quoted by Ian Dunlop, *Louis XIV* (Chatto and Windus, 1999), p. xi.
4   The works quoted here will for the most part re-emerge in later pages.
5   Quoted in William F. Church, *The Greatness of Louis XIV* (D.C. Heath, 1972), p. 75.
6   The debate is summarised by W. Beik in *Past and Present*, August 2005, pp. 195–224.
7   Dunlop, *Louis XIV*, p. xii.
8   Lord Acton, *Lectures in Modern History* (Macmillan, 1906), p. 234.
9   Anthony Levi, *Louis XIV* (Constable, 2005), *passim*.
10 Antonia Fraser, *Love and Louis XIV* (Weidenfeld and Nicolson, 2006). According to Fraser, *Daily Telegraph*, 19 August 2006: 'Any woman – including me! – might be happy as the mistress of Louis XIV.'
11 *Hebrews 12*.
12 Robin Briggs, *Early Modern France* (Oxford University Press, 1990), p. 145: 'A mediocre man in many respects, the king had two great attributes: enormous physical vitality and an exceptionally strong will.'
13 Robert Darnton, *The Great Cat Massacre* (Basic Books, 1984), p. 4. Darnton's bizarre title refers to the practice, unfamiliar to us, of torturing and killing cats as representatives of the devil, witchcraft and the sexual domination of men by women.
14 T.C.W. Blanning, *The Culture of Power and the Power of Culture* (Oxford University Press, 2002), p. 7.

2 THE RISING SUN, 1638–61

1   Anthony Levi, *Louis XIV* (Constable, 2005), pp. 13–20. When I suggested to Professor Levi that DNA would settle the matter, he agreed, but doubted whether the French would cooperate. (Letter 4 September 2004.)
2   R.J. Knecht in *History Today*, April 2004, exemplifies historians' scepticism about Levi's theory. I am grateful to Roger Mettam for the anecdote about Brienne.

3   Geoffrey Treasure's *Mazarin* (Routledge, 1997) is not only the best but the only biography in English since 1903. For a brief coverage see the article on Mazarin by Richard Wilkinson in *History Today*, April 1996.

4   Pierre La Porte, *Mémoires* (Paris, 1839), quoted by J.-C. Petitfils, *Louis XIV* (Perrin, 2002), p. 41.

5   From a lecture delivered by David Parrott in London, 11 March 1994.

6   Roger Mettam, *Power and Faction in Louis XIV's France* (Oxford University Press, 1988), p. 134.

7   Scarron's verse translates: 'Buggering bugger, buggered bugger, Bugger to the supreme degree, Hairy bugger and feathered bugger, Bugger in large and small volume, Bugger sodomizing the State, Bugger of the purest mixture' – quoted by Robert Darnton, *The Forbidden Best-Sellers of Pre-revolutionary France* (Norton, 1995), p. 207.

8   Thus Darnton, ibid. According to the prim Bluche/Greengrass version, 'He kisses her' (François Bluche, *Louis XIV*, trans. Mark Greengrass (Blackwell, 1990), p. 40).

9   I am grateful to Robin Briggs for this point.

10 Colin Jones, *The Great Nation* (Penguin, 2003), p. 13.

11 *Registres du Parlement*, quoted by François Bluche, *Louis XIV vous parle* (Paris, 1988), p. 35.

12 *Cardinal Mazarin's Letters to Louis XIV, On his love to the Cardinal's Niece* (London, 1691).

13 Quoted in V. Sackville-West, *Daughter of France* (Michael Joseph, 1959), pp. 217–18.

14 There have been other examples in history: Wolsey? Cherie Blair?

15 The allegation of homosexual assault has been discussed by Prince Michael of Greece, *Louis XIV* (Orbis, 1983), p. 61, and by Philippe Erlanger, *Louis XIV* (Phoenix, 2003), p. 71. Their source is La Porte who hated Mazarin. But the story is not impossible. It might explain Louis' homophobia.

16 Mark Potter, *Corps and Clienteles* (Ashgate, 2003), *passim*.

17 'A King's Lessons in Statecraft', in *Mémoires* of Louis XIV, edited by Jean Longdon (Fisher Unwin, 1924 [Paris, 1978]), p. 41.

18 Ian Dunlop, *Louis XIV* (Chatto and Windus, 1999), p. 40.

3   THE KING AND HIS SUBJECTS

1   Anthony Levi, *Louis XIV* (Constable, 2005), p. 223.

2   A. Chéruel, *Mémoires sur la vie publique et privée de Fouquet* (Paris, 1862), pp. 325–6.

3   Cf. Revelation 6: 1–8. See Pierre Goubert, *The French Peasantry in Seventeenth Century France* (Cambridge University Press, 1986), p. 91, for the comparison with Richelieu.

4   The row was over Molière's *Le Tartuffe*, a brilliant send-up of religious hypocrisy.
5   Robert Darnton, *The Forbidden Best-Sellers of Pre-revolutionary France* (Norton, 1995).
6   Marc Fumaroli, *The Poet and the King* (University of Nôtre Dame, 2002).
7   For Bossuet, Simon and Bayle, see Paul Hazard, *The European Mind* (Hollis and Carter, 1953), *passim*.
8   Ibid.
9   Antonia Fraser, *The Weaker Vessel* (Mandarin, 1993), pp. 524–5.
10   Wendy Gibson, *Women in Seventeenth Century France* (Macmillan, 1989).
11   John Locke, *A Traveller in France* (London, 1677).
12   Anne Somerset, *The Affair of the Poisons* (Weidenfeld and Nicolson, 2003), *passim*.
13   Robin Briggs, *Early Modern France 1560–1715* (Oxford University Press, 1977), p. 211.

4   THE KING AT WORK

1   Quoted by J.B. Wolf, *Louis XIV* (Gollancz, 1969) p. 133.
2   Lettre de Louis XIV écrit à la reine à l'arrestation de Surintendant Fouquet.
3   Daniel Dessert, *Fouquet* (Fayard, 1987), pp. 256–7.
4   See the essay by M. Fumaroli in J.H. Elliott and L.W.B. Brockliss, *The World of the Favourite* (Yale University Press, 1999). See also Mark Fumaroli, *The Poet and the King* (University of Nôtre Dame, 2002), which explores Louis' relationship with the critical La Fontaine.
5   Letter to the author, 31 August 2005.
6   Louis XIV, *Mémoires*, edited and translated by Paul Sonnino (Free Press, 1970), pp. 23–4, 255–6.
7   Pierre Goubert, *Louis XIV and Twenty Million Frenchmen* (Allen Lane, 1970), p. 96.
8   *Mémoires* (ed. and trans. Sonnino).
9   Prince Michael of Greece, *Louis XIV* (Orbis, 1983), p. 190.
10   *Mémoires* (ed. and trans. Sonnino).
11   Ibid.
12   Ibid.
13   Quoted by Wolf, *Louis XIV*, p. 203.
14   Guy Rowlands, *The Dynastic State and the Army under Louis XIV* (Cambridge University Press, 2002), p. 62.
15   Jean-Baptiste Colbert, marquis de Torcy, *Journal* (London, 1757), entry for 7 January 1710.
16   Sara Chapman, *Private Ambition and Political Alliances* (University of Rochester Press, 2004), p. 133.

17   N. Henshall, *Myth of Absolutism* (Longman, 1992), p. 234. There is a useful summary of the present state of the debate about absolutism by W. Beik, 'The Absolutism of Louis XIV as Social Collaboration', *Past and Present* (August 2005), pp. 195–224.

18   Quoted in the Clément edition of Colbert's correspondence, vol. 2, under 23 December 1672 entry. See also Roger Mettam, *Government and Society in Louis XIV's France* (Macmillan, 1977).

19   Donna Bohannan, *Crown and Nobility in Early Modern France* (Palgrave Macmillan, 2001), p. 224.

20   Letter to the author, 31 August 2005.

21   David Sturdy, *Louis XIV* (Macmillan, 1998), p. 45.

22   Roger Mettam, in conversation with the author, 9 November 2005.

23   John Hurt, *Louis XIV and the Parlements: The Assertion of Royal Authority* (Manchester University Press, 2002), p. ix.

24   *Mémoires* (ed. and trans. Sonnino).

25   Esprit Fléchier, *Mémoires sur les Grand-Jours d'Auvergne en 1665*, edited by Y.-M. Berce (Paris, 1984), pp. 36–9.

26   Wolf, *Louis XIV*, p. 198.

27   The increasing status of the intendants is covered in Sara Chapman's *Private Ambition* and by Anette Smedley-Weill, *Les Intendants de Louis XIV* (Fayard, 1995), *passim*.

28   Dennis Brogan, Introduction to *Memoirs of the Duc de Saint-Simon* (Hamish Hamilton, 1967), p. xix. Louis' image is explored by Peter Burke, *The Fabrication of Louis XIV* (Cambridge University Press, 1995). See also Chapter 5 of this work.

29   Letter to the author, 12 October 2005.

30   See Jeroen Duindam, *Vienna and Versailles* (Cambridge University Press, 2003) and *Myths of Power* (Amsterdam University Press, 2005).

31   E. Le Roy Ladurie, *Saint-Simon and the Court of Louis XIV* (University of Chicago Press, 2001).

5   CULTURE WITH A PURPOSE

1   Quoted by Paul Sonnino, *Louis XIV and the Origins of the Dutch War* (Cambridge University Press, 1988).

2   Mark Bannister, in J.H. Elliott and J.W.B. Brockliss, *The World of the Favourite* (Yale University Press, 1999), p. 127. See also Mark Bannister, *Condé in Context* (Legenda, 2000).

3   Louis XIV, *Mémoires*, edited and translated by Paul Sonnino (Free Press, 1970), p. 28.

4   Molière, *Tartuffe*, Act III.

5   James Gaines, *Evening in the Palace of Reason* (Fourth Estate, 2005), p. 58.

6   It is reassuring to find one's own uneducated impression confirmed by James Gaines, and by David Jay Grout, 'Some forerunners of the Lully opera', *Music and Letters*, 22 (1941). There are CDs of Lully's music, though when my second son tried to buy me one at HMV in Birmingham the salesgirl replied, 'Do you mean Lulu?'

7   Robert M. Isherwood, *Music in the Service of the King* (Comet, 1973), pp. 200–1.

8   Ibid., pp. 202-3.

9   For Louis XIV's embellishment of Paris, see W. Berger, *A Royal Passion* (Cambridge University Press, 1994).

10   Louis XIV to Colbert, 15 June 1669.

11   Quoted by Anthony Levi, *Louis XIV* (Constable, 2005), p. 195.

12   See Peter Burke, *The Fabrication of Louis XIV* (Cambridge, 1989), Louis Marin, *Portrait of the King* (Minnesota, 1988) and M. Fumaroli, *The Poet and the King* (University of Nôtre Dame, 2002) for discussion of Louis XIV's self-promotion.

13   Molière, *The Misanthrope and Other Plays* (Penguin Classics, 1969), pp. 162–3.

14   Quoted by Elizabeth Hyde, *Cultivated Powers* (University of Pennsylvania Press, 2005).

15   Hyde discusses the importance of flowers in the Sun King's propaganda in ibid.

16   Alban Krailsheimer, *Pascal* (Oxford University Press, 1980).

17   Lucy Norton (ed.), *Saint-Simon at Versailles: Selections from the Memoirs* (Hamish Hamilton, 1980), p. 162.

6   RELATIONS AND FRIENDS

1   E. Le Roy Ladurie, *Saint-Simon and the Court of Louis XIV* (University of Chicago Press, 2001), p. 261.

2   Wendy Gibson, *Women in Seventeenth Century France* (Macmillan, 1989), p. 261.

3   Quoted by Lisa Hilton, *Athénaïs, the Real Queen of France: A Biography of Madame de Montespan* (Little, Brown, 2002), p. 5.

4   Antonia Fraser, *Love and Louis XIV* (Weidenfeld and Nicolson, 2006), p. 92.

5   Ibid., p. 78.

6   The rivalry between Louise and Athénaïs is covered by Hilton, *Athénaïs*, pp. 56–65.

7   Fraser, *Love and Louis XIV*, rejects this story because she is unwilling to believe that Louis could be so callous (footnote, p. 114). I see no reason to doubt it.

8   Fraser, in ibid., p. 188, gives an inaccurate account of this episode. See Anthony Levi, *Louis XIV* (Constable, 2005), p. 215.

9   Hilton, *Athénaïs*, objects to Nancy Mitford's description of Montespan as a 'grubby woman' in *The Sun King* (Hamish Hamilton, 1966), p. 58. But Mitford relies on the duchesse de Orléans contemporary account.

10 Hilton, *Athénaïs*, p. 171.

11 Ibid., p. 117.

12 Ibid., p. 49.

13 Ibid., p. 91.

14 Ibid., p. 101.

15 Ibid., p. 238.

16 Fraser, *Love and Louis XIV*, p. 201.

17 See Lucy Norton, *First Lady of Versailles* (Hamish Hamilton, 1978).

18 Fraser, *Love and Louis XIV*, pp. 283–4.

19 Mitford, *The Sun King*, pp. 149ff.

20 See Chapter 8.

21 Michel Verge-Francheshi, *Colbert* (Payot, 2003), p. 379.

7 THE WORLD AT HIS FEET: FOREIGN POLICY, 1661–84

1   Quoted by John A. Lynn, *The Wars of Louis XIV* (Longman, 1999), p. 31.

2   Ibid., p. 105.

3   Mark Fumaroli, *The Poet and the King* (University of Nôtre Dame Press, 2002), *passim*, and in J.H. Elliott and L.W.B. Brockliss, *The World of the Favourite* (Yale University Press 1999).

4   Andrew Lossky, *Louis XIV and the French Monarchy* (Rutgers, 1994), p. 60.

5   Louis XIV, *Mémoires*, edited and translated by Paul Sonnino (Free Press, 1970), pp. 26–7.

6   Ibid., p. 27.

7   See the article by Jonathan Spangler, 'A lesson in diplomacy for Louis XIV: the Treaty of Montmartre', *French History*, 17, 3 (September 2003).

8   *A Dialogue concerning the Rights of her most Christian Majesty*, printed in the Savoy, by Thomas Newcomb, 1667.

9   Peter Robert Campbell, *Louis XIV* (Longman, 1993), p. 63.

10 Quoted by J.C. Rule, *Louis XIV and the Craft of Kingship* (Ohio State University Press, 1969), p. 397.

11 Paul Sonnino, *Louis XIV and the Origins of the Dutch War* (Cambridge University Press, 1988).

12   Jean Racine, *La Précise Histoire des campaigns de Louis le Grands* (Paris, 1681).

13   *Mémoires* (ed. and trans. Sonnino).

14   When the Prussian assault on France was launched on 12 July 1870, Moltke, the chief of the general staff and in effect commander-in-chief, was discovered sprawling on a sofa, reading *Lady Audley's Secret*.

15   Ian Dunlop, *Louis XIV* (Chatto and Windus, 1999), p. 235.

16   Duchess of Orléans, quoted by Lynn, p. 112 *Wars of Louis XIV*, on Louvois' plebeian appearance.

17   See my analysis of Hore-Belisha's role, *History Today* (December, 1997), and *Royal United Services Institute Journal* (1998).

18   See especially Lynn, *Wars of Louis XIV*; Guy Rowlands, *The Dynastic State and the Army under Louis XIV* (Cambridge, 2002; George Satterfield, *Princes, Posts and Partisans* (Brill, 2003; Carl J. Ekberg, *The Failure of Louis XIV's Dutch War* (University of North Carolina Press, 1979).

19   David J. Sturdy, *Louis XIV* (Macmillan, 1999), p. 139.

20   *Mémoires* (ed. and trans. Sonnino), p. 223.

21   François Bluche, *Louis XIV*, trans. Mark Greengrass (Blackwell, 1990), p. 289.

22   J.H. Elliott, *Imperial Spain* (Penguin, 1975), pp. 311, 373.

23   Bluche, *Louis XIV*, chapter 15, 'The Tedium of the Armed Peace'.

8   LOUIS XIV AND RELIGION

1   François Bluche, *Louis XIV*, trans. Mark Greengrass (Blackwell, 1990), p. 385.

2   Joseph Bergin, *Crown, Church and Episcopate Under Louis XIV* (Yale University Press, 2004), p. 346.

3   Quoted by J.H.M. Salmon, 'The King and His Conscience', *History Today* (May, 1965), p. 336.

4   See G. Coutton, *La Chair et l'Ame* (Presses Unitaires de Grenoble, 1995), pp. 56–7.

5   Bergin, *Crown Church and Episcopate*, p. 248.

6   Louis XIV, *Mémoires*, edited and translated by Paul Sonnino (Free Press, 1970), p. 51.

7   Elisabeth Labrousse, *La revocation de l'Edit de Nantes* (Payot, 1990), pp. 159–60.

8   Warren Scoville, *The Persecution of the Huguenots and French Economic Development* (University of California Press, 1960).

9   Archives Nationales, serie TT243, liasse 14, 'Interrogatoires, information et judgement concernant l'assemblée de hobereaux convertis', 5 au 6 Janvier 1692.

10   *Journal of the Huguenot Society* (August, 1991).

11   Jacques-Bénigne Bossuet, *Political Treatise*, Readings in European History (Boston, 1906).

12   R. Mousnier, *Louis XIV* (Historical Association, 1973), p. 17.

13   John McManners, *Oxford Illustrated History of Christianity* (Oxford University Press, 1990).

14   Graham Tomlin, *The Power of the Cross* (Paternoster, 1999), p. 219.

15   David J. Sturdy, *Louis XIV* (Macmillan, 1998), p. 81.

16   Ronald Knox, *Enthusiasm* (Oxford University Press, 1950), p. 339.

17   David L. Smith, *Louis XIV* (Cambridge University Press, 1992), p. 40.

18   Mark Fumaroli, *The Poet and the King* (University of Nôtre Dame, 2002), *passim*.

19   Bergin, *Crown, Church and Episcopate*, chapters 3 and 4, *passim*.

20   Robin Briggs, *Communities of Belief* (Oxford University Press, 1989), p. 244.

21   Philip F. Riley, *Lust for Virtue* (Greenwood Press, 2001), *passim*.

22   Bluche, *Louis XIV*, p. 593.

23   Paul Hazard, *The European Mind* (Hollis and Carter, 1953), p. xv.

24   L. Greenfield, *Nationalism* (Harvard University Press, 1992), pp. 129–33.

25   Dale Van Kley, *The Religious Origins of the French Revolution* (Yale University Press, 1996), p. 16.

9   NEMESIS: FOREIGN POLICY, 1684–1715

1   David Sturdy, *Louis XIV* (Macmillan, 1998), p. 141.

2   John Lynn, *The Wars of Louis XIV* (Longman, 1999), pp. 363ff.

3   Ian Dunlop, *Louis XIV* (Chatto and Windus, 1999), p. 308.

4   Geoffrey Treasure, *Louis XIV* (Longman, 2001), p. 245.

5   François Bluche, *Louis XIV*, trans. Mark Greengrass (Blackwell, 1990), p. 432.

6   *Lettre du Roi, écrite à Monseigneur l'Archéveque de Paris, por faire chanter le Te Deum* (Paris, 1697).

7   Jean-Baptiste Colbert, marquis de Torcy, *Memoirs* (London, 1757).

8   Louis XIV to William III, 8 December 1700.

9   Torcy, *Memoirs*, p. 107.

10   Mark A. Thomson, 'Louis XIV and the origins of the War of the Spanish Succession', paper read to the Royal Historical Society, London, 14 November 1953.

11   Bluche, *Louis XIV*, p. 529.

12   '*Con-capitaine*' and '*con-lieutenant*' are hard to translate. The literal 'cunt-captain' etc. is more offensive in English than in French. 'Bitch-captain' is not offensive enough.

13   Claude C. Sturgill, *Marshal Villars and the War of the Spanish Succession* (University of Kentucky Press, 1965), p. 155.

14   Ibid., p. 85.

15   W. Doyle, *Venality* (Oxford University Press, 1996), p. 56.

16   Quoted by Bluche, *Louis XIV*, pp. 541–2.

17   Torcy, *Memoirs*, p. 236.

18   Marlborough should not have paid him the compliment of being heir to the British throne, as he had been debarred as a Catholic by the Bill of Rights and the Act of Settlement.

19   Torcy, *Memoirs*, pp. 236ff.

20   Sturgill, *Marshal Villars*, p. 113.

21   See the beginning of Chapter 7.

22   This interpretation is developed by Philip Bobbitt, *The Shield of Achilles: War, Peace and the Course of History* (Allen Lane, 2002), pp. 522–7. I am grateful to Dean Petters for directing me to this source.

23   Lynn, *Wars of Louis XIV*, pp. 355–9; Bluche, *Louis XIV*, p. 572: 'Louis XIV's wars had cost the lives of 500,000 men.'

10   THE SUN KING AND HIS PEOPLE, 1684–1715

1   In due course, 'Marianne' would personify France, just as John Bull personified Britain.

2   Jean de la Bruyèree's comments are quoted by V. Mallia-Milanes, *Louis XIV and France* (Macmillan, 1986), p. 39.

3   Boisguilbert, *Détail de la France*, quoted by H.G. Judge, *Louis XIV* (Longmans, 1965), p. 104.

4   Ibid.

5   Sebastian Vauban, *La Dîme Royale*, Jean-Marc Daniel edition (L'Harmattan, 2004), p. 216.

6   Quoted by François Bluche, *Louis XIV*, trans. Mark Greengrass (Blackwell, 1990), p. 542.

7   J.-C. Petitfils, *Louis XIV* (Perrin, 2002), pp. 704–5.

8   Ibid.

9   David J. Sturdy, *Louis XIV* (Macmillan, 1998), p. 49.

10   See Pierre Goubert, *The French Peasantry in the Seventeenth Century* (Cambridge University Press, 1986), *passim*.

11 On the Rohan conspiracy, see Lionel Rothkrug, *The Opposition to Louis XIV* (Princeton University Press, 1965), pp. 164–5, footnote 52.

12 Quoted by Kathryn A. Hoffmann, *Society of Pleasures* (New York, 1997), pp. 154–5.

13 *The Most Christian Turk*, printed in London, 1693.

14 For Christian agrarianism, see Rothkrug, *Opposition*, and Sturdy, *Louis XIV*, pp. 66–7.

15 See Anne Somerset, *The Affair of the Poisons* (Weidenfeld and Nicolson 2003), *passim*.

16 Mme de Maintenon, *Dialogues and Addresses*, edited and translated by John J. Conley (University of Chicago Press, 2004), p. i.

17 Robin Briggs, letter to the author, 31 August 2005.

18 See Mme de Maintenon, *Dialogues and Addresses, passim*, but especially pp. 122–3 and 146–7.

11 CONCLUSION

1 Alfred Cobban, *A History of Modern France* (Pelican, 1965), vol. 1, p. 17.

2 *Lettres de Louis XIV*, edited by Pierre Gaxotte (Talendier, 1930).

3 Philippe Erlanger, *Louis XIV* (Phoenix, 1988), p. 449.

4 Geoffrey Treasure, *Louis XIV* (Longman, 2001), p. 331.

5 François Bluche, *Louis XIV*, trans. Mark Greengrass (Blackwell, 1990), p. 607. The king's death is well described by Bluche on pp. 605–13.

6 Treasure, *Louis XIV*, p. 340.

7 Bluche, *Louis XIV*, pp. 464–5.

8 Mathieu Da Vinha, *Les Valets de Chambre de Louis XIV* (Perrin, 2004), p. 322.

9 Robin Briggs, *Early Modern France* (Oxford University Press, 1990), p. 165.

10 J.R. Green's moral judgement went as follows: 'Foul as hell is, it is defiled by the even fouler presence of King John.'

11 The title of a book by David Sheppard, bishop of Liverpool.

12 J.-C. Petitfils, *Louis XIV* (Perrin, 2002), p. 700.

13 David Ogg, *Louis XIV* (Oxford University Press, 1963), p. 214.

14 Pierre Goubert, *Louis XIV and Twenty Million Frenchmen* (Allen Lane, 1970), quoted in W.F. Church (ed.) *The Greatness of Louis XIV* (D.C. Heath, 1972), p. 183.

15 Quoted by Briggs, *Early Modern France*, p. ix.

INDEX

absolutism 6–7, 68–76
Académies 87
agriculture 35, 46–7, 198, 206
Aix-la-Chapelle, Treaty of 127–8
Alexander VII, Pope 125
ambassadors' staircase at Versailles
    92
Amsterdam 131
Anjou, duc de, *see* Philip V of Spain
Annat, Père 146
Anne of Austria, Queen of France
    Plate 9, personality 11, control
    over Louis XIV's childhood
    13–22, 34, 51, 57–9, 98, 143–4
Apollo 3, 76
Army, French 52, 71, 75, 152,
    170–8, 184–5
Artagnan, Charles sieur d' 58–9
Asiento 182
Augsburg, League of 171–2
Auvergne, Grand Jours de 41, 72–3
Avignon 147, 171

ballets at Court 23, 86
Barbézieux, marquis de 62, 65, 177
Bavaria, Maximilian Elector of 186
Bayle, Pierre 49
Beachy Head, battle of 174
Beaufort, Francois de Vendome, duc
    de 14, 63
Beauvais, Mme de 27, 29
Beauvillier, duc de 66, 70
Bentink, Earl of Portland 176, 224
Bernard, Samuel 43, 80
Bernini, Giovanni 89
Berwick, James Duke of 3, 185

Blenheim, battle of 186, 188
Boisguilbert, Pierre de Peasant de
    199, 206
Bolingbroke, Viscount 193
Bontemps, Alexandre 94, 144, 223
Bossuet, Benigne, Bishop of Condom,
    then Meaux 4, 49–50, 68, 70,
    90, 95, 100, 104, 108, 123,
    132–5, 154, 158, 161–2, 204
Boufflers, Louis-François, duc and
    marshal 185
Bourdaloue, Père 6–7, 95
Bourgogne, Louis duc de 11, 205,
    222
Bourgogne, Marie-Adelaide of Savoy,
    duchesse de 77, 81, 116–7,
    death 119
Bourgeoisie 41–2
Boyne, battle of, 173–4
Brienne, Lomenie de 12
Broussel, Pierre 19
Burnet, Bishop Gilbert 231

Camisards 153
Canal du Midi 69, 74, 203
capitation tax 67, 80, 175, 189
Carlos II Plate 1, 120, 126, 140,
    155, 176, 178–9, 181, 196, 227
Casale 139
Cassel, battle of 133
Catinat, Marshal 170, 185
Caulet, bishop 147
Catholic Church 38–40
Chamillart, Michel de 185,
    188–9,223
Charles II, king of England 129, 145

Charles, Archduke, later Emperor
    Charles VI 187
Chevreuse, duchesse de 51
Church, French 163–7
Clientage 77
Colbert, Jean-Baptiste 5, 31,
    41–2, 47–8, rivalry with
    Fouquet 58–60, leading role in
    government 61–65,
    reprimanded by Louis XIV 65,
    70, 80, 83, 89, 97, 106, 121,
    130, 137–8, 171, 173, 202–3
Cologne 148–9, 172
Concini, Concino 20
Condé, Louis de Bourbon 18–21, 23,
    30, 84, 131–2
Conseils 61–3
Coronation of Louis XIV at Reims
    23–4, 34, 145–6, 197, 221
Court 1, 76–81, 110–11, 209, 219
Corsican guards affair 125, 147
Couperin, François 88
Croissy, marquis de 62, 66, 138,
    169, 179
Cromwell, Oliver 22, 26

Daguesseau, procureur general
    215–6
Dangeau, Philip de 96
Daquin, Antoine 115–6
Dauphin, the Grand, Monseigneur
    50, 82, 96, 98–100, 172, 204
Denain, battle of 186, 189, 193
Descartes, René de 49
Desmarets, Nicolas 62, 189
Devolution, War of 126–8, 141
Dîme Royale 206
Dixième 80, 189
Dover, Secret Treaty of 51, 120, 129
Dragonnades 151–5
Dunes, battle of the 26
Dunkirk 26
Dutch war 123, 129–38, 141

Elizabeth Charlotte of the Palatinate
    (Liselotte), duchesse d'Orléans
    46, 52, 79, 96, 101, 112,
    117–8, 120, 144, 172
Estates 38–41
Eugene of Savoy, Prince 160, 185–6,
    189, 193

Fagon, Guy-Crescent 216–221
Fénelon, François de Salignac de la
    Mothe 43, 95, 123, 129, 141,
    158, 161–3, 205–6
Fontanges, Marie-Angélique,
    duchesse de 111
Fontainebleu, Edict of, see Edict of
    Nantes
Fouquet, Nicolas 25, 56–60, 74,
    123, 162–3
Fronde, the 17–22, 24, 94, 124
Furstenberg, William Egon von
    148–9, 171

galleys 152–3
Gallicanism 147–8
Gallican Articles 147–9
Généralités 70
Genoa 140
Gondi, Cardinal de Retz 18–9, 22,
    39, 157
Guyon, Jeanne Bouvier de la Motte,
    Mme 160–3

Hague, The, Peace talks at 190–2
Harlay de Champvallon, Archbishop
    of Paris 154, 164
Heinsius, Anthony 192
Henri III 2, 77
Henri IV 2, 12–13, 17, 43, 56, 103,
    112, 145, 229
Henriette-Ann (Minette), duchesse
    d'Orléans 51, 101, 104, 110,
    120, 129
Heurtebise 133

Huguenots 34, 38–9, 49, 149–55, 208

hunting, 1, 82–3

Innocent XI, Pope 140, 147–9,

Innocent XII, Pope 149, 206

Intendants 69–70, 197

Invalides 79, 89, 133

James II, king of England 120–21, 138, 173, 182

James Stuart, the Old Pretender 182, 194

Jansenism 2, 39, 50, 81, 155–60, 166, 206, 208

Jesuits, the Society of Jesus 146, 156, 167

Jurieu, Pastor Pierre 204, 228

Kerouailles, Louise de 120

La Chaise, Père 107, 114, 144, 146, 154

La Fontaine 92–3, 123, 163

La Porte, Pierre de 15–6

La Reynie, Nicolas de 73, 110–11, 165

La Rochefoucauld, 115

La Vallière, Louise de Plate 7, 58, 103–6, 127,

Lauzun, comte de 109–10

Le Brun, Charles 58, 91, 94

Le Nôtre, André 58, 94

Le Tellier, Michel 56, 61, 124, 151, 172

Le Tellier, Charles-Maurice, Archbishop of Reims 164

Le Tellier, Père 146, 219

Le Vau, Louis 58

Leopold I, Emperor 128, 138, 140, 173, 175, 179, 195, 230

Lionne, Hugues de 56, 61, 124, 128, 130

London 125

Louis XIII 10, 13–4, 20, 229

Louis XIV Plates 2, 3 and 4 (plus front cover) appearance 1, 32, 215–8; personality 2–4, 221–6; loss of temper 65 (with Louvois), 78 (because of de Maine's cowardice), 109–19 with Lauzun, 215 with Daguesseau; birth 11–12; legitimacy 12–13; childhood 15–7; illnesses 16, 25–7, 115–6; death 216–221; and the Fronde 17–22, 25–6; coronation 23–4, 34, 143–6; debt to Mazarin 29–33; sex education 26–8; attitudes to women 50–3, 165–7, 224–6; sexual standards 101–113; *memoirs* 35, 124–32; gluttony 46, 115; personal rule 55–67; and Fouquet 57–60; employment of aristocrats 62–3; letter reprimanding Colbert 65; absolutism 68–76; cult of Apollo 76–8; motto (*nec pluribus impar*) 85, 125; devotion to duty 77, 80–1, 216–7; opens courtiers' mail 78–9; outdoor pursuits 82–3; personifies the *honnete home;* befriends Molière 86; enthusiasm for music 87–8; love of gardens, flowers and vegetables 1, 94; and family 98–101, mistresses 103–112, political effects of mistresses 120–1; and war 122–3, 127, 133–6,187–9, 226–9; foreign policy objectives 126, 169–73; religious priorities 143–4, 209–214; relations with Rome 146–9; and Huguenots 149–55; with Jansenists 155–60, 166, 229–30; with

Quietists 160–3; blunders 181–3; kept his nerve 190–3; assessment of foreign policy 195–6; and *soulagement* 197–201, 227–230; and reactions to criticism 203–7; and nationalism 189–91, responsibility for the French Revolution 230, overall assessment 225–31; sense of humour 221–2; courtesy 1–231, figure 2 explaining French expansion, figure 3 detailing Louis XIV's palaces
Louis XV 6, 103, 112, 145
Louvois, François Michel Le Tellier, marquis de 60, 62, rivalry with Colbert 64–5, 74, 84, 97, 112, 114, 127, crucial role in expanding the French army 130–6, 139, 151, 165, 180, 182, 185, 208, 210–3, 222, 225
Louvre, The 11, 89
Lully, Jean-Baptiste 58, 87–8, 139
Luxembourg, maréchal-duc de Plate 5, 96, 110, 132–3, 135, 174–8

Mademoiselle, la grande duchesse de Montpensier 21, 23, 109–110
Marie-Anne of Bavaria 208
Maine, Louis Auguste de Bourbon, duc de 78, 102, 109, 114, 206, 217
Maintenon, Françoise d'Aubigné, marquise de Plate 8, 29, 43, 51, 66, 79, 80–1, employed by Mme de Montespan 88, 96, 102–3, 108, background and marriage to Louis XIV 113–120, 129, religious influence 144–6, 151, 165, 180, 182, 185, 208, case-study 210–3, 222, 225

Malplaquet, battle of 189
Mancini, Mary 26–8
Mansart, Jules Hardouin 89
Marguerite of Savoy 26
Marie-Louise d'Orléans, Queen of Spain, first wife of Carlos II 120
Marie-Adelaide de Savoy, duchesse de Bourgogne 77, 81, 116–7
Marie Thérèse, queen of France Plate 9, 27–9, 51, 98–9, 105, 107, 114, 120, 126–7
Marlborough, John Churchill, Duke of 185–6, 192,
Mary-Beatrice of Modena 120–1, 222
Mazarin, Cardinal Jules 12, 14–5, 17–21, 27–32, 59
Mazarinades 19–20, 48
medical profession 16, 25–7, 115–6, 119, 208, 216–221
Mémoires 124–5, 127, 132
mentalité 9, 77, 122–4, 146, 155, 162, 213
Mignard, Pierre 95
Molière, Jean Baptiste 58, 86, 93, 95
Montmartre, Treaty of 125
Montespan, Françoise Athénaïs de Montemart, marquise de Plate 6, 79, 93, 95, 99, 103, 105, *mistress en titre* 106–114, involved in poison affair 110–112, 127, 212, 225
Montespan, Louis Henri, marquis de 107–8
Motteville, madame de, diarist 28–9

Namur 175
Nantes, Edict of, revoked 149–55
navy, French 35, 42, 62, 152, 170, 173–4, 184–7
Neerwinden, battle of 175
Nijmegen, treaty of 136–7

Noailles, Louis-Antoine de, cardinal archbishop of Paris 207, 219
Noblesse d'epée 40–1
Noblesse de robe 40–1

Offices and officiers 17, 40, 67, 69, 75
Ordinances, civil and criminal, 73
Orléans, Gaston, duc d' 11, 23
Orléans, Philippe duc d', Monsieur 15–6, 19, 23, 43, 51, 77, 100–1, 104, 133, 145
Orléans, Philippe duc d', Louis XIV's nephew 101, 118, 166, 185, 205–6, 217
Oudenarde, battle of 186, 188

Palatinate 171–2
Paris 2, 18, 22, 41, 154
Parlements 18, 25, 38, 41, 45, 58, 71–3, 89, 137, 181, 215–6
partition treaties 179
Pascal, Blaise 96, 157–8
patronage 67, 69
Pavillon, bishop 147
Pellison, Paul 4, 35, 96
Péréfixe, Hardouin de Beaumont de, Archbishop of Paris 158
Phélypeaux 62
Philip II, king of Spain 8, 57
Philip IV, king of Spain 13, 29, 123, 125
Philip V, king of Spain 155, 179, 184–6, 194
Philippsburg 172–3
poison 110–1
Pomponne, Simon Arnauld, marquis de 66, 137, 159, 179
Pontchartrain, Jerome de 62, 66, 67
Pontchartrain, Louis Phélypeaux, comte de 62, 66–7, 175, 189
population 36–7
Port-Royal, Paris 155, 158
Port-Royal-des-Champs 155,159

Propaganda 65, 96–7, 126–7, 141, 166, 171–2, 176, 181, 190, 200
Protestants, *see* Huguenots
Pyrenees, peace of 126

Quesnel, Pasquier 159
Quietism 160–3

Racine, Jean 5, 93, 95, 131, 133, 211
Ramillies, battle of 186–7, 193–4
Rastadt, treaty of 160, 187
Ratisbon, truce of 140–1, 168–9, 172
rebellions 17–25, 153, 201
régale, the 147
Reynie, Nicolas de la 42–3
Retz, Cardinal de, *see* Gondi
Reunions 139–142
Richelieu, Armand-Jean de Plessis, Cardinal de 10, 12, 14, 17–8, 38, 46, 48, 64, 124
Rigaud, Hyacinthe 49, 95, 218, and Plate 2
Rochefoucauld, duc de 78
Rohan, Armand-Gaston-Maximilien, Cardinal de 11, 219
Rohan, Louis, chevalier de 74, 203
Ryswick, treaty of 175, 182

Saint-Cyr 117, 212–3, 220, 231
Saint-Simon, Louis de Rouvroy, duc de 40, 63, 77–8, 90, 96, 116–8, 159, 205, 220
Savoy, Charles-Emmanuel, duc de 175, 222
Scarron, Paul 19, 113, 163, 211
scrofula 38,145
Séguier, Pierre, Chancellor of France 19, 56, 59, 94–5
Seignelay, Jean-Baptiste Colbert, marquis de 62, 169, 173–4

Sévigné, Marie de, marquise de 38, 52, 96, 104, 109
Soulagement Plate 10 of *The Baker's Cart* 34–5, 75, 189, 197–201
Spanish Succession, war of the 184–193, figure 1
Steenkirk, battle of 175
Strasbourg 139
Subversion 203–5

Tallard, Camille, marshal 188
Talon, Omer 19, 22
Tartuffe 86, 93
Torcy, Jean-Baptiste Colbert, marquis de 62, 64, 66, 96, 179, 186, 189–92
Toulouse, Louis-Alexandre de Bourbon, comte de 67, 102, 217
Tourville, Anne-Hilarion de Cotentin, admiral 174, 178
Turenne, Henri de la Tour d'Auvergne, maréchal de 22, 25, 26, 63, 74, 130–32

Unigenitus 67, 72, 120–1, 159–60, 206–7, 215
Ursins, Anne-Marie, princesse de 118–20, 185, 187, 211
Utrecht, treaty of 193–4

Vauban, Sébastien Le Pretre 43, 70, 127, 133, 139, 152, 170, 174, 178, 195, 199–200, 206
Vaudois 170
Vaux-le-Vicomte 48, 58
Vendôme, Louis de Bourbon, duc de 175, 178, 185–6, 188, 192
Ventadour, Charlotte duchesse de 119
Vermandois,Louis de Bourbon, comte de 79, 106, 210

Versailles 2, 48, 65, 68, 76–81, 89–93, 215–231, figure 4
explaining cabals, 81
Victor Amadeus of Savoy 170
Villars, Claude Louis Hector, duc de 153, 185–94
Villeroy, Nicolas, marquis de 15,
Villeroy, François de Neufville, duc et maréchal 80, 185, 218
Vineam Domini 159
Visconti Primo 2, 9, 96, 110–1, 115
Voltaire, François Marie Arouet de 5–6, 32, 90, 175

Westphalia, peace of 30, 138
William of Orange, from 1688 William III, king of England 131–2, 138, 153, 173, 175, 178, 195, 230
Witt, Cornelius and Jan de 123, 130–1
wolves in the Ile-de-France 82
women 50–53, 165–6, 207–13

Henry VII

Sean Cunningham

This new biography illuminates the life of Henry VII himself, how he ran his government, how his authority was maintained, and the nature of the country over which he ruled since he first claimed the throne in 1485.

Sean Cunningham explores how Henry's reign was vitally important in stabilizing the English monarchy and providing the sound financial and institutional basis for later developments in government, and tackles key questions in the debate:

- Was Henry VII a conventional late medieval nobleman?
- How did his upbringing affect his later kingship?
- What was the nature of Henry's marriage to Elizabeth of York?
- How and why did he become the main rival to Richard III following the disappearance of Edward V and his brother in July 1483?

Up until now the details of Henry as a person and as a king, his court and household, his subjects, and his country have remained little known. This book remedies that lack, and brings to the forefront the life and times of the very first Tudor king.

978-0-415-26620-8   (Hardback)
978-0-415-26621-5   (Paperback)

Mary Queen of Scots

Retha Warnicke

Mary Queen of Scots

In this new biography of one of the most intriguing figures of early modern European history, Retha Warnicke, widely regarded as a leading historian on Tudor queenship, offers a fresh interpretation of the life of Mary Stuart, popularly known as Mary, Queen of Scots.

Setting Mary's life within the context of the cultural and intellectual climate of the time and bringing to life the realities of being a female monarch in the sixteenth century, Warnicke also examines Mary's three marriages, her constant ill health and her role in numerous plots and conspiracies. Placing Mary within the context of early modern gender relations, Warnicke reveals the challenges that faced her and the forces that worked to destroy her.

This highly readable and fascinating study will pour fresh light on the much-debated life of a central figure of the sixteenth century, providing a new interpretation of Mary Stuart's impact on politics, gender and nationhood in the Tudor era.

978-0-415-29182-8 (Hardback)
978-0-415-29183-5 (Paperback)

Routledge History

The Enlightenment World

Edited by Martin Fitzpatrick, Peter Jones,
Christa Knellwolf and Iain McCalman

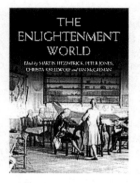

'It is simply the best study of the Enlightenment World ever produced' – *H.T. Dickenson, Sir Richard Lodge Professor of British History, University of Edinburgh*

'A fine team of contributors…The imaginative range of topics is particularly impressive…An Enlightenment project that definitely succeeds!' – *John Hedley Brooke, Andreas Idreos Professor of Science and Religion, University of Oxford*

'The rich scholarship on the Enlightenment is critically and constructively invoked throughout, making this a fine reference work' – *Knud Haakonssen, Boston University*

The Enlightenment World offers an informed, comprehensive and up-to-date analysis of the European Enlightenment (circa. 1720–1800) as both an historical epoch and a cultural formation.

This prestigious collection begins with the intellectual origins of the Enlightenment, and spans early formations up to both contemporary and modern critics of the Enlightenment.

The chapters, written by leading international experts, represent the most cutting-edge research within the field and include:

- The High Enlightenment
- Polite Culture and the Arts
- Reforming the World
- Material and Pop Culture
- Transformations and Exploration.

Covering topics as diverse as government, fashion, craftsmen and artisans, philanthropy, cross-cultural encounters, feminism, censorship, science and education, this volume will provide essential reading for all students of the Enlightenment.

978-0-415-215756   (Hardback)
978-0-415-40408-2   (Paperback)

The French Revolution, 2nd Edition

Gary Kates

This fascinating book studies all aspects of the French Revolution, from its origins, through its development, right up to the consequences of this major historical event.

Bringing together key texts at the forefront of new research and interpretation, Gary Kates challenges orthodox assumptions concerning the origins, development and long-term historical repercussions of the Revolution.

Completely updated to include discussion of new research and articles, this welcome second edition includes articles discussing colonialism and family legislation, and emphasizes approaches that focus on class, gender, and race.

Including a clear and thoroughly updated introduction, this is the perfect reader for students studying the French Revolution.

978-0-415-35832-3   (Hardback)
978-0-415-35833-0   (Paperback)

The Wars of the French Revolution and Napoleon, 1792–1815

Owen Connelly

Written by an experienced author and expert in the field, *Wars of the French Revolution and Napoleon*, 1792–1815 provides a thorough re-examination of the crucial period in the history of France for students of history and military studies.

Based on extensive research, and including twenty detailed maps, this study is unique in its focus on the wars of the both the French Revolution and Napoleon. Owen Connelly expertly analyzes them both to provide a broader context for warfare. Examining the causes of the Wars, Connelly looks at how the practices of warfare during this period were to influence modes of combat throughout the nineteenth and twentieth centuries, establishing trends discernable in the First and Second World Wars.

Hbk 0-415-23983-4   Pbk 0-415-23984-2

France and 1848: The End of Monarchy

William Fortescue

An extensive and authoritative study that examines the economic, social and political crises of France during the revolution of 1848. Using analysis of original sources and recent research, Fortescue here offers new interpretations of events leading up to and after the second republic was declared.

Looking at Louis Philippe's overthrow, the proclamation of manhood suffrage and the unexpected success of the right-wing in the subsequent elections, this book evaluates the political history of France in 1848 and the French political culture of the time.

This should be read by all students of nineteenth century history, political scientists and all those with an interest in the historical development of French political culture.

Hbk 0-415-31461-5   Pbk 0-415-31462-3

French Revolution and Napoleon

Philip Dwyer and Peter McPhee

The upheavals, terror, and drama of the French Revolutionary and Napoleonic period restructured politics and society on a grand scale, making this the defining moment for modern European history.

This volume collects together a wide selection of primary texts to explain the process behind the enormous changes undergone by France and Europe between 1787 and 1815, from the Terror to the Counter-Revolution and from Marie-Antoinette to Robespierre and Bonaparte. While bringing the impact of historical events to life, Philip Dwyer and Peter McPhee provide a clear outline of the period through key documents and lucid introductory passages and commentary. They illustrate the meaning of the Revolution for peasants, sans-culottes, women, and slaves, as well as placing events within a wider European context.

Students will find this an invaluable source of information on the Revolution as a whole as well as the international significance of the events.

Hbk 0-415-19907-7
Pbk 0-415-19908-5

Glory and Terror
Seven Deaths Under the French Revolution

Antoine de Baecque

Glory and Terror is a vivid and often gory history of the darker side of the French Revolution. Through an examination of contemporary visual and literary representations of executions, funerals, processions and ceremonies it brings the often horrific events of the time to life.

Among the seven real life cases on which the author focuses are:

- the public autopsy performed on the corpse of Mirabeau
- the exhumation and transportation of Voltaire's body to the Pantheon
- the public torture, murder and subsequent mutilation of the Princesse de Lamballe
- the agonizingly slow death of Robespierre.

Hbk 0-415-92616-5
Pbk 0-415-92617-3

To Speak for the People

Jon Cowans

Although there is now a great deal of literature on the concept of public opinion in the 18th century France, it is almost entirely devoted to the pre-revolutionary years. No book has tackled the concept of public opinion in the French Revolution itself. *To Speak for the People* is a lucid and innovative study that finally fills this gap. Historian Jon Cowans adds a strong and genuinely original voice to the historical debate over the problem of legitimacy during the Revolution drawing on the works of such luminaries as Jürgen Habermas, Keith Baker, François Furet, and Nancy Fraser. He then examines the uses of terms such as "public opinion," "the public," and "the people" in political debates during the Revolution and analyzes those terms' changing meaning and the role they played in attempts to secure political authority. While shedding new light on the Revolution itself, the book raises broader issues by addressing the problem of legitimacy that has haunted all revolutionary and democratic governments throughout the modern period.

Hbk 0-415-92971-7   Pbk 0-415-92972-5

French Revolution
Rethinking the Debate

Gwynne Lewis

This is the first short introductory history of the French Revolution which covers social, economic and cultural aspects of the period as well as intellectual and political matters. It:

- combines interpretative narrative with thematic analysis
- incorporates traditional and recent studies into a new synthesis
- engages in past and present controversies
- concentrates equally on the popular classes and the privileged elites.

The French Revolution provides students with an accessible and challenging resume of the revolution and its historians.

Hbk 0-415-31461-5   Pbk 0-415-05466-4

The Governing of Britain

Peter Jupp

Focusing on the institutions and players of central and local government during an era of great transformation, Peter Jupp examines the cohesive nature of the British state, and how Britain was governed between 1688 and 1848.

Divided into two parts, bisected by the accession of George III in 1760, this study:

- examines the changes to the framework and function of executive government
- presents an analysis of its achievements, the composition and functions of Parliament
- explores Parliament's role in government
- looks at the interaction between the executive, Parliament and the public.

Providing new insights into the formulation of notions and traditions of legislation, the public sphere and popular politics, *The Governing of Britain* is an essential guide to a formative era in political life.

Hbk: 978-0-415-22948-7
Pbk: 978-0-415-22949-4

LOUIS XIV

Richard Wilkinson

Routledge
Taylor & Francis Group

LONDON AND NEW YORK

First published 2007
by Routledge
2 Park Square, Milton Park, Abingdon, Oxon, OX14 4RN

Simultaneously published in the USA and Canada
by Routledge
270 Madison Avenue, New York, NY 10016

Transferred to digital printing 2010

Routledge is an imprint of the Taylor & Francis Group, an informa business

Typeset in Great Britain by Saxon Graphics Ltd, Derby
Printed and bound in Great Britain by
Antony Rowe, Chippenham, Wiltshire

British Library Cataloguing in Publication Data
A catalogue record for this book is available from the British Library

Library of Congress Cataloging-in-Publication Data
Wilkinson, Richard.
    Louis XIV / Richard Wilkinson.
        p. cm. -- (Routledge historical biographies)
    Includes index.
1. Louis XIV, King of France, 1638–1715. 2. France--History--Louis XIV,
1643–1715. 3. France--Kings and rulers--Biography. I. Title.
    DC129.W55 2007
    944'.033092--dc22
    [B]

2006035860

ISBN 978–0–415–35815–6 (hbk)
ISBN 978–0–415–35816–3 (pbk)

The Routledge Companion to Britain in the Eighteenth Century, 1688–1820

John Stevenson and Jeremy Gregory

The Routledge Companion to Britain in the Eighteenth Century is an invaluable compendium of facts, figures, lists and chronologies on all aspects of British life between 1688-1820. A vital resource for students and scholars of the era, this *Companion* is crammed with information on the monarchy and outlines of British military campaigns, and also includes key events in literature, science, philosophy, religion and the arts during the era. Complete with a section of biographies of key individuals, a glossary of key terms, an annotated bibliography to aid further research and a map section, it provides a one-stop shop for those with an interest in this fascinating period of British history.

Hbk 0-415-37882-6
Pbk 0-415-37883-4

Gladstone and Disraeli

Stephen J. Lee

Gladstone and Disraeli surveys and compares the careers of these two influential Prime Ministers. Stephen J. Lee examines how Gladstone and Disraeli emerged as leaders of the two leading parties and goes on to consider their time in power, analysing many different aspects of their careers.

Using a wide variety of sources and historiography, Stephen J. Lee compares and contrasts the beliefs of Gladstone and Disraeli, their effect on the economy, social reform, the Irish problem and parliamentary reform, and on foreign policy.

Hbk 0-415-32356-8
Pbk 0-415-32357-6

The Island Race: Englishness, Empire and Gender in the Eighteenth Century

Kathleen Wilson

Rooted in a period of vigorous exploration and colonialism, *The Island Race: Englishness, Empire and Gender in the Eighteenth Century* is an innovative study of the issues of nation, gender and identity. Wilson bases her analysis on a wide range of case studies drawn both from Britain and across the Atlantic and Pacific worlds.

Creating a colourful and original colonial landscape, she considers topics such as:

- sodomy
- theatre
- masculinity
- the symbolism of Britannia
- the role of women in war.

Wilson shows the far-reaching implications that colonial power and expansion had upon the English people's sense of self, and argues that the vaunted singularity of English culture was in fact constituted by the bodies, practices and exchanges of peoples across the globe. Theoretically rigorous and highly readable, *The Island Race* will become a seminal text for understanding the pressing issues that it confronts.

Hbk 0-415-15895-8
Pbk 0-415-15896-6